There's No Place
Like Home

DECORATING BOOKS BY CARLETON VARNEY

You and Your Apartment
The Family Decorates a Home
Carleton Varney's Book of Decorating Ideas
Carleton Varney Decorates Windows
Decorating with Color
Decorating for Fun
Carleton Varney Decorates from A to Z
Be Your Own Decorator

There's No Place Like Home

Confessions of an Interior Designer

Carleton Varney

The Bobbs-Merrill Company, Inc.
Indianapolis   New York

Published by The Bobbs-Merrill Company, Inc.
Indianapolis   New York

Library of Congress Cataloging in Publication Data

Varney, Carleton.
    There's no place like home.

    1. Varney, Carleton.   2. Interior decora-
tors—United States—Biography. I.   Title.
NK2004.3.V37A2   1980   729 [B]   80–1020
ISBN 0–672–51872–4

Designed by J. Tschantre Graphics Services, Ltd.

Manufactured in the United States of America
First printing

To my wife, Suzanne, who lived so much of this book—and for Dr. Max, who helped open the doors of the real homes in my head.

Acknowledgments

I wish to acknowledge those people who helped make my book *There's No Place Like Home* a reality. Rosalind Cole, who believed in the idea from its very beginning; Jim Fisher, who chose to publish my work; Grace Shaw, who edited the book and stood with me from first draft to finished product; Irene Frank and Richard Horn, who suffered through the first dictations and the very earliest manuscript; Corrigan Earnshaw, who suffered extreme head and finger cramps through the second draft, and was able to decipher my handwriting; the talented Catherine Revland, who spent hours with me in the preparation of the final manuscript; Darinka Papich, who took me into her confidence and told me of the last days of life on earth for Joan Crawford; Florence Walsh, who encouraged Ms. Papich to meet with me; photographers Bettina Cirone, Richard Champion, Ellen Graham, and Danilo Nardi, who supplied some of the photos in the book; Irene Glynn for her copyediting of the manuscript; Linda Worden at Bobbs-Merrill, who watched and assisted as I made last-minute manuscript changes; and my sons Nicholas and Sebastian, who gave up life with Daddy on more than a few occasions so that Daddy could write this book.

Contents

There's No Place
Like Home

"Gorgonzola." The Fair-Haired Boy, Dorothy Draper, and Leon Hegwood manage a smile for the camera during a short truce in the Draper wars.

Chapter 1

Dorothy Draper and Me

People often ask me how I managed to become president of Dorothy Draper and Company at the tender age of twenty-nine. "How did you do it?" they want to know. "Did you push Mrs. Draper down an elevator shaft?" The truth is, I did not. On the other hand, I think Dorothy Draper may have given the matter some thought, with me, the fair-haired boy, as victim.

Before a quirk of fate made me a decorator in the late 1950s, I spent a lot of time in Greenwich Village where I was a graduate student at New York University. It was a haven for the artistic and beat generation in those days, but I was no beatnik. I was a proper Bostonian whose goal was to become the ambassador to Spain, but I had discovered that the quaint jumble of Village streets was a fascinating harbor for people with a variety of interests who wanted to turn one another on. With ideas, I hasten to add, not dope—this was the Eisenhower era. I was going to graduate school, my major was Spanish (how would I become ambassador to Spain unless I spoke flawless Spanish?), and I found living in New York like going to the circus. I loved it.

My upbringing took place in a Boston suburb, a comfortable childhood. At school my grades were all As—I was a perfect student and a good little boy. Like most of the residents of Nahant, Massachusetts, my goal in life was to be like the Lodges, those exemplary WASPs, and my particular role model was Henry Cabot Lodge. Yet, when it came time to choose a college, I was beginning to feel the constraints of New England. I was tired of the Lodges, and of the Yankee environment, and I decided to go to college in another part of the country. It was a timid first step. I chose Oberlin College in Ohio primarily because it was coed and because they had offered me a full-tuition scholarship, but also because it wasn't in New England. Oberlin was nice, but it was no melting pot—to say nothing of fleshpot. In fact, I found the Midwest only about one step above New England when it came to broadening my horizons. Consequently, I was overjoyed when I got to spend my junior year abroad at the University of Madrid. The brother of a rejected role model awaited me there; the American ambassador to Spain was John Lodge. Nevertheless, in every other way Spain was vastly different from Nahant, Massachusetts, and Oberlin, Ohio. I became enamoured of a life style I had rarely seen in my eighteen years.

During my junior year in Madrid, I met a new role model, one who was as different from the old hero as Henry VIII was from Oliver Cromwell. I met Errol Flynn. He was staying at a villa, El Moli, on the island of Mallorca and had a boat called the *Zaca*, on which he lived with his beautiful wife Patrice and their year-old daughter, Arnella. Flynn it was who pointed out to me that the drawing-room approach to courting young women, which I had been taught, was not the only way to go about it. In fact, he quickly demonstrated that his way was far superior. Many an evening, as soon as the sun went down, I with Errol and some of his friends went to the *tascas* of Serrono, and he would show me how the local damsels (as well as some imported and more exotic flowers) could be wooed, won, and abandoned. What a role model. I hear these days he is being called a homosexual. All I know is that Errol Flynn emanated pheromones for a hundred yards in every direction—and if he wasn't sending, a hell of a lot of women out there were receiving. I know no details of Flynn's intimate life; I do know that when it came to women, he was awe-inspiring.

I also learned much about flamboyance from Errol Flynn. Many screen idols are a disappointment when you meet them because they are so much smaller than their gigantic screen size. Not so with Errol. He was every bit as brawling and colorful in real life as he was as the celluloid swashbuckler. Most of the time he seemed on the verge of being out of control. One day some friends drove with him to the Palma de Mallorca airport where he was going to catch a plane to London to make a film. His leg was in a cast, and he was roaring drunk. When an announcement came over the loudspeaker that the plane he was taking was going to be late, he started waving his crutches and yelling, "Call Howard Hughes! Errol Flynn will not be kept waiting!" Flynn also loved good design, beautiful paintings, and quality furnishings. His boat reflected his elegant tastes.

Having replaced the Lodges with Errol Flynn as my inspiration, I came back to the United States and finished college. And as the ink dried on my diploma I was packing my bags for New York. I didn't know what I was going to do when I got there, but whenever I'm in doubt, I always give myself an ambitious goal. I would go to Gotham and give myself a year in which to make my fortune. I arrived with a few bags and a lot of nebulous dreams; I was nineteen years old and ready to take on the world. First, however, I would have to get a job to keep me afloat.

I decided to try for something solid, preferably in a job that would require using Spanish and fine arts—my major and minor. I paid a visit to a teacher-placement office on 42nd Street. There I was interviewed by Miss Mary Watkins, who looked appropriately like a schoolmarm with her neat gray bun, Jane Eyre outfit, and crackling skin. "Young man," she said, "I think I have a job for you." She gave me some complicated train instructions, and I was on my way to my first interview.

By the end of the day I was employed. "You will teach fifth- and sixth-grade history," intoned Paul Firestone, the headmaster of the New Rochelle Academy. "You will teach Spanish and French. You will teach ninth- through twelfth-grade Spanish. You will teach Spanish and French in the lower school, grades one and two. And you will be paid $3,600 a year." I thought the salary low, even for 1958, but I had visions of becoming a Bostonian Mr. Chips. I was also overjoyed at having landed my first job. By the end of the school year my joy had abated. Teaching was fun, but commuting and the heavy schedule filled my time to the extent that I was not able to devote any efforts to my one-year timetable to a Master's degree and fame and fortune—to say nothing of trying out some of Errol Flynn's seduction techniques on the glorious women of Manhattan.

The following year I decided to go to graduate school full-time and not hold down a job at all. I rented a small garden apartment on East 64th Street for which I paid $127 a month. Whoever is living there now probably pays six times that amount. I painted the walls of the apartment sandalwood and covered some studio couches in black corduroy. The draperies were yellow felt. A few strolls down Second Avenue resulted in the purchase of a stool with a cane top and some Queen Anne chairs with rush seats. I really liked that apartment. My tastes were still more in the Lodge style—play safe, avoid risks—than reflective of the swashbuckling flair I later adopted as my trademark, but the place made me happy. Besides, I didn't see much of it.

I met all kinds of people on the Upper East Side of Manhattan and in the Village. After class I'd have an espresso and a canoli with friends at the Figaro or the Borgia right across the street, and I'd watch beautiful blackstockinged women come and go. I felt right out of *La Boheme.* One of the many actors hanging out in the Village at the time was Tony Musante, who had been a classmate of mine at Oberlin. He was one of the unknowns in that charmed circle of friends circa 1958 who went on to fame. Another member of the circle was already well known, decorator Leon Hegwood. One night I was at a party, and Leon and I got to talking about what we were doing. When I told him I wasn't sure what I would do with my Master's degree, he said, "Have you ever thought about going into interior design?" I said no, I hadn't. It was the farthest thing from my mind.

But I did have a good business head, a strong arts background, and an appreciation of quality. A friend of my mother's, Daniel Farr, was a New York antique dealer from whom we had acquired some beautiful pieces: tambour desks, Jacobean side tables, some Queen Anne chairs, and Korean dolls that sat in our dining room. So you see, from an early age I had been exposed to many different styles as well as quality furnishings. And I had gotten an *A* in seventh grade mechanical drawing and did minor in fine arts at Oberlin. If I couldn't design sets with Cecil Beaton or get that ambassador's job, I might as well give decorating a thought. "How would you like to work in the Draper office?" Hegwood asked. I thought "Draper" was a clever name for a decorating firm. "Believe me," he added, "all those stories you hear about how fabulous she is as a decorator are true. But you'll meet her. I've bought the firm, but she still consults with the office."

In fact, I didn't even know who Dorothy Draper was, but I figured I had a little time to find out before I reported to work. When I discovered that she was Her Serene Highness, the Queen of Interior Design, I had a heady sensation I was on my way to fame and fortune. Even if I weren't, I didn't have anything to lose.

After so many years of widespread imitation of her style, it is hard to reconstruct the impact Dorothy Draper had on interior design. Suffice it to say that having Dorothy Draper as your decorator was like having Yosuf Karsh take your picture or having Luciano Pavarotti sing at your wedding. She was *IT*, society's most prestigious imprimatur. Whether she designed a single room or a whole hotel, Dorothy Draper's name was the one you wanted to drop. Did you ever wonder why woodwork from coast to coast is enameled white? Because Dorothy Draper decided it should be. After World War II she was riding high, throwing windows wide open and flooding rooms with sunshine, flinging color around like a mad painter. She transformed the dismal military gray/green/beige color scheme of the postwar era.

When she did a job, she would first paint everything white—walls, woodwork, wainscotting, even whole paneled rooms. (Today, restorers all over this land curse her name on the way to the hardware store for another gallon of paint remover.) Then she might paint the ceiling pink, put down a green carpet, bring in a red chair and a black Parsons table, and cover the sofa in a chintz with big blowsy cabbage roses. The result was magic.

Hotels were revolutionized by the wizardry of Dorothy Draper. Before she came along, lobbies all over the country looked pretty much the same: drab walls, Oriental-style rugs, potted palms, and scratchy upholstery. In came Dorothy to "Draperize," a word that was coined to mean give something "the look," fresh, sparkling, and bright, as if a spring breeze were about to billow the curtains. Old, seedy, single-bed hotel rooms were transformed into magnificent places that looked like rooms in a great English country home.

Dorothy Draper's career really took off in the 1920s when she was hired to decorate the Hampshire House in New York City. It was the first major job to display her inimitable style, and the largest decorating job awarded a woman at that time. She installed a plaque on the outside of the hotel, which declared: *Hampshire House, dedicated to the charm of yesterday and the convenience of tomorrow.* Those were not idle words. The sliding-glass shower doors she installed in the bathrooms were copied everywhere, as were the ornate baroque plaster moldings and wallpaper featuring great clusters of her beloved cabbage roses. She went on to Draperize the Essex House in New York City, the Quintandinha Hotel in Petropolis, Brazil, the Arrowhead Springs Hotel in California (a favorite watering spot for movie stars in its day), New York's Plaza Hotel, and the cafeteria of the city's Metropolitan Museum, one of her most successful jobs. There she installed white birdcage chandeliers, painted the walls aubergine, and gave the ceiling a canopy. It earned the nickname The Dorotheum. Today The Dorotheum is repainted beige; the magic has been destroyed. Draper's crown jewel was the Greenbrier Hotel in White Sulphur Springs, West Virginia, where she transformed a hotel used to house Japanese prisoners of war into what many call the most impressive hotel in America.

When she couldn't find the furnishings she needed, she improvised. It was Dorothy Draper who first cut off the legs of oak tables and converted them into low coffee tables. She had cabinetmakers manufacture Parsons tables before they were in style, and she installed big rhododendron hardware on chests to give them a little majesty. Many of her ceilings were painted a light sky blue she called Blue Blossom, and all her jobs were awash with color and lots of it. Mrs. D., as we called her, would often ask us which of two gift packages we would select, one wrapped in plain brown paper and twine or one wrapped in red and white striped paper and tied with a big green bow. Naturally everyone wanted the package à la Draper. She looked at rooms the way she talked about those packages, covering the walls with green and white striped paper, laying Christmas red carpeting on the floor, and covering the furniture in floral splashes of red flowers, green leaves, and aqua bows on a white background. To this lady, everything was a Christmas package. Timid she was not.

From the day she was born Dorothy's father called her "Star." This self-fulfilling prophecy was helped along a little by Dorothy's having been born into one of America's best families. The Tuckermans went back to colonial Connecticut and the signing of the Declaration of Independence. One of Dorothy's nieces is Jacqueline Kennedy Onassis's spokesperson. They had been school chums. Other well-known relatives included Paul Draper the dancer and Ruth Draper the monologist. After Tuxedo Park came Campobello, for Dorothy's husband, George Draper, whom she married in 1912, was Franklin Delano Roosevelt's personal physician. The Drapers were divorced in 1930, at about the time Dorothy was lighting up the field of interior design like a roman candle.

From her successful decorating of residences and hotels Dorothy branched into auto and airplane interiors, and even a floating hotel; and she designed and marketed her own fabrics.

Everything she took on was produced with meticulous attention to detail, from matchbook covers to the brass nailheads (always Number 9) for her beloved black patent leather chairs. And discipline: once she was at the top of her profession, she took a course in how to present merchandise, for she was always eager to learn how to do things better.

Her residential clients were the cream of international society, among them the Duke and Duchess of Windsor, Hope Hampton, and oleomargarine heir Micky Jelke, who later went to jail. A typical Draper Christmas at home featured a living room full of family as well as *Who's Who*. That living room, in the Carlyle Hotel, was one of the most magnificent I have ever seen. The high-ceilinged walls were painted eggplant with white trim. There were beautifully fringed beige draperies at the windows, a peacock blue satin sofa, white carpets on a dark stained floor, and two bright red velvet chairs in front of the fireplace. Basil Rathbone sat in one of those chairs at every Christmas party and read Dickens' *A Christmas Carol* to the distinguished guests seated around him, champagne in hand.

Dorothy was a star, all right, and she was determined to remain one after rising to the top of her industry. When her public relations man, the late Benjamin Sonnenberg, was unable to get her on the cover of *Life* instead of her clients the Duke and Duchess of Windsor, relegating her to the inside pages, people in the office said she was very disappointed, and it was years before she forgave him.

The Draper reputation was one thing; the Draper presence another, and even more awesome. When I joined the firm, Dorothy was in her early seventies; she struck me as a Roman gladiator of a woman, more handsome than pretty. Of course, she had decorated her offices in her unmistakable style. The conference-room walls, for example, were white cane, which contrasted with a black ceiling and a sparkling emerald green carpet. The desks were white laminate with black bases, and the chairs were upholstered in black patent leather. Everything went together to form the perfect background against which interior design presentations could be dramatically spotlighted for the most dazzling effect. The ceilings were illuminated by magical downlights on our interior design sketches, which were strategically placed on easels. The sum total of the room was a dramatic serenity rare to conference rooms, and a foil to the overheated conferences often held there.

Dorothy Draper's presence overpowered any room. In her later years someone had apparently persuaded her to have her nose altered. She had a perfectly beautiful nose to begin with, very classic. That new nose was the only dainty thing about her. She would arrive in the morning in her azalea-colored hat and her azalea, green, and beige tweed cape; she would swoop into her office, remove her long white gloves, and cry, "Who wants me? Who wants me?" Having a conversation with her was nearly always disconcerting. She heard what she wanted to hear and then she tuned out.

Understatement was not her style, and her business tactics matched her forthright personality. She was a fierce competitor. At the time, decorating was one of the few businesses in which women had risen to the top, but no spirit of comaraderie prevailed among the lonely few at the pinnacle. To the contrary. Rather than pull one another up and help each other stay there, the women who headed the top firms were every bit as ruthless as the men. One of Dorothy's rivals was Elizabeth Draper, who was not ruthless, and who had the additional handicap of being the second Mrs. George Draper. The penultimate wife showed her no mercy. As Elizabeth Draper delicately put it, "There was a certain hostility toward anyone with whom she shared the Draper name."

Elizabeth had designed a bank on the corner of 59th Street and Park Avenue, near the offices of Dorothy Draper and Company, and every time we passed it Dorothy would say, "How *dare* that woman use my color combination. The *nerve* of her! It just shows you how little imagination she has of her own." Red and black being Dorothy Draper colors, she apparently regarded anyone else who used the combination guilty of plagiarism, especially if the thief happened to be the woman who had succeeded her as Mrs. George Draper. Elizabeth once crossed Dorothy's path when Elizabeth's firm had a contract ready to sign for a New York hotel job. With everything ready for signatures, Elizabeth got a telephone call from the client-to-be. "Sorry, wrong Draper." Then it was Elizabeth's turn, for Dorothy felt her rival had begun to impinge on her *Who's Who* monopoly. One day we got a call from Barbara Eisenhower. "Could your office send over some of your red and cream chintz, the one Mrs. Draper named the Eisenhower toile?" Mrs. Eisenhower asked. "I want it for my house in Gettysburg." It was Elizabeth Draper who had designed the Eisenhower toile, and it was Elizabeth who was the choice of the Eisenhower family at large for their interiors. By the time we realized Barbara Eisenhower had mistakenly called the wrong Mrs. Draper, Dorothy's wounded ravings could be heard all over the office. In a few years the decorating world would see yet another firm bearing the name of Draper thrown into the fray, but the real tooth-and-claw was yet to come.

As for myself, I was still very much the apprentice, soaking up the look, learning the magic. Yes, it was magic, but the magic had a formula, one that few people understood. It was a combination of scale and color that made incongruous things work. For example, we are all taught in school that red and green are terrible together, except at Christmas, and that only people with a tendency toward the gauche combine yellow and blue or red and purple. Dorothy could combine a red carpet with a green bedspread and a royal blue chair and with the right wall color, the proper scale, and the essential piece of black, she could make it all work. The key was the unexpected, that note in the symphony you're not ready for, the one that startles but never clashes. I understood the unexpected, and since I was a large size myself, I was also at home with the broad sweep, the flair, the willingness to be daring that either comes naturally or doesn't work at all. During those early years at Dorothy Draper and Company I immersed myself in her style, then learned how to make it the basis for my own. Those first paychecks of $326 every two weeks were like a tuition in reverse, for I was getting the very best top-speed advance course in the field of interior design.

I was in awe of Dorothy Draper then. We all were. She was famous, and her life was studded with the *haut monde*. I still didn't know where Sutton Place was, and when I found it, Dorothy had already Draperized a goodly number of the stately residences there. I worked in an office directly opposite hers and was a member of her loyal entourage. When she came out of her office with her coat and hat and announced, "It's time for lunch," we ran for our coats and escorted her out the door. Dorothy was forever dieting, although her announcements of a new diet were often followed by a quick trip downstairs to Schrafft's for four of their big popovers. Having lunch with Dorothy could be a surprise, for you didn't always eat what you had ordered. Once several of us went out to lunch on a Friday. We ordered, and Dorothy said she'd have the Friday Special, which was broiled fish. "I'm dieting," she explained. Someone else ordered a steak.

When the food came, the waiter served Dorothy her fish, and she said, "No, no. He gets the fish. I'm having the steak." One did not argue.

The old-timers in the office told me that Dorothy had a somewhat unusual relationship with her three children. Rumor had it that they didn't live with her much during their growing-up years because Mother was too busy for them. Nevertheless, they were devoted to her, and when Elizabeth became the second Mrs. Draper, they responded to her kindness as well. One evening I went to a restaurant dinner with Dorothy, her eldest daughter Diana, and Leon Hegwood. After dinner we dropped Leon off at his apartment, then took Mrs. Draper to her Carlyle home. On the way Diana whispered to me, "Let's get rid of the old lady and go for a nightcap." It was a bit like sticking out one's tongue at the empress's back, and one of the few demonstrations of a lack of respect on her daughter's part that I can remember. No one was disrespectful then, and certainly not Dorothy's children or her employees.

When Dorothy's young personal secretary became engaged, the office talk was that she and her fiancé stayed in her single girl apartment prior to the wedding. Dorothy was not crazy about the arrangement, being an advocate of a more traditional etiquette. "Why can't that man stay someplace else?" she would complain. "Does he have to check in before they're even married?" However Dorothy may have fulfilled the role of motherhood, her children as well as the young people on her staff seemed to have a genuine affection for her, and knew how to ignore the bluster.

There was a girlish side to Dorothy as well. When Edward R. Murrow was to interview her for his "Person to Person" television show, she broke out in a fit of giggles as the technicians wired her for sound. Another time, we were staying at the Greenbrier and sat one night in the Old White Club, and when the band struck up "The Fabulous Shack in the Hills of West Virginia," one of Dorothy's favorites, incongruously enough, she asked me to dance. It was a memorable scene: the stately Mrs. Draper in the arms of her twenty-two-year-old decorating assistant, a man she had yet to brand her enemy. There were other good moments, but most of the times I remember were not good, unfortunately, and even these rare lighthearted moments were soon to vanish. It was a halcyon period, those years I spent as a loyal courtier to the High Priestess of Decorating.

In spite of my respect for her design talents, it was obvious to me that Dorothy Draper was not adept at running the financial end of her business. Historically, people in design firms do not have the best business heads, but Dorothy's cavalier attitude toward money stood out in a field already overcrowded with spendthrifts. She went through a $150,000 fee for designing the interior of the Convair 880 jets like Grant took Richmond. The problem was, when she went through her money, she simply called her brother on Wall Street and told him to send up some more. This became a habit, and her extravagance was one of the main topics of discussion at office confabs. Mrs. Draper, it seemed, was getting more and more difficult to handle, and her cost overruns could not go on.

Other disturbing behavior patterns seemed to be intensifying. She had always been a little scatterbrained. I remember one afternoon when she announced to one and all that we were going to see *Gone With the Wind* with her that evening. It had just been rereleased, and she was enchanted all over again with the use of color and the antebellum atmosphere of the film, and wanted to demonstrate how we could adopt some of the style. The lecture was not forthcoming. The credits rolled as we all sat in dutiful silence, awaiting the *GWTW*-in-the-living-room lecture, but by the time Scarlett had met Rhett in the library, Dorothy was sound asleep. The music swelled, and she woke up and exclaimed, "Oh! I've seen this movie before. Let's go." And we all marched out to her waiting limousine.

The forgetfulness was becoming more and more noticeable. Late one afternoon her chauffeur called the office. Although Dorothy Draper and Company was then located at 5 East 57th Street and Bonwit Teller was right across the street, she always had her chauffeur drive her over to Bonwit's for a little lunch-hour shopping, wait in the limousine, then drive her back to her apartment or office. It was past four o'clock when the chauffeur called, and he was concerned. Mrs. Draper had gone into Bonwit's at 12:30 and had not come out. Did we think someone should go looking for her? We called her apartment at the Carlyle. Madame was at home. She had finished shopping hours ago, had taken a taxi home, and was having high tea.

So far, her idiosyncrasies had been minor, more a matter of inconvenience than anything else. When her memory losses started jeopardizing the business, however, we began to worry. Dorothy was increasingly hostile to some clients and approached others with total amnesia. The office had just completed a Stouffer's restaurant in Garden City, Long Island. It was a big chain, and an important account. Dorothy had designed the restaurant in Victorian, unusual for the time, and it was spectacular with its red flocked walls, tufted chairs, and big-ball light fixtures. One day Mrs. Draper swooped into the restaurant with several of the staff in her wake and shook hands with Vernon Stouffer, who had been waiting for the Draper group to arrive for a final tour of the completed job. It is said that Dorothy had been vague all day. She walked around the restaurant with a look of distaste on her face, then turned to Mr. Stouffer and said, "Oh, Vernon, I must say it—this upholstery is so—it's wrong! The fixtures are all out of scale. Vernon, I must do this restaurant." To which Mr. Stouffer replied, "Mrs. Draper, you've just done it."

One day I made a trip with her by train to Philadelphia to help publicize Cooper River Plaza, a high-rise apartment complex in Pennsauken, New Jersey. The office had decorated lobbies, corridors, and model apartments, and we were to be interviewed by Grace Madley, the decorating editor of the *Philadelphia Enquirer*. Several public relations people from Cooper River Plaza came with us to lunch. Dorothy had been far from her best of late, and to compound her disgruntled mood she wasn't crazy about decorating the lobbies of Cooper River Plaza anyway; she felt the job was beneath her. The owners, she complained, were capitalizing on her name and taking too much of her time for what she considered a nuts-and-bolts job. Such was the proliferation of Draper rooms that the lunch just happened to be held in a dining room she had decorated, in the Barclay Hotel. She sat on one of her beloved black patent leather chairs, surrounded by one of her typical color schemes of pale blue, citrus green, and black, and was more than vague and less than charming. She was also very tired.

After the luncheon we boarded the train for New York, accompanied by one of the Cooper River PR men. "I read your column last week, Mrs. Draper," he said, referring to her widely syndicated "Ask Dorothy Draper." "I thought your ideas about color coordination were most interesting."

"Really," she said, and by the look in her eyes I knew she was tuning out.

"But what did you mean by . . ." As the conversation continued I realized that Dorothy had never seen, let alone written, the column the man was talking about. Of course, her column writing had always been done in conjunction with members of her staff, and she rarely put words on paper herself, but I assumed she was still telling the writers what to write. Obviously she was not. It was just one more indication that she was losing touch.

The more I learned from Dorothy Draper, the more I traveled with her, soothed her, and learned to outwit her craziness, the more I realized she was losing her grip. As she became less and less in touch with reality, I somehow began to emerge as the enemy. She now regarded me as Leon Hegwood's henchman, an employee who dared to critize her and who was a threat to her hegemony. At first her animosity toward me was communicated by a chill wind every time she passed my desk. Later her displeasure showed in more obvious ways. One Christmas she passed out gifts to everyone on the staff but me. I was getting the message that war had been officially declared on the fair-haired boy.

Then Dorothy's forgetfulness really began to go public. Senility is always hard to witness, especially in a loved one, and even in someone who has declared you her enemy. We cannot help taking senility personally—after all, if we live long enough, it happens to all of us, that terrible frustration of being unable to function in small, ordinary ways. In many old people the confusion of senility has an endearing quality to it, but in Dorothy's case her memory loss made her angry and ill-tempered. Dorothy was not confused when her memory took a siesta; she was furious. And in her fury she did harm. One of her most famous jobs was the Greenbrier Hotel. The office had just completed decorating the elegant Crystal Room in the hotel, and the management arrived at the 57th Street office for a meeting with Mrs. Draper. She acted toward them with such hostility that the Greenbrier executives were obviously upset. When Truman Wright, general manager of the hotel, criticized a color scheme she had chosen, Dorothy threw her arms in the air and shouted, "Well, Truman, maybe *you'd* like to do the room."

Leon Hegwood found it impossible to criticize her. He adored her for what she stood for in the business, and regarded himself as her most loyal associate. No one, it seemed, could come forward and simply tell her to behave herself. Well, not quite. There was someone who would, and did. Me. You can imagine how she took to being criticized by "Leon's fair-haired boy." It was obvious to me why the business was faltering, and I talked to Hegwood daily about her destructive activities and utter disregard for money.

When I came to the office in 1960, the firm had just been sold to Hegwood and two other investors. Although Dorothy was still chairman of the board and a director of the company, she did not own it. She owned only the nonvoting first preferred stock of the corporation. Selling the company had come about at the urging of her brother. The money she had spent on decorating and design staff, personal office, secretaries, the vast apartment at the Carlyle, and, at times, limousines around the clock had alarmed the money nannies in charge of her trust fund to the point where they would not let her high-handedness go on any longer.

While Dorothy seemed to be losing her grip on reality, I also suffered a personal tragedy. I lost both my parents within a short time. Their deaths came suddenly, and the loss left me reeling. My mother was only forty-nine when she died of injuries incurred falling down a flight of stairs in our Nahant home. A year and a half later, my father died at age fifty-four, having been unable to get over the loss of my mother, on whom he was both mentally and physically dependent.

My parents' will left me with enough money to acquire two-thirds of the common stock in Dorothy Draper and Company. When I agreed to purchase the common stock from Leon Hegwood, I believed that I was literally investing in my own future. Meanwhile, the skirmishes had begun in earnest. Mrs. Draper was being urged by her brother to get out of the business completely, to retire and enjoy the fruits of her well-earned fame (as well as keep out of serious financial trouble). She wouldn't hear of it. Hegwood and the firm's lawyers, accountants, and other experts suggested to her that she give up her first preferred stock. If she relinquished the stock, Hegwood was willing to let her do whatever she pleased. She could decorate lampposts, she could redo the whole of south shore of Long Island, she could sit in a sunny room all day and draw wallpaper designs. She could do whatever her heart desired, and give full attention to her wishes without the burdens of managing the business. Because of Mrs. D.'s age, Hegwood and I thought she would do none of these things. We were wrong.

Mrs. Draper had developed a close ally, a former staff member I shall call Ivan, who whispered in her ear, "Do what they want, Mrs. Draper. Give up the first preferred stock, and then you'll be free. We'll open a new Dorothy Draper and start all over, free and clear of those terrible people who want to ruin you!"

Dorothy was all ears; the designer pressed on. "We'll get them coming and going," he chortled in the privacy of her study. "We'll relinquish to them Dorothy Draper and Company's first preferred stock and use the firm Dorothy Draper Enterprises in competition with them." (Dorothy Draper Enterprises had been established for her column and other related activities.) "We'll write all your clients and tell them there's been a little change — you're now known as Dorothy Draper Enterprises. How can we lose?"

Towering over him like a gladiator, Mrs. Draper went everywhere on the arm of Ivan. And the maneuvers went on and on. Hegwood was at wit's end. Finally, just when it looked as if the white cane walls of Dorothy Draper and Company were about to fall in, Dorothy agreed to relinquish the stock. She was to lose her first preferred stock in the corporation but was to go on doing whatever she pleased, not limiting her activities exclusively to the creative end of the business. Ivan was to run the business part of Dorothy Draper Enterprises.

Every day Mrs. Draper and Ivan sailed in and sailed out of the 57th Street office, getting ready to start their new venture. Meanwhile, "Ask Dorothy Draper" appeared on schedule, and all over the world people continued to receive the Dorothy Draper touch. Then one day Dorothy and Ivan didn't show up at the office. Neither did her secretary. By the end of the day we discovered what had happened: not only had Mrs. D. walked out as a consultant to the design firm, she was now head of a competing interior design firm, Dorothy Draper Enterprises Inc. And at her side was the ambitious Ivan. Dorothy had even taken office space for her new firm in the Turtle Bay area of the East 40s.

Her coup had taken us by surprise. At first her tactics seemed rather petty, as if she was piqued but not really able to make an effective counterattack. Then came the storm. She wrote a haughty letter informing us, among other things, that if we ever used her picture in our company activities she would sue. Her secretary came in with two large Bonwit Teller shopping bags and began stripping the place of Mrs. Draper's personal belongings. And that was only the beginning. One morning we came in and found the files had been rifled. Boxes and boxes stuffed with file folders had apparently been spirited away in the night to a waiting Mrs. Draper, her fury now unslakable. Then our mail stopped coming. We found she had cut off our letters at the post office and had them rerouted to her apartment, where she or her apartment staff went through every piece and passed on to us only what they didn't want. Staff stealing was rampant. Dorothy promised potential defectors the earth in a bright red bow, and many could not refuse. Others in the office were discovered to be undercover agents for Dorothy Draper Enterprises, passing on vital information to Control Central at the Carlyle. And her company somehow got listed directly *above* our name in the Manhattan Yellow Pages. There was simply no end to it.

Dorothy then announced she was an industrial design firm as well as an interior design firm, which translated to mean she could do absolutely anything she wanted and not be guilty of breach of contract. She could take on Celanese as well as the Windsors. She could design three-dimensional products. She did go on to do beautiful fabrics and wallpapers for Schumacher called the Viennese Collection, and a second collection, also Viennese, for Henredon. She took to calling herself "*Mrs.* Dorothy Draper." I don't know what the current Mrs. Draper did to distinguish her decorating firm from Dorothy's and ours, but she must have had to call herself "*Mrs. Elizabeth* Draper." The confusion bordered on madness. How diabolically clever of her, I thought, to dub herself Mrs. Dorothy Draper, leaving the obvious impression that she was the famous head of Dorothy Draper and Company as well as its subsidiary, Dorothy Draper Enterprises! The legal battles were endless. I sometimes thought her tactics worthy of a Bonaparte.

Worst of all was the client stealing. She swooped down, by mail and telephone, on the heads of just about every hotel, castle, mansion, and estate Dorothy Draper and Company had ever decorated. She wanted them back, every one. Many were the horror stories she served up to her clients about that terrible Carleton Varney and that awful Leon Hegwood. Going out on maintenance trips became forays into free-fire zones; you never knew whether the client was on the side of Draper or Draper. I paid a visit to the Greenbrier not long after the general manager had returned from the meeting in New York at which Dorothy had told him if he didn't like her color selection, he could do the job himself. At first it appeared that her fence mending had been successful. I was approached by the hotel's social hostess, who said to me in a decidedly antisocial way, "I could kill you, you hear?" Of all Dorothy's treasures, those far-flung oases of sparkling white enamel and sunny chintz, the Greenbrier was quintessential Draper, the most highly prized jewel in her crown. And she wanted it back.

But the Greenbrier stayed with our firm, and after a prolonged siege we also retained Dromoland Castle; but as the Draper wars went on year after year, we lost some and held on to others. It was exhausting, to say the least. I felt like I was in the London blitz: I knew the next bomb was sure to come, but I didn't know where or when.

Dorothy's tactics soon got too downright wicked not to be noticed and condemned by people in the decorating trade, and her mental and physical states were deteriorating more rapidly than ours. Most damaging to her cause was her increasing senility. Had it evidenced itself in a more charming manner, I think some of her clients would have clung to her out of loyalty, but she was by now so angry, as well as befuddled, that she did herself in. One evening she attended the opening of the new wing of the International Hotel at JFK airport, which she had designed—that is, which Dorothy Draper and Company had designed. All the dignitaries were there for the gala opening, forming a semicircle around the guests as they stepped out of their limousines. Out of one limousine, looking haughty, came Mrs. Draper and her Ivan. Their attendance, of course, was more than ceremonial. It was a deliberate ploy to foster more confusion in the minds of everyone present, client and potential client, as to who was what at Dorothy Draper and Company.

She was dressed with her usual flair, complete with flowered hat and long gloves. She and Ivan approached the waiting brass to shake the hand of the chairman of the board of Knott hotels, owners of the property. They had met many times during the design phase of the job. As he shook her hand, she said imperiously, "Who are you and what are you doing here?" It was not the way to win over a client.

The Draper wars lasted nearly eight years. Dorothy spent the last of them, through Dorothy Draper Enterprises, fighting to discredit Dorothy Draper and Company from a nursing home in Cleveland. To the outside world all seemed well. "Ask Dorothy Draper" appeared as usual in newspapers all over the country. The industry and the public had no idea that Dorothy Draper was in a nursing home, attending to the simple things in life. These were trying years. Toward the end, her campaign was reduced to the ravings of a Lear, mad and somewhat pathetic. When she died at age seventy-nine, her highly successful confusion tactics concerning who was the real Dorothy Draper finally backfired. As the syndicated column cancellations came pouring in, a reporter for the *New York Times* called me about her obituary. Could I clarify some things? It was an error of identification that may have helped the company. I explained that he had reached the wrong Dorothy Draper, and then I explained why. I told the *Times* reporter the whole sad, crazy story. When the obituary appeared, the reporter had left out the story of the Draper wars, but he did write: "Associates in her company said Mrs. Draper's enthusiasm led to widespread publicity for her, but the company was not a financial success. . . . It is now operated by Carleton Varney, a well-known industry figure. For a time Mrs. Draper operated a smaller concern called Dorothy Draper Enterprises."

Those words helped keep the firm from going under. The survival rate of interior design firms succeeding once the founder dies is minimal. Like the descendants of Elizabeth Arden or Helena Rubenstein, I was now in a position of carrying on after the giantess had fallen. Hardly anybody in the industry gave me a chance of surviving. The fact that I lasted I attribute to the stamina of youth. Now I find I need to sleep every night.

Only the family was invited to the private funeral ceremony at Newport, but I sent a special floral piece that I knew she would have loved, a massive cabbage rose made out of rose petals. Like the lady herself, and like her concept of design, the funeral ceremony had its unexpected moments. A close friend of the family told me that Dorothy's son, at one time a newspaper foreign correspondent, played "Mine Eyes Have Seen the Glory of the Coming of the Lord" on the harmonica. The hymn was a favorite of Mrs. Draper.

As for Mrs. Draper's daughters, the eldest, a warm, funny, and appealing woman, committed suicide. The younger daughter lives in the Midwest and is involved in educational pursuits. I understand she is a credit to her illustrious family. Dorothy's former husband, George Draper, died after spending nearly a decade in a wheelchair. Elizabeth is still active and a remarkably youthful eighty-one. As for Dorothy, she lives on; vestiges of her legacy can be found all over, in unlikely places and at unexpected moments.

She was a great decorator—maybe the greatest!

In 1976 I was designing and decorating an Egyptian night-club called Ibis on 50th Street near the Waldorf Towers. The decor was to be tongue-in-cheek nouveau Egyptian because the club's opening coincided with the King Tut craze inspired by the Metropolitan Museum's exhibit. To celebrate the club's opening, a charity gala was to be arranged, "Fourth of July in Old New York," in honor of the Bicentennial, with Angie Biddle-Duke as guest speaker. Following his little talk there would be some sultry dancing by the Ibis dancing girls, including club owner Samiha Koura's special holiday number, belly dancing with a lighted chandelier on her head.

Ibis just happened to be on the site of the glorious old Versailles restaurant, which had been one of Dorothy Draper's early projects. Edith Piaf had sung there when she was the chanteuse of New York, and I had seen pictures in the company files of the restaurant in its heyday in the 1930s. Between the Versailles and the Ibis, the place had been many other things, including a pizza parlor and a spot called Hippodrome. As we went to work clearing out the place, I found vestiges of all its earlier incarnations in stratified layers. First, workmen uncovered remnants of its 1960s image, early hip discothèque. Next to be exposed were Neapolitan murals, artifacts of its pizza parlor days. And underneath it all, the Egyptian atmosphere having by then permeated my brain, I felt something like a thrill of an archeologist discovering a pharaoh's burial chamber as the workmen exposed a vivid lime green wall and ornate plaster moldings of heroic size. Authentic early Draper. Unlike the poet lamenting over shattered visages in the sand, I didn't stand there and contemplate the ephemeral nature of human accomplishment. How could I when, a few steps away, in many a Waldorf Tower room the Draper touch lived on, as bold and bright as ever?

Here's a toast to Dorothy Draper, the person who bravely liberated the country from its self-imposed drabness. In spite of all my wounds I'm proud to be president of a company that still bears her name. Wherever she is, I hope it is a place full of bright color and roses.

Photographed by Joe Griffith

Ethel Merman. Is this Chinese porcelain really a crystal ball? The young decorator contemplates the future.

Photographed by Bettina Cirone

"How my tabby cats would love to get their claws into these threads."
Van Johnson plays client to my decorator in the Carleton V New York
Showroom.

"The Party's Over"—no one can sing that song like Polly Bergen. And
few can top her relaxed intimate parties either.

Photographed by Bettina Cirone

Chapter 2

Three Stars in My Crown:
Ethel Merman, Van Johnson, Polly Bergen

America's greatest Broadway musical comedy star came into my life when I was still learning the ropes at Dorothy Draper. The morning I was to meet her, I put on my most serious business suit, for I wanted to appear older than my age. At ten o'clock I went to my client's apartment at the Old Park Lane Hotel, and she greeted me at the door dressed in a black satin shimmy-style dress with a deep collar and long fringes. As I had been brought up to believe that fringe was best worn after dark, I was a little awestruck. On the other hand, how would such a flamboyant lady look in a sedate black suit? Now, *that* would have been a shocker.

In spite of her bold look, I soon discovered that my client was keeping her distance. I had a feeling she instinctively mistrusted strangers until they had proven themselves trustworthy. I was later to learn that my observation had been especially keen.

It was 1964. Ethel was moving out of the Park Lane because it was set for demolition, and she had just leased a two-bedroom apartment in the Berkshire Hotel on Madison Avenue and 52nd Street. The windows all looked uptown, and the view was terrific, the perfect nighttime backdrop for a star. The Berkshire at the time was owned by the Knott Hotels Corporation, and as interior design consultant for them, I was given the assignment of redecorating Ethel Merman's apartment. The Knott people had agreed to supply carpeting, draperies, and some furnishings to her taste, coordinating them with the furnishings she wanted to bring to her new home.

I admit I was in awe of my client. I had seen her in *Gypsy* when I had first come to New York and had fallen under her spell. Nor could I ever forget her *Annie Get Your Gun* at Lincoln

Center and that big, brassy voice of hers that no one in the world could imitate. Ethel, on the other hand, was "on stage" most of the time I spent with her. She was very wary of her decorator, as she was with most people she didn't know well.

Ethel reserves her enormous store of affection for a select few. She was closer to her parents than anyone I have ever seen. Pop Zinmerman was a handsome white-haired man, the sort of granddad everyone wanted, and Ethel's mother was warm but more proper and straitlaced than Pop. Her parents doted on their Little Eth, as they called her, and Ethel was the world's greatest daughter. She later had me decorate another apartment in the Berkshire for her Mom and Pop, directly below her own so that she could be close to them. When her mother was dying, Ethel sat with her throughout her final illness, along with a round-the-clock companion and nurse, Catherine. Later, when Ethel's father was dying, she lavished the same care on him. She was not about to send her beloved Mom and Pop to a nursing home, for she doted on them as much as they doted on their Little Eth.

That first apartment I decorated for her in the Berkshire was to be chapter 1 in the mellowing of Ethel Merman. Appropriately, the predominant color was fire-engine red. Later, she softened her color schemes to reflect her changing personality, but in the beginning her color scheme was bold, bright, and brassy, a true *Hello, Dolly!* apartment. The rug was red, the draperies were white, and the sofas were upholstered in a light blue tweed. Big red velvet wing chairs provided further visual stimulation. I called that apartment her red, white, and blue star-spangled all-American home. All it lacked was drum and bugle music for a doorbell.

The second apartment I did for her was still colorful, but softer and less violent. It had a frosted pink ceiling in the bed-room and chintz draperies of frosting pink, white, lilac, and emerald green flowers. The carpet was strawberry. In the living room she chose a bright yellow ceiling and yellow and black and green chintz in the draperies and furniture. All the apartments I did for her had a lime green library where a big painting from the *Showbill* cover of *Panama Hattie* hung over the sofa. The painting had been a gift to Ethel from Robert Levitt, her first husband. The second apartment didn't set off alarm bells like the first one did. Instead, it was like a big sweet tropical ice-cream confection.

Her current apartment is even softer. It was 1978, and Ethel had been through many heartbreaks since the first apartment had been completed for her in 1964. The latest apartment is basically white with soft lavender and hunter green. Gone are the electric colors. Gone too is Ethel's wariness and impatience, and as the years pass she becomes more lighthearted and easier to be around. When it comes to paying her bill, she's apt to say, "OK, let's take a look at the national debt."

I've had one falling out with Ethel Merman over the sixteen years I've known her, and it resulted from her suspicions that I was trying to use her. The lady is not one to be used as a stepping-stone for greater rewards, and over the years she has had ample reason to be suspicious. She's met just about everyone in show business, but she clings to old and trusted friends. When she went on a tour to promote her autobiography, a friend from Babylon, Long Island accompanied her, a girl Ethel had met during the days she worked as a stenographer.

If I was trying to use Ethel, it was only my error in assuming that she was among society's legions who believe in exchanging favors. I was doing my designing work at Ibis, the club where I had unearthed vestiges of my mentor, Dorothy Draper, and I involved Ethel in a charity event. I had great hopes at the time that Ibis would become the new El Morocco, a place for East Siders, show people, and columnists to drop in every night. The club was planning to celebrate its opening by holding a charity gala. The club owners had agreed to donate the club and a good portion of the food costs to the Bicentennial committee, for which the event was being held, and I was asked to turn out some stars. I put together a list of fifty or sixty people to invite, all of whom I thought would lend glamour to what I felt would be a glamorous evening. Among the stars on my list was Ethel Merman. I invited her and a date as my personal guests, and Dorothy Draper and Company paid for the $100-a-head tickets. I knew Ethel's presence would guarantee a mention in every society page in town, and the club would be off to a fine start.

Ethel agreed to come if I would seat her at my table. When the day arrived for the celebration I wanted to spread the stars around so I placed Ethel at a table with my friends Donald and Janet Chipman, art dealer Marjorie Reed and a male decorator who is warm and funny and rather outrageous. I thought Ethel would enjoy his humor, but I was wrong. I was on the dance floor with my wife when Ethel stormed up to us and hissed, "Don't you *ever* put me in this position again. You have seated me with people I don't even know, and here I've come as your guest to have a good time!" With that she left the Ibis, huffing and puffing, with her bewildered escort, a New York public relations man who handled a Puerto Rican rum account. She created quite a stir, but there was nothing to do but reassemble the seating and go on, Ethel or no Ethel, and hope somehow to mend her outraged feelings.

Aside from the mellowing, another wonderful thing about Ethel is her incredible energy. She keeps herself busy doing concerts with the Philharmonic and symphony orchestras, The Boston Pops, making records, appearing on talk shows, and going all over the country to promote her records and autobiography. But she will no longer take on a long and tiring Broadway run. Ethel is now seventy-one, and her entire life, she says, has been "theater to hotel to sleep to matinee to hotel to rest to theater." She never stops, and her energy is all her own special supply of adrenalin. She's one of those rare performers who takes no drugs, whether alcohol or weed or pills, to perform. Merman is sane at all times, and all I've ever seen her drink is her beloved Almaden Chablis wine. Why not? Like Van Johnson and Polly Bergen, Ethel has no need to put on the dog. What you see is what you get when you walk into her living room. Everything reflects her and no one else.

Ethel has never forgotten her origins. In fact, when she moved to Manhattan, she took a little of Astoria with her. She surrounds herself with Victoriana and china figurines. Her tabletops overflow with the bibelots one associates with Astoria around 1930. She loves statuary and lamps with quaint porcelain bases and equally quaint shades. Her big brass bed is accesorized with dolls. And then there are her pictures. She has them everywhere, so many it takes a full day to hang them all. Some of her oils are very good, and others she hangs for sentimental value. Over the years I've become her favorite picture hanger, and I amaze her every time. "How do you get them just right without measuring?" she says as I line them up with one eye and a finger on the wall. "How do you hit high notes?" I answer. Practice makes perfect.

Another feature common to all her apartments is an elaborate supply of locks on all the doors. One evening when she was living in the Berkshire Hotel apartment, she came home from a performance of *Hello, Dolly!* to find her apartment in a shambles. The bedroom had been torn apart, her safe opened with a blowtorch. Gone was all her jewelry. She was never comfortable again in that apartment, and soon moved into another in the same hotel. The new apartment had only one set of keys—hers—for all those locks, and maids had to arrive at a time when Ethel or the hotel manager was there to let them in.

One reason Ethel likes hotel living is the services. The lady is definitely not the domestic type. In fact, over the years her kitchens have become more and more minimal to the point where they have all but disappeared. In that first apartment her kitchen cupboards were filled with row upon row of canned meatballs. I don't know whether Ethel ate them for late-night snacks or whether they were left over from a cocktail party. Her custom, for as long as I have known her, is to entertain at home only for cocktails, then take her guests out to dinner. Now Ethel has relinquished cooking and all its accouterments completely. When I moved her into her current apartment she insisted that the stove be removed. Not only doesn't she cook but she's also afraid of gas. The stove was sent to the basement, and the gas pipes were capped. "All I need is something to boil water on," she says, and the only cooking appliance in her present kitchen is a small hotplate.

Ethel is one star who doesn't need to put on the dog. She drinks Almaden wine because she likes it. She doesn't care that her furnishings are considered passé, that bronzes and china figurines are currently out. She likes what she likes, and in time her tastes may be all the rage. Already antiques investors are taking a new interest in bronze sculpture. Ethel's rooms work for her because the objects she lives with have a meaning and a purpose. Everything says "Ethel Merman," and the overall effect is successful because its statement is strong and truthful.

Although Ethel herself may have changed, her show business career has remained the same—vibrant and successful. Unfortunately, her private life has been full of disappointments and tragedy. Just about everybody knows about her brief, disastrous marriage to actor Ernest Borgnine. She handled that marriage in one page of her autobiography: blank. But there were other disasters in her life that are not so well known. Her first husband, Robert Levitt, brother of the late New York State comptroller Arthur Levitt, committed suicide. Their daughter, Ethel, died in 1967 in Colorado at the early age of twenty-four, leaving behind a husband and two small children. The death may or may not have been unintentional. Ethel's son, Bobby Levitt, a wonderful man, lives in California or Hawaii in a house/bus. Shortly after Ethel's daughter died, Bobby's wife, actress Barbara Colby, was shot to death in a Hollywood parking lot by an unknown assailant in July of 1975. She had been attending a meditation meeting. Yet another of Ethel's marriages ended in divorce, the one to Bob Six, president of Continental Airways. Ethel implies that she was the one who paid most of the bills. One time I asked Ethel to introduce me to Bob Six as I hoped to do some airplane interiors for him. "Don't use my name with that man," she said flatly. "It'll get you nowhere."

In one way, Ethel has come a long way from Astoria, and in another way she never left it. She brought enough of it with her to always feel at home. In the meantime, as the strong-willed and ambitious Ethel Zinmerman has matured and mellowed, she's learned to be more tolerant of the outside world. I remember one night when she was at our apartment for dinner. After dessert we retired to the living room, and I put a Merman record on the stereo. As the old familiar "Have an egg roll, Mr. Goldstone" filled the room, several guests started to dance. At first Ethel looked displeased. The star dislikes hearing her own voice on records and never plays her own music in her home. People weren't supposed to get up and dance when Ethel Merman sang. They were supposed to sit still and listen. But as the number went on and the dancing did too, she started to relax. In fact, she seemed to be enjoying herself. After all, she seemed to have concluded, why shouldn't people dance to Ethel Merman?

         *   *   *

Van Johnson is probably the most unpretentious movie star in the world. What else can you say about a man who names his cats Sam, Kitty, Fred, and Bo? "Is that spelled Beau?" I asked him.

"Nah. Bo. Like in Derek."

Van is apt to deflate any and all puffery with boisterous good humor. Hearing someone speak of spending the summer in Westhampton, he's liable to raise one eyebrow and say incredulously, "Not East Hampton?" With equal gusto he ridicules his own past pretenses. "In California I had all the status symbols," he said. "Houses in Palm Springs, Santa Monica, at the beach, in the desert. Nine meals were served—the staff, the help, the kids, whoever—before I ever came down for my own. I had tennis courts, swimming pools, projection rooms, Cadillacs—ludicrous! I look back on all those years and I laugh my head off."

But Van Johnson is a man who has little desire to mull over the past. He forgets his accomplishments like other people forget old telephone numbers. "When were you the top box-office attraction?" I asked him once. "Wasn't it in 1947?"

"I wonder," he replied. "I really don't remember. I remember Pearl Harbor and my birthday and that's about it." Even last week's accomplishments do a fast fadeout. I recently had lunch with him at New York's Chantilly on East 57th Street, after he had just finished a film in California with Ava Gardner and Hal Holbrook. "What's the name of the picture?" I asked. "The President's Been Kidnapped—Somebody Kidnapped the President—something like that," he said.

Van Johnson is consumed with the present, which he ingests with gusto and discrimination through all his senses. He's not a shy man by any means, but when it comes to providing details of his personal style, he draws a curtain around his privacy. I'm afraid *Architectural Digest* will never photograph his Sutton Place penthouse. "I don't want any cameras in my private life. All the privacy I've got left in the whole world are those four walls." If a question seems to invade areas of his life that are closed to public scrutiny, he abruptly changes the topic. When I asked him whether his mother, who abandoned the family when Van was very young, had ever remarried, his response was, "Yes. Several times. Have you ever been to Brooklyn's Gage and Tollner restaurant?"

Ask Van about his origins, the kinds of questions that send other people into rhapsodic sagas, and you're likely to be answered with a joke, a nonsequitur, or just plain nonsense. *What was Rhode Island like?* Small. *Where was he born?* In a house, in a trunk at the Princess Theater, on Ayrult Street, Newport, Rhode Island. His father, Charles E. Johnson, was a plumber, "the best plumber in Newport." Van was an only child, something he regards as an act of mercy on his parents. "Thank God, one like me was enough." His mother left the family after three years of marriage. "She flew the coop very early. I was brought up by my father and my little Swedish grandmother."

"Why did she fly?" I asked.

"I think she was bored."

Life as the son of the best plumber in Newport, Rhode Island, meant seeing the inside of a lot of marble palaces. "I used to sweep up the bathhouses at Bailey's Beach for ninety dollars a week. My father took care of all the big houses around Newport, summer cottages as they called them." It was Charles Johnson who turned off the water every fall at the "cottages" of the Vanderbilts and Whitneys. "I realized there was a whole world outside Newport, and I wanted some of it," Van told me.

Although he didn't stay put for long, he remains proud of his New England roots. Like his father, who died in the ancestral home in Newport, Van is still a true New Englander. "Just the smell of a fish net makes me go berserk," he says. "Anything New England I collect—shells, seaweed, lobsters. . . . I love to go to Maine. I love the people. I love ship models. I love the crashing of the ocean against the rocks."

But, like his mother, Van left Newport early to see the world. Right after high school graduation in 1934, he came to New York. "I wanted the theater, I wanted to be a New Yorker. I wanted that eight-thirty curtain. It's much more civilized than getting up at five A.M. I had no thought of the movies at all." His first show was *Entre Nous* at the Cherry Lane theater in Greenwich Village. "That was before off-off Broadway was chic." One year after his arrival in New York, Van made it to Broadway. The cast of *New Faces* included such future stars as Imogene Coca, Henry Fonda, and Gypsy Rose Lee. Next came vaudeville on the borscht circuit in New York's Catskill Mountains. "Jan Murray was the emcee. We did everything—danced, sang, did sketches." Then back to New York and Agnes DeMille's *Oklahoma*. During his bachelor years in the theater, he began a lifelong custom of living in hotels. In those days it was the Knickerbocker, long closed. Next came Hollywood and a poignant airport farewell from the *Oklahoma* cast. And the rest is film history.

Many stars of that era talk about the studio system as a form of slavery in which their lives were regulated by evil movie moguls. Not so with Van. "How controlled were you at Metro?" I asked him. "Completely, thank God," he answered. "If you had to be controlled by somebody, Louis B. Mayer was the finest."

But Van scoffs at the idea that Mayer controlled his private life. He insists he never got called in and reprimanded about anything he did with his life. "How could I? I was too busy doing six pictures a year to do anything scandalous. I didn't have the strength!" He talks about going out in a group with Judy Garland, June Allyson, Gloria DeHaven, and other stars as if they were chaste kids on a school holiday. "Film stars today are a different breed. It's a whole new business. I don't know them. I really don't want to know them."

"But didn't you object to the dictatorial aspects of the studio system?" I protested.

"No. I'm a servant. I like being told what to do. I need it."

During his Hollywood years, as a family man Van lived in a series of lavish houses in Palm Springs, Santa Monica, and Beverly Hills. I asked him whether he found living in houses during this period caused him to put down some West Coast roots.

"In California? Never. There are no roots in California. I was always glad to walk in the front door, but I knew one day I'd be back East where I was brought up. I missed the seasons terribly when I lived in California. I'm not knocking it. It's just that I have my roots in New England." Those houses were furnished without the help of a decorator. "I just went into stores and bought things," Van recalls. "The look was Early Cluttered. Even Sutton Place is getting too cluttered." He has a penchant for all things from England, Old and New, and collects pewter, English antiques, and English painters.

One of the problems about asking Van about his style preferences is that he loves so many things. I asked him about his favorite homes during those golden Hollywood years and his favorite people to visit. "Oh, there were so many! I loved to go to Doris and Jules Styne's because they had such good taste, all those English pieces from Partridge's. Jack and Anne Warner had a beautiful formal French château-type house. I loved to go there too. And Mr. Mayer—he had impeccable taste."

But his favorite? "Roz and Freddie's." That would be, of course, the late Rosalind Russell and her husband, Freddie Brisson. "I always knew I'd have a great time there. It was a special place to really relax. The best food: Mary Benny's! I always had a marvelous time there because Barbara Stanwyck, all the people I loved best, would be there. Mary always ran a movie. The best food . . ."

Food is an all-consuming passion. Van becomes downright eloquent when the subject is where to go around the country for the best food. When you live the life of a theatrical gypsy, knowing where to find a good restaurant becomes crucial. Over lunch we reminisced about a marvelous Chinese restaurant in Corning, New York, and about where to get the best food in New Orleans. When the hors d'oeuvres came around, he groaned, "Oh my God, that lamb is gone already." He ordered a lobster appetizer, being a professed collector of all things from New England, and I ordered shrimp. I'm a passionate eater myself, so as we ate, we talked about food. Van said, "I love to talk about food. I love reading about food. The first thing I do when I check into a hotel after I've unpacked is jump into bed and read all the room-service menus."

I told him I had put on twenty pounds after Dr. Tarnower, my diet warden, was shot to death, and to shed some weight, I ordered a piece of cold roast chicken and a salad.

"What discipline." He laughed and ordered his chicken with a Béarnaise sauce.

I said one of my problems in keeping my weight down was having kids around me eating all the time. They've even introduced me to the glories of peanut butter and ice cream. "We were on a boat coming back from La Samanna, and they'd come to me with their peanut butter and jelly sandwiches—"

"Oh, I smell it," Van said, rolling his eyes.

"— and I found myself putting them away like I was a disposal unit."

Being friends with Van is easy when it's time to send gifts. I give him food. Every Christmas he gets an apple pie from the New York Athletic Club, and whenever I'm in the Middle East (although these days that's all in the past tense), I bring him back the richest caviar and the best vodka. Over the years, I have learned to mistrust anyone who does not love to eat. Van I would trust with my life.

After twenty years in Hollywood, Van returned to Broadway, starring in *Come on Strong* with Carroll Baker. His life had taken many turns. Left behind in California were the houses, the marriage, and his beloved daughter. Once again Van started living in bachelor apartments and hotels, as he had done in those early years in New York. His father had died, and Van sold the family homestead, or as he put it, "I dumped it." After many years, I know that he treats matters close to his heart with tough-guy language. Van was not about to return to Newport. Instead, he lived in the Delmonico Hotel. "Park Avenue, naturally. Status. Then to Sutton Place and my penthouse. I've lived there ever since. I'll die there," he said ominously.

Would he ever return to California? "Never. Two things I miss about California, though: the outdoor life and the Farmer's Market."

My friendship with Van began over the decorating of his Sutton Place apartment. Years later he told me, "When I first saw your smiling face in the *New York Post* over your column I said to myself, 'I've known that guy all my life.'" I met Van at a party devoted, appropriately enough, to food. Every year Joanne Winship, wife of Freddy, a senior editor of United Press, gives a chile party. It is an event of such social importance that the *New York Times* not only covers it but has even published Joanne's chile recipe. Everyone had been seated and the chile had been served when in walked Van. He could not enter a room unnoticed even if he weren't famous. His voice booms, and his six-foot-two frame towers over a gathering. He is definitely larger than life. As soon as he was ushered into the room, he cried out, "Where is Carleton Varney, where is Carleton Varney? I've been looking for him all my life!" We were hastily introduced by the hostess, and Van began to down his chile, all the while telling me how he was a fan of mine, always read my column, and only came to the party because he had heard I was going to be there.

Van was wearing his famous red socks, but was otherwise dressed fairly conventionally. By the time he was wolfing his chocolate mousse, I had agreed to design his apartment. Our first business meeting was at the New York Athletic Club overlooking Central Park. I have been a member for many years; I like the dining room where I always ask to be seated by a window. Even better than the view is the food. That day, however, I was on one of my many diet regimens, this time, Dr. Stillman, a particularly hard taskmaster. As I drank club soda and ate cantaloupe, Van had corned beef and cabbage with horseradish sauce and deep-dish apple pie. Van's approach to weight loss is to indulge, then suffer for a few weeks at a fat farm.

"Bob Considine always told me to come here as his guest and use the pool," Van told me. "No way." Club members don't wear suits in the pool, and movie stars, Van explained, are vain creatures. Unless he's just returned from a weight-reducing spa, he wouldn't jump nude into anyone's pool. "Not with a body of my vintage."

Van told me he had lived in his 54th Street penthouse on the East River for many years with an ever-growing number of enormous tabby cats. He wanted me to help him do the place over with more of a New England feeling. The first time I saw the apartment, I was immediately aware of his good taste. The apartment had a definite English country look with its wood beamed ceilings, magnificent plank floor, and wood bar. There were Chippendale wing chairs around the fireplace, and large antique model ships mounted on the walls. On every sofa and club chair and bench were needlepoint pillows made by Van himself, and through the rooms stalked the huge tabby cats. I knew at once that working with Van would be a pleasure. He knew what he wanted; he just wanted professional advice on making some refurbishing changes.

Van is also a great photograph collector. Among the pictures of Greta Garbo and other legends was a photo of a young girl who looked so much like Van it startled me. "That's Skylar," he said gruffly. I could tell by the look in his eyes that his daughter, from whom he is apparently estranged in the aftermath of an unhappy divorce, is one subject that is excluded from conversation.

Over the next few months, we fit in several trips to New York showrooms around his busy touring schedule. At the time he was playing in *Send Me No Flowers* and *Boeing-Boeing* to well-attended houses all over the country. I quickly learned that going anywhere with Van attracts attention. Not only his size, his booming voice, and his familiar face gather a crowd, but he can't go anywhere without clowning. Frequently, men are uncomfortable picking out furniture and looking at swatches of fabric. Not Van. He turned the experience into a piece of theater never to be forgotten on New York's showroom circuit. Regardless of his sometimes outrageous behavior, Van was approaching his task seriously, and after shopping around for just the right fabric for draperies in his living room, he selected a burgundy and cream toile printed fabric to go with a Victorian rug of bright red roses on a black background.

During one of our decorating lunches we talked about Joan Crawford. Van knew she was a client of mine. He had an autographed copy of *The Films of Joan Crawford* signed, oddly enough, "To Van, from Joan's Bones." When I asked him what that meant, he said, "Joan thought she was too skinny those days when we were on the Metro lot." Van was a little afraid of La Crawford, as he is of all women with strong personalities. He once complained to me of her habit of never being on time when he was escorting her to dinner. They would end up hours late and the food would be cold or, God forbid, gone. Being late to dinner is an unpardonable sin in Van's rulebook, and when I would relay messages between Joan and Van, he never called her as she requested. I think Joan was disappointed and couldn't understand why he didn't come around. I never told her why.

Van's Sutton Place penthouse is a homey place. His good taste is reflected everywhere, and if you close your eyes, you can almost hear the surf. It was hard for me to believe that I was the only decorator he had ever consulted. Wasn't there someone who influenced him? "Barbara D'arcy at Bloomingdale's," he answered at once. "I couldn't *wait* for those new rooms to be opened."

These days, Van Johnson lives mostly on the road. "Twelve months a year," he says, and he has become expert at changing impersonal hotel rooms into something like home. I asked him what his favorite hotel was. He named about twenty. "Wherever I go, the first thing I do is call a florist and tell him to flood my rooms with flowers and plants. Right now at the Astor in Chicago, where I'll be going on the weekend, it's mums. I always carry a couple of little throw carpets with horses and ships on them, and maybe I'll put up a poster I've bought of the South of France or some château. I take along some photographs and some needlepoint pillows too." His only regret is not being able to pursue his painting while he travels. "I've really neglected that. It's not easy to carry paints around."

The life of a theater gypsy is not glamorous in the least, according to Van. He rarely goes out in the evenings after a performance. "I go right home, soak in the tub with a glass of wine, and fall into bed." Mornings are taken up with public relations activities like television interviews, then back to his hotel room for a four P.M. nap, except for the two days a week he has matinees. "I'm off to Chicago to do *Send Me No Flowers* at the Playhouse Theater with my group. I travel with my own troupe of Ethiopians. Then we'll tour up and down the Cape—Westport, Maine, Skowhegan, Falmouth. I'll love every minute of it."

Most of all, he regrets that his hectic touring schedule doesn't allow him time to see friends in the area. "I do want to drive up to Milwaukee to see Lynn Fontanne. She lives up around there, you know. I love to walk, there's all those marvelous restaurants to try out. I love the art galleries, I'd like to see Dolly Moore's dollhouse. I love Chicago. I love the road. I love hotel life, the feeling of people all around me checking in, checking out . . . transients."

"What fascinates you so about hotel life?" I asked.

"One bill," was his answer. "If a light bulb needs changing, I pick up the phone and somebody comes up and fixes it. If they need any money when I want something done, they can always stop by the front desk and draw ten bucks on the way out. I love to push buttons. And I sleep better in hotels than I do in my apartment in New York. Hotels offer me a kind of security."

I found that interesting because I don't sleep well in hotels at all. When I said this to Van, he remarked, "You've seen too many of them too fast, Carleton. You can't treat a hotel room like a one-night stand. You're in and out. Me, I hole up for six weeks at a time."

If somebody told me I had to spend six weeks in a hotel, I'd go right through the ceiling. I find hotel life very confining. I do recall one exception. At the Greenbrier I always take the same room and don't let them change my decor. That way I walk into something that at least looks familiar even if it's not home, and it doesn't feel as if I'm interrupting the continuum of my life.

When it comes to room temperature, Van is a true New Englander. He likes his rooms just this side of frigid. "I hate heat. I never turn a radiator on. In a hotel room the first thing I do is turn the heat off, and then I open the windows and turn on the A.C. In New York my air conditioner is on all year round. I can't get a room cold enough."

We talked about hotels, new ones and old ones and long-gone ones. The conversation was stimulating to me because I have spent much of my career designing hotel interiors, and Van has spent much of his life in them. We both regard good hotels much the same way we regard fine wines or great cars, a part of life in which you exercise much discrimination and keep your standards high. "Just walking through the Waldorf gives me a thrill," Van said with an expansive gesture. True hotel lovers cultivate their hosts, and I found that Van knew them all. We spoke of Gustav at London's Connaught, and whether O'Neill was still at the Ritz. The desecration of the grand old Ambassador West in Chicago dismayed him. "Why take away that rich wood look?" he said sadly. Obviously, if you have to spend a great deal of time living in hotels, the only way to feel at home is to plunge into the local life and absorb all the details. Van knows hotel-keepers around the world like other people know their doormen or their next-door neighbors, and when he arrives in yet another town, familiarity is waiting for him.

Van has visited my wife and me many times. "I like your apartment," he said. "It's a happy house. Every time I go there, it's got good vibes. I'm very sensitive to good vibes, even in hotel rooms."

"Since you were at our house last, everything's been changed," I told him. He was dismayed. "Again? No more strawberry wallpaper in the boys' rooms?" I said we hadn't done much entertaining since the latest redecoration, but we would love to have him come up to our house in the Hudson River Valley. This was in April, and the first free time Van would have to visit was late summer. "I'll be up," he said, "but just you and Suzanne. None of that star stuff. It makes me very nervous."

"When you come, you owe me a needlepoint pillow," I reminded him.

"Oh, do I? You'll get one. 'Van loves Carleton.' Did you see the red one I did for Ethel Merman on the pink chair?"

Of course I had. It was prominently displayed on a wingback chair in one of the pictures of her home that appeared in *Architectural Digest*. "Van loves Ethel." All his pillows to his friends read "Van Loves Somebody." Since the topic seemed to be love, I asked him, "Who did you love? Who do you really love?"

"Suzanne Varney," he said with exaggerated lust.

Van says the reason he works so much is to keep from going under. Alimony blues. "But what do you know of such problems," he asked, "sitting in a boat eating peanut butter sandwiches with your kids?" We parted with an agreement to have lunch one day at Brooklyn's Gage and Tollner's. "In winter when the snow falls," he specified. "I'll take you this time."

Van loves the snow. He loves the winter. He probably loves Brooklyn. He loves hotels. He loves the sea. He loves his friends and sends them pillows that tell them so. He's a hard man not to love in return.

*   *   *

Like Van Johnson, Polly Bergen has lived the gypsy life, but her travels began in childhood.

"I averaged ten schools a year from the age of six," she told me. "The shortest stay was in Slidell, Louisiana, where we lived for three weeks." Her father was a construction engineer who built homes for other people but never for himself. Polly, a sister ten years her junior, and their parents lived all over the country in furnished apartments. "Anything we owned had to fit into the trunk or the back seat of the car." Polly's childhood was true gypsy, American style, but she doesn't feel deprived. "I was perfectly thrilled with my childhood. I thought it was sensational. To me it was normal, growing up all over the United States."

Life on the road means the excitement of always discovering what's on the other side of the mountain, but it also means never planting a garden, or building a treehouse, or playing with the treasures in Grandma's trunk in the attic. It means spending your school years as the perpetual new kid and an endless stream of instant friends, soon to be left behind with the urgent vows of childhood to write letters that never get written.

Nomads travel light. There were no large or cumbersome possessions in Polly Bergen's childhood—no bicycles or treasure troves in the lilac tree. The only continuum between the ever-changing furnished rooms was a car. An automobile's back seat can be confining but it can also be a cozy, womblike place, a small room on wheels that contains everything a child treasures. Nevertheless, when fame arrived, allowing Polly Bergen to indulge herself in buying whatever she wanted, she chose to live in a seventeen-room house in Beverly Hills. She proceeded to fill all those rooms with treasures, making her expanded nest a permanent storehouse of everything she wanted and needed. She soon became an enthusiastic collector.

"My life at that time was ruled by *things,*" she recalled. "I never had a place, a block, the same friends, the same furniture. I wanted to have it all. I wanted to learn the names of my neighbors, plant a tree, stay put, and collect anything my heart desired." One of her indulgences was textured walls. "I used to put more money into walls than anything else, which is a stupid thing to do because you can't take the walls with you when you move. Instead, you leave that fortune in fabric behind for the next people, who always hate it."

But moving was the last thing on her mind during those expansive years. Along with the delayed satisfaction of staying put and spreading out, she confessed to developing some strong "Craig's wife" tendencies. "Everything had to be perfect. Certain rooms in my house were treated like rooms in a museum. The only thing lacking was the rope in front of the door. I ran around holding ash trays under my guests' cigarettes. I dashed out to the kitchen for towels if anything spilled. I must have made my guests really uncomfortable, and it took a concentrated effort to break myself of that habit. Now if someone spills a glass of red wine on my white carpet, I'm cool about it. People are more important to me now than things."

Having so many rooms, she found, can be a problem. How can seventeen rooms to rattle around in be a problem to a woman who once had to fit all her possessions into a car? The answer is that, to Polly, a room is not something to pass through but to live in, to nest with every creature comfort at hand. "That house was so darn big I didn't know what to *do* with all those rooms, so I made one of them into a library and another into a den. What happened next is what always happens to people who have dens—they live in the den! Meanwhile, the living room becomes a place where you might as well hang a sign that says *For Display Purposes Only*. How silly it is to take the biggest and most conducive room for entertaining in your home and reserve it for guests. Now I believe in having everything you enjoy in the room you use most—books, TV, fireplace, collections of pictures. . . ."

Suddenly, at age forty-one, after having been married most of her adult life, Polly Bergen was single again. She decided it was time to consolidate and scale down, a process that was very painful at first, as collecting is a habit that dies hard. "I had moved a hundred and fifty times when I was growing up, and now I was on the move again." To make matters even more complicated, this time she was moving in and out on two coasts. "In the last couple of years I moved from a seventeen-room house in Beverly Hills into a one-bedroom apartment in New York. Then I moved into Ryan O'Neal's house and bought another house in Malibu and had it done over. Before it was finished, Ryan came back from doing *Barry Lyndon* and so I moved into yet another rented house in Malibu, and then finally into my own."

If that hadn't been enough packing and unpacking, Polly also moved out of her tiny New York apartment and into the River House for six months, then back into the tiny apartment while she looked for another. Finally she got her life in order. The frantic readjustment period was over, and once again she had a permanent California residence with neighbors, time to find out what bloomed in the backyard, and a New York address to give to the stationers for a new order of letterheads. But as her personal life had changed drastically, she determined to alter her surroundings as well.

"I had moved out of seventeen rooms, and now I wanted a much simpler scale. I wanted to stop being *owned* by a lot of possessions that needed taking care of." I asked her what possessions she found she could not live without when the scaling down began. She knew without having to search her memory:

There was an old oak table she had bought years ago in an antique shop. She had the legs cut coffee-table height, Dorothy Draper style, and it sat in a 70- x 45-foot projection room. "I couldn't part with it, nor could I get rid of two jardinieres I adored, or the Persian screen I bought in a dusty old antique shop in California. The screen was very cheap, and the jardinieres were very expensive."

Price was not the deciding factor when she began to make her decisions about what to keep and what to dispose of. "I'm the kind of person who wears a two-thousand-dollar gown one night and a sixteen-dollar dress the next day. It's the same with furniture. The most valuable piece I own is a chest with a mirror, a real museum piece. Sitting on top of it are four fake pre-Columbian figures that cost about forty dollars each." Some things were kept because they had sentimental value, others for their sheer beauty—but her collection of Porthault linens came along for another reason. "Call it animal comfort. I keep sending the towels out to be rebound, and I have the little holes sewn up in the sheets."

But the collecting instinct has by no means been extinguished. "I'll buy a whole collection at a time if I like it—hands, match strikers, Fabergé. . . . I finally sold my Fabergé because I got tired of worrying about it. I want to walk out my front door and not fret about valuable things being stolen while I'm gone." Another collection Polly didn't relinquish was a mass of photographs of friends that spanned her quarter-century show business career. Her personal picture gallery comes with her, although it too has been reduced in size.

Moving from a big place to a not-so-big space eliminated the dilemma of not knowing what to do with all those rooms. Her present house in Malibu does not have a den, library, or family room. The dining room is an area at one end of the living room and features a hand-painted Chinese table and six cane chairs Polly found she could not live without. In her new life, Polly has moved everything she loves most into her bedroom. In fact, she all but lives there. "When I was married, the look in my bedroom was more formal, and I spent far less time in it. Now my children are grown. Living rooms are for couples, and as a single I've found my bedroom is where I feel most cozy. I even do my work there. I have a desk there too, but I rarely use it. I use my bed. I eat in my bedroom too. Usually I get up, fix my own breakfast, put it on a tray, and take it back to bed. Essentially I'm very lazy. That's why I stopped using bedspreads a long time ago. Who needs all that wrinkling? I use blanket covers or top sheets."

Her bedroom is all white. Gone are the dark, heavy fabrics she used to prefer, to create a sort of womblike atmosphere. "Now I prefer sunshine. I do my exercises in the bedroom; I rehearse, read, watch TV. In fact, if I come home at night with two or three friends, we sit in front of the bedroom fireplace and have brandy or a late coffee." The centerpiece, of course, is the bed, which is heaped high with pillows, ten in all. She sleeps on two of them.

Should a couple's bedroom be feminine or masculine? "That's an interesting question," she said. "People say when you're married, you shouldn't have a bedroom a man will feel uncomfortable in, and I agree. But even for a single woman, a bedroom is where a man might end up, and I think it should reflect that too. I personally love the look of a man's bedroom. I think it's a room that definitely should reflect who sleeps in it." Once she came close to buying something truly masculine, a lucite and chrome headboard. "I opted for pillows instead because I decided all the linens I've collected over the years would look silly on that headboard. What I'd really like to have is a bed that's all beige satin sheets with a marvelous brown fur comforter. . . ." I have a feeling that Polly will be changing her bedroom scheme frequently, as the room has become the center of her life, the place where she's most comfortable and which must accurately reflect her evolving style. "Two years from now I'm sure it will be different," she predicted. "I'm changing all the time."

In the constant adaptation that goes on in her life, Polly has done away with womblike enclosures. "I used to have draperies at the windows, but now I have blinds. Draperies not only cut out light but they're dust carriers. They just hang there and catch dirt. Now I use bamboo or natural linen blinds. They're more interesting. My floors are bare or I use area rugs."

Another important room in her life is the kitchen, and it gets a great deal of attention. "My husband used to say, 'Why do you fuss so much over kitchens? You never spend any time in them.' It's not true that I don't cook. I cook very well, but I'm always working. I did all the cooking in my family from the time I was eight or nine to when I was seventeen because both my parents worked. I could make Christmas dinners, pies, turkey and stuffing—I'm a good all-around country cook. But I've worked so hard for the last twenty years or so that I don't spend a lot of time in the kitchen. To me, the time I spend cooking is a luxury."

Her kitchen decor reflects her cooking: country. It is old brick, wood, copper pans hanging from the walls, everything clean and shining. Plants are everywhere. "I'm from California, remember? I'm used to greens and flowering plants. Any florist would love to have me in the neighborhood because I spend more on plants than anything."

One evening Polly invited my wife, Suzanne, and me to a dinner at her apartment on East 79th Street. She served her guests, who that night included *Cosmopolitan* magazine's Helen Gurley Brown and actress Hope Lange, in the kitchen right from the stove, each of us standing in line with our plates. The food was piping hot, the way it should be, and the wine chilled in a sink full of ice. "Why don't people use their kitchens more?" Polly says.

That intimate beginning set the mood for the evening. Polly doesn't like her dinner guests to sit across a wide expanse of lengthy table. She wants them closer together in small groups for easier conversation. Her long dining room table is in sections that can be split into four 36-inch-square card tables that can seat four or a cozy two. "You don't feel lost that way," Polly says, "and when you want one big table, you just join them together."

Polly is an inveterate card player, and the tables are an ideal size for a night of bridge or backgammon. One evening, shortly after she had devised her new seating plan, she invited a group of friends over for dinner. "Phil Silvers came in, looked over the dining room, and said, "I'd like a table for four near the orchestra."

Nor does Polly feel obligated to serve her guests on matching china. Each plate at a Bergen dinner party is unique, as are the cups and saucers. As a result, each setting looks like a work of art instead of a study in uniformity. I found the arrangement at her dinner party very conducive to relaxed conversation and a convivial atmosphere. There's something very uptight and regimental about being seated in two long rows, alternately male and female, and something akin to kitchen-table intimacy about eating at a small square table.

At the time of that party, Polly was very much into being a single woman about town. Hers was one of the faces you'd see at every opening, whether it was the opera or a charity benefit for Project Hope or JOB. It seemed as if Polly was out every night. It may have been too soon after her separation for her to feel like a whole person when she was alone at home. As with so many of my friends who have gone through the agonies of a marital breakup, the first step toward readjustment is fleeing all those memories of the cozy twosome at home. Polly was apparently still in that phase.

After dinner one evening, Polly and I talked about an article I was planning to do on her for *Family Circle*. Fabulous photographs by Richard Champion would show Polly on the Porthault and the pillows with a cat curled up beside her. She looked devastatingly sexy. While I was writing the story, Polly asked me to do her a favor: decorate just one small room. She told me about her wonderful South American maid, who was soon to return from a visit to her home. Could we do up her room before she returned and surprise her with a sort of lady-in-waiting decor? Although our company rarely does one room, in Polly's case I said I'd love to.

The walls were covered in a yellow and white floral print. There were balloon shades at the windows and quilted bedskirts to match. Polly chose thick wall-to-wall carpeting for the floor and insisted on just the right overhead lighting to illuminate the desk, club chairs, and throw pillows. When it was completed, Polly laughingly pronounced it the most expensive maid's room of all time.

Decorating maids' rooms is one of the occasions when my profession provides me with a peek at the truth behind the facade. I have had clients for whom money was no problem (except deciding how to get rid of it) who lavished their living-room walls with watered silk but chose linoleum for the floor of the maid's room, all without the slightest twinge of embarrassment. Many times in my career, the wall-to-wall has stopped at the maid's room door. Matching gingham spread and curtains from Macy's is good enough for the live-in help of many a Park Avenue scion. When a client lavishes not only money but time on a maid's room, debating for hours whether she'd be happier with chintz or channel quilt, draperies or blinds, then I know I'm in an alliance with a truly generous person, the kind who doesn't stint where it doesn't show. After all, there is a difference between giving out Georg Jensen table favors and laying down superpile carpet in the maid's room!

There is something about Polly Bergen's lack of pretension that is not only refreshing but that compels someone like me, who is so often hired to lay on the status, to want to understand what makes her so different. I keep thinking about that young girl in the back seat of the car with her sister, both parents always within reach in the front seat, and her memories of those years, which were, in her words, thrilling. Because she had no roots, she became adept at making temporary homes provide her with comfort and a sense of belonging. Obviously she was successful at it, and her childhood circumstances seem to have put her more in touch with her surroundings than most people are. Polly Bergen evolved from the tight little environment of the family car to the sweep of a large house in Beverly Hills to a bed heaped high with pillows and the finest linen. It's almost as if she's uncomfortable in a large space.

"It's important if you're in a room that's fairly large that you decorate a corner that's small and cozy. For two people in a room this size, which is thirty-five feet long, there would be a feeling of getting lost in all that space if there weren't a cozy area in it for intimate conversation." When Polly describes her former homes, she remembers the exact dimensions of the rooms, as well as the overall square footage. She's space-conscious. And what's too big for comfort, she makes small.

Many people are not attuned to their relationship with space. They don't know whether they like the wide-open feeling or the cozy nest, and because they haven't investigated their preferences, they spend years redecorating room after room, wondering why they're never really comfortable. Life experiences taught Polly Bergen to be consciously aware of how she feels about space. And comfort too. "I like things soft and cozy, the kind of place where you can put your feet on the table. A home should be a place to live, not a showplace."

Had Polly's been the typical star-with-a-deprived-childhood story, I doubt if she ever would have had the confidence to serve celebrities from the stove! More likely, she would have preferred gloved footmen behind each chair. Polly's down-to-earth good nature confirms her insistence that her so-called underprivileged childhood was thrilling. Wherever she goes, Polly succeeds in duplicating the feeling of that intimate atmosphere she remembers—riding the open road with her family, perpetual vacationers over the face of America—from the comfort of her tiny nuclear world in the back seat of the family car.

Chapter 3

Joan Crawford Was Not Just "Mommie Dearest"

In our society the most unforgivable thing a woman can be is a bad mother. Yet, aside from a few dissenters who are either extremely fortunate or not telling the truth, nearly everybody admits to a few nightmarish memories of parents out of control; and nearly all parents (saints excluded) regret a shameful episode or two when they lashed out at their children, moments they would do almost anything to erase. Because of these strong and nearly universal memories, we all love a good monster tale about parents who are far worse than anyone *we* know.

Transference is what psychiatrists call the projection of our own fears of being bad on to someone else, and it usually results in a delicious sigh of relief that conveys, "What a terrible person! Who ever heard of such behavior?" The Greeks loved to watch Medea, the killer mother, throw her murdered children at their father's feet; Elizabethans flocked to theaters to gasp at bad parents who served up their babies in pies; and Victorians thrilled to stories of parental depravity in the *Police Gazette*. For a little relief, our own generation can turn to the *National Enquirer*, Rupert Murdoch's *National Star*, or Christina Crawford's *Mommie Dearest*.

Christina's remembrances of her mother were published in late 1978 and created an instant furor among the reading public, who loved it, and among Joan Crawford's circle of intimates, who despaired and grieved over it. Since then it has been nearly impossible to talk about Joan as the many-faceted human being she was. Instead, post–*Mommie Dearest* Joan had been reduced to that awful woman who once broke a can of Bon Ami over her little girl's head and then made her clean up the mess in the middle of the night.

I would never, God knows, have wanted to be Joan Crawford's child, but I remember a much more complicated woman, an endlessly fascinating, irritating, stimulating, strong, feminine, and above all, inspiring woman. Joan may have been one of the world's lousiest mothers—I don't know if she was or she wasn't, and she's not around to defend herself—but I know she was a lot of other things as well, also all in the superlative, and I fear it will be a long time before the real Joan Crawford in all her complexity will reemerge to replace the monster image left by her daughter's book.

Before Joan, Hollywood's image of the divine woman was someone soft, warm, and pliable—like Melanie in *Gone With the Wind,* who later became the quintessential symbol of the "good woman." Bad women in pre-Crawford years, such as the legendary Theda Bara, usually ended up severely punished for their naughtiness, and many a final frame found them sprawled on a staircase or over a steering wheel, shot through their wicked little hearts. Along came Joan, and a new image of the divine female flashed across the world's movie screens. Here was a beautiful woman who could also be tough, mean, selfish, strong-willed, and even cruel—but in spite of her unlovable qualities, she still got what she wanted! That was Joan's legacy. She never forgot it, nor did she ever relinquish that image of the strong woman forever in control, no, not even when she was dying.

Death was a while in coming. Only a handful of people were in contact with Crawford those last eighteen months during which she fought for life. Because she had become virtually a recluse near the end, rumors began to fly in a tempest of wild guesses after her death: she had drunk herself to death; she had committed suicide; she had died of her own meanness, or of an "overdose of loneliness"; she had gone to her Maker terror-stricken and alone, having alienated everyone who had ever cared for her. And there were other rumors too silly to repeat. Only a few people knew the real story, and none of them wanted to expose themselves to the terrible crossfire of charges and eventual lawsuits that came after the reading of Crawford's vengeful will and Christina's equally vengeful book.

One of those people who knew but refused to tell was Darinka Papich, a close friend of Joan's and the only person with Joan when she died. For nearly three years Darinka refused to talk to the press or satisfy the curiosity of the publicity hounds.

Then one blustery March afternoon this year she met me at "21," one of Joan's favorite haunts, and shared with me the story of those last days.

What follows is a recollection of my twelve-year friendship with Crawford, how she lived, how she related to me as a client and a friend, how she withdrew from life and why, and how she died. Even in the final battle she handled her life in her own iron-willed way, refusing to relinquish control over how she would die to doctors and drugs. She even refused to allow anyone to indulge in sentimental pathos and pity, which she deplored, by keeping her terminal illness a secret from everyone. Yes, even from her children. Joan Crawford was one gutsy lady.

*   *   *

On a chilly November morning in 1965 the entire fourth floor of New York's gigantic Coliseum was reverberating with excitement, for word was out that Joan Crawford was arriving there at eleven o'clock. The Grand Dame of the Pepsi Generation was to pose for pictures in The Drummer's Inn. This was one of the restaurant interiors I had designed for a display called "Designs for Dining," for the National Hotel and Motel's 100th Anniversary Exposition held that month. The other restaurant displays I had designed were The Rugby Bar, a cocktail lounge definitely "macho" in style; a discothèque patio; a Spanish restaurant called La Caseta; and an elegant French restaurant called Au Bob Chef.

The Drummer's Inn, where I stood waiting for Joan, was a coffee shop done in yellow and green check and guarded by life-size *papier-mâché* toy soldiers. During the design and production period of "Designs for Dining," our office had worked with the show's producer to get top manufacturers to back the showcase and share in production and building costs. In exchange, their products would be very much on display and would be seen by thousands of restaurant and hotel people when they visited the Coliseum during Hotel Show Week. Pepsi-Cola was one of the companies that responded. Needless to say, when I put the finishing touches on The Drummer's Inn, Pepsi flowed from every spigot on the soda fountain. Joan Crawford herself was coming to visit my little coffee shop and pose for pictures, bottle of Pepsi in hand. As the designer of the display, I was to greet her and pose for pictures with her.

I was getting a little nervous that morning; I had never met

Joan Crawford. She was at the point in her life when she had gone from the tumultuous success of her comeback in *Whatever Happened to Baby Jane?* to corporate superstardom as chief spokeswoman for Pepsi, assuming that mantle after the death of her husband, Alfred Steele, who had been Pepsi's chairman of the board. When Crawford was in her heyday, I was a kid who had eyes only for Betty Grable, June Haver, and other light-hearted stars. Joan Crawford was for the more serious-minded moviegoer, like my mother. I had a vivid memory of my mother talking to a friend about how much she admired Crawford, and perhaps that was why I had a preconception of Joan as a mother figure. Nevertheless, I was excited about meeting her, as well as a little anxious, for everyone, fan or not, knew La Crawford was unpredictable, to put it mildly.

In booths displaying everything from refrigerators to lamps, manufacturers went about their business that morning with one eye on the door. I was arranging some orchid blooms in the interior of Au Bob Chef when I noticed that the room had suddenly become very quiet. I looked up and saw a tight group of people walking toward me, and in the middle of the knot was Joan Crawford. She's so tiny, was my first thought. From her films I had always imagined her a big, broad woman to match that fierce face; but not so. We shook hands, and for me it was a strange kind of love at first sight. I was a young bachelor at the time, and my parents had both recently died. Something came from Joan, a kind of unqualified human warmth and affection for a perfect stranger, and I responded to it. She must have sensed this, because the rapport that developed between us that morning remained strong until her death.

At the display, Joan made sure many pictures were taken of us together. She seemed especially impressed with a two-seater tête-à-tête chair I had designed for the coffee shop. "Come sit here with me, Carleton," she said, and I did, heart thumping, and while we sat looking at each other the photographers kept on snapping. Joan said she was impressed that I was president of Dorothy Draper and Company at such a young age. "I remember Dorothy Draper," she said, "as a lady who always wore big hats." Dorothy, of course, had a considerable reputation in Los Angeles. As I mentioned earlier, she had decorated the glamorous Arrowhead Springs Hotel in the San Fernando Valley, a favorite watering spot of Hollywood stars and would-be stars in the 1940s.

As Joan talked, I watched. First there were those eyes that said they knew a lot. Then the lips; on anybody else they would have looked too thick and harsh, but on Joan they were an important ingredient of that unusual face. Then there was the sense of command that I remembered from her films, especially *The Best of Everything*. No doubt about it, I was starstruck. I thought I was even a little bit in love, but it was an unusual feeling, a combination of the emotions a man has when he looks at a desirable woman and those he has for his mother. I didn't know which feeling was stronger, but it hardly mattered. This was 1965, and the older woman with the younger man was years away from being accepted on the social scene.

When the picture taking was over, we all headed for the Commodore ballroom for lunch and a keynote speech by Crawford. There were about a thousand of us, hotel men and women of America, display people, and participants; and when we arrived at the huge dining area, I found myself as the designer for the exposition's showcase sitting at a front table with some Pepsi executives.

Joan stepped to the podium to speak and acknowledged the thunderous applause, which she obviously enjoyed. Dessert was still being served in the back section of the ballroom, and so there was the usual post-dinner rumble of conversation and dish rattling. Suddenly Joan stopped talking mid-sentence and stared straight ahead of her. I turned around to see what those penetrating eyes were focusing on and came to the conclusion that Joan was glaring at the waiters, since there was nothing unusual going on in the back of the room. As the noise continued, she went rigid with annoyance. "I will not continue until the noise of the dishes and conversation has stopped," she said. Then she waited, looking out over the audience with those savage eyes while the embarrassed waiters tiptoed back and forth with their overflowing trays. The guests, humbled into silence, sat like schoolchildren at their desks as Joan surveyed the scene with a tiny smile on her lips. Several times she looked directly at me, and after she resumed her speech, I was left with the impression that she was talking to me and me alone the entire time. That's star quality, I guess, being able to make someone feel as if he's the only one in the room.

I was not surprised, but pleased, nevertheless, when several weeks later Crawford's New York secretary, Florence Walsh, called me and said Mrs. Alfred Steele would like to talk to me.

Joan wanted to see me. Could I come that afternoon at four? I said I could, although on the way over I couldn't imagine what she wanted. I thought perhaps she would ask me to design an office for Pepsi-Cola.

I arrived at her Fifth Avenue apartment building at 2 East 70th Street at four on the dot, and the elevator man delivered me to her door. Mamacita, Joan's German maid, greeted me with one small Shih Tzu dog in her arms and another barking fiercely beside her on the floor. From within the apartment I heard a familiar voice call out, "Come on in, Carleton," and Mamacita motioned me toward the library, a room with a view overlooking the front garden of the beautiful Frick Museum.

Joan was sitting at her desk, her back to the window. She was dressed in a sleeveless mumu-like housedress. She wore no makeup, and her orange-colored hair was pulled back behind her ears and secured with a rubber band. As she got up to receive me, I noticed that she wore rubber flip-flops (to protect her highly polished floor, I later learned). She greeted me affectionately, offering me first her right cheek to kiss and then her left, then she offered me a drink, which I accepted. She was having one herself, a vodka on the rocks, in a large plastic barrel-shaped glass with a fly-casting symbol on it, the kind of drinking glass fishermen take on trips. The sight of Joan in a mumu, hair in a rubber band, and fishermen's drinking glass in hand, was to become a familiar part of life with Crawford over the next twelve years. Only people who are very secure about who they are can receive guests with such lack of pretension.

I was eager to have a look at Joan's large penthouse, a well-known apartment on the New York social scene, but before I took another step, Joan asked me to remove my shoes. She didn't want any of the black polish from my shoes to get on her white rugs.

Her entire apartment had been architecturally planned and designed by Skidmore, Owings and Merrill. Her late husband Alfred, whom she once described to me as the only man she ever loved, had added the second floor to the penthouse to make room for a bedroom befitting a superstar. The apartment was extraordinary. The floor was pink marble, like the inside of an exquisite shell, and the view of Central Park framed by an all-glass wall was spectacular. As we walked from room to room I thought about what this space represented: Fifth Avenue in the 70s, high above the greatest city in the world, a view that spanned a panorama of the park from the Plaza Hotel on the left to the Metropolitan Museum on the right. Were someone to write a movie script of such an apartment in a rags-to-riches story about a poor but beautiful young girl from Texas who made it to the top, it would be thrown out—too much of a cliché to be believable.

The late William Haines, a friend of Joan's who had been in films before he turned to interior design, had been the creator of Joan's penthouse, and the decor throughout was like a movie set built in New York: blond modern 1950s Beverly Hills glamour, but expensive. Billy Haines had very costly tastes, even for those fat years, and when he did Joan's penthouse he had apparently indulged his most expensive decorating fantasies. The result was a sort of "Hollywood Rises over Central Park." The rooms were filled with long sweeping sofas and silk upholstered chairs with legs that angled out in a crazy way. All the furnishings were covered in lemon yellow, beige, or white biscuit-quilted fabrics, and everywhere I looked the furniture was covered in clear plastic. There were more objects wrapped in plastic in Joan's apartment than in an A&P meat counter. This first look at her penthouse was also my introduction to Joan's obsessive tidiness. The lady wanted everything in her life to be clean!

And neat: In the dining room an enormous table was bolted to the floor and surrounded by cabinetry that opened discreetly at the touch. Joan had storage space everywhere for her silver, dishes, porcelains, and accessories. There was an entire room for shoes and another for hats. As I walked through the rooms I was impressed by a feeling of order, spartan cleanliness, and an absence of flamboyance, even of bright color. It was an austere place that didn't fit the personality of the owner, I thought.

Her bedroom was another matter. All the bedrooms I was to design for her featured pink and white, the colors of that penthouse bedroom, for she thought that color scheme was very flattering. Alfred Steele's bedroom, which was next to Joan's, had not been altered since his death. If the rest of the apartment had been decorated in Hollywood Modern, Alfred's bedroom had been done in Hollywood Motel. Again the furnishings were blond 1950s vintage, and the Hollywood bed had fitted covers and a bolster back upholstered with gold Lurex threading its glistening way through a black material. The wall-to-wall carpeting was emerald green, and the pillow accents on that Hollywood bed were bright, bright yellow and orange. For a chairman of the board of Pepsi-Cola, the room was a shocker. It was not in the least what I had expected to see. On that same floor, along with the room for shoes and the room for hats, was a massage room where Joan lay on a big table to get her daily massage. Mamacita once told me that Joan had a regular schedule for the beauty treatments for which she was a great advertisement. Joan's body was in super shape when I met her. She was then around fifty-eight.

Upstairs, downstairs, and all over the apartment were those white rugs. Everyone—from prime ministers to delivery boys—took off his shoes before gaining entrance to Joan's apartment. For cocktail parties she sometimes left Chinese slippers neatly stacked near the doorway. There were, of course, times when people kept their shoes on, but I'm sure that on those occasions Joan was not at ease.

Crawford also had definite rules about the management of her household, and everyone who entered her home or her life had to obey them. She even carried a small box of tissues with her as she went about the apartment so that if one of her dogs did its duty in the wrong place, she could clean it up fast. She then used another tissue to wipe the dog. Whether it was New York dust sifting its way through the windows or a visitor's dirty shoes or her little housebound dog's offending behind, Joan was ready with her crew of cleaners, personally leading the way with a box of tissues and eradicating uncleanliness wherever she found it. Mamacita was her field marshal. She was in charge of giving orders to the floor cleaner, rug cleaner, window cleaner, and all the regular household help. Not only did she see to it that everything in the star's life was clean but also that it matched. Mamacita was fastidious about laying out Joan's wardrobe, whether Joan was at home in New York or traveling. If Joan planned to wear a pink dress, Mamacita laid out shoes, hat, gloves, and jewelry to match, all taken from closets catalogued and labeled in an organized manner that rivaled the Dewey Decimal System. Pink and turquoise blue were two plentiful colors in those closets.

Over the years I knew Joan, Mamacita left the actress's employ only twice, both times to visit her family in Germany. Joan did not always talk nicely to Mama, but Mama was ever indulgent, never failing to call her "Miss Crawford" in the most respectful terms, and going about her daily chores with a great deal of energy. She never slept in a maid's room, for Joan gave as much attention to the decoration of Mama's room as she did to her own. After all, Mamacita was her companion. When the secretaries and cleaners had departed and the phones had stopped ringing, it was Mama who sat with Joan late at night in the sterile white kitchen, and it was Mama on whom she depended. Her name was no accident. I regret that Mamacita left Joan's employ before her death. In those last years, when Joan was at her most difficult, apparently Mama finally came to the decision that she had had enough, and upon the insistence of her daughter returned to Germany.

After I had taken a look around, wondering what my function was to be, Joan said in a calm voice, "I'm selling this apartment." She explained that she simply could no longer afford the nearly $3,000 monthly maintenance, and her lawyer was urging her to sell and move into something smaller. I was later told by La Crawford herself that before Joan married Alfred Steele, his life insurance had to be signed over to his first wife, Lillian, as part of her agreement to a divorce. Without Steele's life insurance, even "that movie star bitch," as Joan told me Lillian was wont to call Joan, could not afford $3,000-a-month maintenance.

Joan had invited me to the penthouse because she wanted me to see how she lived before I assisted her in decorating her next apartment. She had to find something soon. I looked around at the spacious rooms and the magnificent view and thought how anybody with a penchant for the finest would find moving from a penthouse at Fifth Avenue and 70th Street, particularly a place with as many happy memories as this one must have, a deeply wrenching experience. But Joan's face revealed nothing as she glided through the rooms, cheerfully pointing out this chair and that night table, asking me questions and telling me charming anecdotes. Little did I know that under that placid exterior, trouble was brewing.

A buyer for the apartment was readily found, the sister of an industrialist-diplomat. One morning the lady had an appointment to go through the apartment with her designer, and Joan asked me to be there. I arrived first. Joan greeted me in her usual at-home attire of housecoat and beach thongs, hair done up in the familiar rubber band and in need of a touch-up from her colorist. All that was missing that morning was the plastic barrel of vodka.

The owner-to-be and her decorator arrived, and as they walked around the apartment I noticed the woman seemed to be thoroughly enjoying herself and pleased to have purchased the

home of the great Joan Crawford. Ascending the modern staircase, she said to her decorator, "This has to go too. I don't care
for modern things." From the general tenor of their conversation,
it was evident that the new owner was planning a more traditional approach, and the execution of her plans would require
many changes. As they murmured in a corner, discussing altera-
tions, I caught a glimpse of Joan's face. It conveyed more than
forty pages of the best screen writing—the intense emotional effect of having a person come into one's beloved home and act as
if she already owned it. It was obvious that Joan's emotions were
beginning to catch up with the fast-moving events of her life,
and her eyes were filled with hostility and pain as she led the
woman and the decorator through her rooms and heard how they
were going to be "improved."

At one point the buyer complained of a slight chill in the
apartment (an understandable reaction, although I don't think
she was aware that the chill was emanating not from the weather
but from Mrs. Alfred Steele). Joan swept into the room, opened
wide one of her closets, and exposed a long row of furs.
"Choose," she said in velvet tones. "There must be something
here to keep you warm." Before the buyer could answer, Joan had
wrapped her in silver fox.

By the time the usurpers departed Joan was very shaky, but
she managed to pull herself together with the help of some 100
proof from the plastic barrel. I think she had only begun to
realize that she was really moving out of that beautiful apartment
with the spectacular view, the marble floors, the memories of her
late husband, and the undeniable magic of Fifth Avenue. It was
not the first time I had witnessed that poignant moment when a
person confronts a sudden change in environment, always more
wrenching when it comes out of necessity rather than choice.
Deep is the anguish of standing by while perfect strangers march
through one's bathrooms flushing the toilets to check for water
pressure, roll marbles across the floor to measure levels, and chat-
ter enthusiastically about all the wonderful ideas they have for
making the place more livable. Grief is grief, whether it's the
sadness of moving from the family homestead into a con-
dominium or from a luxurious Upper East Side penthouse into a
luxurious but smaller Upper East Side apartment. I felt sorry for
Joan that day.

She had a few months before she had to vacate the penthouse, and during that time we met often to discuss what could

be brought to the apartment she had rented in the nearby Imperial House on 69th Street off Lexington Avenue. The new apartment consisted of nine rooms and a large entryway, two terraces, and four baths—not small by any means, but in the rarefied milieu of Upper East Side real estate, a far cry from Fifth Avenue and 70th Street.

What she didn't want to give away or use in the new apartment was sent to Sotheby Parke Bernet, where the furnishings were auctioned. None of the pieces were particularly good, and they went for little money. I think her massage table brought ten dollars, and her hatboxes, each initialied J.C., brought a couple of dollars. Joan was disappointed at the results of the sale. I think she believed that anything belonging to her was of value because of its provenance. Her belongings didn't even rate the main SPB auction rooms, but were shunted off to the less prestigious PB-84; it's a bit like being seated in the second tier at the opera. Had Joan been able to see the pandemonium at the Plaza Gallery after her death, when her effects were auctioned off, I think she would have been amused and gratified. Police guards kept back the screaming crowds as Crawford bedsheets sold for $800, scrapbooks for $2,000, and even her false eyelashes brought fabulous prices.

Some of Joan's belongings were boxed and stored for years. Other boxes were filled with memorabilia and marked for Brandeis University, which had established a Joan Crawford School of Dance. Furnishings went to the Archdiocese of the City of New York, and Cardinal Cooke himself got the plastic-covered yellow-tufted sofa. Joan later decided that other memorabilia was to go to Brandeis, and her costume jewelry to the Fashion Institute of Technology in New York, but these decisions were made when she was dying, and her will was not changed in time.

Joan and I planned her new nine-room apartment down to the last shelf. Custom-made cabinets were designed to house all her china, silver, and glassware. We turned the former maid's room into a hat and shoe room. A second bedroom became Joan's dressing room and was outfitted with wall-to-wall closets. A third bedroom was for Mamacita. We planned to decorate the apartment in—you guessed it—lemon yellow, white, and beige. I was to use many of the Billy Haines pieces, but I did manage to convince her to stain the blond tables a rich ebony. Because there was no room for her long dining table, we made a new lemon yellow lacquer piece. Joan instantly covered it with a top of yellow felt to protect it from becoming scratched. "People are so careless with ballpoint pens," she explained.

All the windowsills in the apartment were covered with white plastic laminate so that they could be cleaned without damaging the paint. Joan didn't like to disrupt her orderly life with painters. History has recorded how Joan was a cleanliness nut, and I've read all the stories about how she tried to scrub away her background. Some of the theories are a little sinister, comparing her attempts to obliterate filth to Lady Macbeth's handwashing routines, but I don't think it was all that complicated. The lady was Mrs. Clean all right, but she herself used to joke about it, comparing herself to Craig's wife, an ultra-clean woman she portrayed in the film by that name. Joan was no psychopath about dirt. She really enjoyed being neat, clean, and tidy. Her mania never prevented her from living well, if you disregard the bother of having to "break the seal" on rising from a plastic-covered couch in warm weather.

Joan tended to do everything in life above-and-beyond. She was the only person I ever knew who sent a thank-you note to a thank-you note. In my files I have hundreds of letters from her on her light blue-green paper, and they all begin, "Carleton Dearest." I once received a note from Christina, also on pale blue-green stationery. I don't remember how she addressed me, but Mommie's favorite salutation inspired the title of Christina's book. But, true to her strong feelings of love and hate, she wrote on the same kind of stationery Mommie Dearest used.

Joan's new dining room carried out the scheme of something old, something new. In the white-painted room I used green and white palmlike patterned drapes at the windows. Black framed chair seats were covered alternately in lime green and lemon yellow washable vinyl. The room was good-looking in spite of the plastic, but it was rarely used for a sit-down dinner. Joan usually took her guests out for dinner, but on occasion she did invite some Pepsi people over for her boiled beef and salad dressed with pure lemon juice. For these dinners she would sometimes hire waiters and a bartender from "21." Otherwise, Joan's guests ate out, and when she was at home she ate sparrow-fashion on a tray with Mama in the kitchen or alone at her desk. After her death I was amused to read that she kept the memory of her late husband alive by the rather macabre habit of setting a place at the table for him. Except for the Pepsi dinners, Joan *never* set the table. When we got hungry, she would order food from Casserole

Kitchen, one of her favorite places. We'd eat the take-out food in the kitchen and wash it down with vodka for her, scotch and soda for me, and talk for hours. I felt at home with her during those times. Once she asked me if I would be her permanent escort. I think she was under the impression she was doing me a favor; I would have the opportunity to escort her to the best parties, and she could open many doors for me in my business. I don't know what her feelings were for me or what kind of fantasies I was having about her, but I often wished she were thirty years younger.

During those months I got a good idea of what life was like in that spectacular penthouse of hers. She gave a few cocktail parties to which I was always invited. One was in honor of the engagement of Franchot Tone's son Jeff. Joan invited what she called "the young set" and intermingled a few of her old pals like Burgess Meredith and his new young wife. At the party Joan gave Jeff many engagement presents, including silver pieces that her former husband had given her during their marriage. As all Hollywood historians know, Franchot had been Joan's second husband. One of the pieces she gave Jeff was a silver cigarette case inscribed in Franchot's hand, *To Joan—with love, Franchot.*

Among the many guests Joan introduced to me at that party was her daughter Christina. She had recently been divorced from Harvey Medlinsky, a producer, and was looking for an apartment of her own in New York. She was not living with Mommie but was staying at the Mayflower House on Central Park West. Joan had talked to me at length about the things she would give Tina for her new apartment as we sorted out her belongings in preparation for the big move. "Do you think Tina will want the pink dressing stool?" she'd ask. "Do you think Tina can use these chairs?" Despite the fact that Joan was on the move herself, she was concerned about her daughter's search for an apartment. One evening the three of us went to see a rental apartment next door to Joan's Fifth Avenue building. Tina loved the apartment, but there was a waiting list and she didn't get it. Finding an apartment in New York is a trial, even if your mother is Joan Crawford. Tina kept looking.

As Joan and I sorted and planned, our friendship grew. she regaled me for hours with fascinating stories about Hollywood in the days when she was one of its brightest stars. In my naiveté I once asked her if she knew Mary Pickford, and she replied, "Carleton, I was once family!" I was not aware that Pickford had been Joan's mother-in-law when Joan was married to Douglas Fairbanks, Jr., and Pickford was married to Douglas Fairbanks, Sr. Joan occasionally spoke about her own family, especially about a brother who had also gone to Hollywood in those early days to make his fortune. Instead, he ended up a bit player. She said he used to come up to her and hiss, "Why are *you* a star when I'm so much better-looking than you are?" When she saw that her brother meant only to hurt her, she cut him out of her life. That was her way. She refused to see anyone who hurt her. She also had no patience with people who unintentionally caused her pain because they did not follow her directions or disagreed with her ideas. Nor did she have any use for the sex stars of the time. "Who wants to watch a couple of butts pumping it out on the screen? It's gross and inartistic," she would rail. Although wild horses could not drag her to see *Last Tango in Paris*, she passed judgment on Marlon Brando anyway, and said she was appalled that an actor of his stature had reduced himself to such a low level. After all, Joan Crawford had worked hard to make a lady out of herself and, "Goddamn it, any friends of mine are going to be ladies and gentlemen, or else!" she said.

Her apartment revealed mementoes from three friends who did pass the Joan Crawford morality test. One was a picture of Noel Coward, who never came to town without seeing her. Another picture was of Barbara Stanwyck, whom Joan called Missie, and on her night table sat a pair of porcelain hands that Helen Hayes had given her. She also had a custom of transforming fans into devoted friends. During the months of preparation for the move to 69th Street, I often met a red-haired woman who was helping Joan organize the move. One night I invited Christina to the Jamaica Arms for dinner, and she brought up the redheaded woman. "What do you think of her?" she asked. "Do you think she's a lesbian?" I was taken aback by this comment and sputtered out something she apparently took for encouragement.

"Well, what do you think?" she persisted. "Do you think she and Mother are having an affair?"

Joan loved to be surrounded by her fans. Some were straight, some were gay. Not having spent any time under her bed, I know nothing of her preferences, but I was a little startled at how ready Christina was to make judgments. But more than anything else, in the face of Christina's curiosity and suspicion, I felt like saying, "Who cares?"

Joan spent the next weeks arranging dishes, ordering more

cartons, and ordering people. Her lawyer, Bud Morris, was delighted that Joan was conserving and moving into a rental. I was happy with the way the new apartment was turning out. There was lots of sunshine and a feeling of space; particularly pleasant was the big sunroom with the two terraces on either side. We had also made a few architectural changes, opening walls to let in more light, and removing all the bathtubs and putting in stall showers instead. "I don't like to sit and soak in my own dirt," said fastidious Joan. I also convinced Joan to get rid of the white rugs and live a little, and we laid custom-made green rugs with yellow borders.

One day we went over to 69th Street to decide where the furniture would be placed. Joan and I blocked out areas on the floor with white masking tape where pieces were to be located, and Joan walked from one piece of imaginary furniture to another as if she were on a movie set going through her blocking. I stared at her in amazement. She was play acting, I thought, as if someone else were about to move into that apartment.

During that readying phase I had to go to Scottsdale, Arizona, on a job, and I gave Joan a number where I could be reached. One day she called, sobbing. She said she had no money. At first I was astonished, but it soon dawned on me that the sale of the penthouse had not yet gone through. Joan kept apologizing. "I can't pay for the rugs, and I can't pay for the carpeting work. I'm so terribly embarrassed." She asked me to wait for the money. I did, and every bill was paid in full. Never again did she discuss money with me after that temporary sojourn into poverty. What she wanted she bought, and that was all there was to it. And she only bought things she liked, never to impress others.

Moving day loomed. The rugs were down, the walls painted, and the draperies installed. Everything was in place except the furniture—and the occupant. Joan, wearing the fox coat she had once loaned to the new penthouse owner, Tina, and I left the duplex on 70th Street to check out the new apartment one last time before moving in. Although we had to walk only a few blocks, Joan insisted on getting a limousine. I sensed what was coming, and I think she did too. We all got out of the limousine and went through the revolving glass doors of the Imperial House. On the way to the elevators she collapsed, and Tina and I carried her back to the limousine. Joan was absolutely beside herself. She couldn't bear to give up the life style she had become accustomed to as the wife of Albert Steele.

Christina and I took Mommie Dearest back to her duplex. She was still very shaky, but after a sip or two from her plastic cup she started to settle down and was soon slumbering in fantasyland. I left her there, wondering what on earth to do next. My mind was reeling; it was like watching a movie played backward. I saw us repacking all the boxes at the new apartment, taking down the draperies; taking up the rugs; repainting the penthouse walls; bringing back the furniture, the massage table, and the hatboxes; bleaching the ebony-stained modern furniture; and giving the new owner her money back with our deepest regrets for any inconvenience. No, it couldn't be done. There had to be another way—but for the moment I was too exhausted to be creative enough to find it.

Florence Walsh, Joan's secretary, thought it would be best for Joan not to be around to see the actual move, but Crawford wouldn't hear of it. In fact, when the time came, she was magnificent. The burly men from Manhattan Storage arrived, took the boxes filled with her treasures, and struggled with the oversized furniture. The most harrowing moment came when a couch had to be lifted twenty-two stories by crane. The night before, I had thought moving that couch would be nothing compared to moving Joan out and in, but I was wrong. She behaved very well, but she never fully recovered. From that day onward, the sipping from the plastic barrel became more and more frequent. By no means was she an alcoholic; she functioned like a managerial wizard in her business dealings and in her private life. But after the move to Imperial House she relied on alcohol to the extent that there were times when she embarrassed herself in public.

Besides her Pepsi commitments, Joan was engaged at that time in a promotion tour for the Hat Institute and was also writing a book, *My Way of Life*. The hat people were often in Joan's apartment, seated at that yellow felt-covered dining-room table drawing up demanding itineraries with those troublemaking ballpoint pens. They expected Joan to be up by five A.M. and be somewhere in Philadelphia by nine o'clock. "*I'm* the one who has to do all this, not them!" she'd complain. She didn't like being controlled by anyone, but she *loved* to work. Work, work, and more work—it kept her going.

When she traveled, she was very specific about her needs.

Wherever she went, Joan wanted to be comfortable. Once, when she was to speak at a Pepsi convention at the Greenbrier Hotel, the Pepsi public relations people forwarded a list of "necessities" to the hotel before her arrival: six boxes of tissues, to be placed by the bed; Sano cigarettes; and her favorite brand of vodka, always 100 proof.

Joan lived in her nine-room apartment for about seven years. Then Imperial House became a cooperative. She decided to pare her life style once more and bought a two-bedroom apartment just down the hall. The cooperative market was in a decline at the time, and she was able to scoop up a real bargain, buying the apartment for something like $85,000. I was to plan the decor, but this move was not as upsetting as the first. Again we installed the stall shower and covered the windowsills with plastic laminate and planted a plastic garden of bamboo shoots lighted from below. Joan loved plastic plants and flowers—they didn't shed and were so easy to clean. She also liked fresh flowers, and the floors of her apartment always held a few vases of blooms sent by admirers. Under each vase was a neatly folded terrycloth towel to keep the floor from getting water-stained.

But more than the neatnik homebody, the businesswoman, or the Hollywood personality, Joan was above all the actress. One of her greatest frustrations was the dearth of good roles for a woman her age. In the early years of our friendship I was thinking of writing a novel about the decorating business starring a Dorothy Draper character. When I mentioned it to Joan, she said, "Write it! We'll sell it to the movies, and I'll play Dorothy Draper." Whereas some women yearn to play Desdemona or Camille, Joan's all-time favorite role was the tycoon. Playing the successful businesswoman represented for her the ultimate opportunity to be womanly, well dressed, and powerful all at the same time. More than anything else in the world, I think she would have loved to have succeeded her late husband as chairman of the board of Pepsi-Cola. Mrs. Alfred Steele, the first lady of the Pepsi Empire. Another role I often thought of her as playing was Eva Peron.

She never got her most coveted role. Soon after she was widowed she began to get messages from the Pepsi hierarchy, unspoken but not subtle. She stayed on, playing *The Best of Everything* to the hilt, and her secretaries continued to answer her telephone with a crisp "Mrs. Steele's office." Being a businesswoman climbing to the pinnacle is a different kind of power from being a movie star, but it also creates a heady lust for more that becomes unquenchable to just about everyone who gets a taste of it. Like cola, it never quenches for long, and I knew Joan didn't *ever* want to stop being Mrs. Pepsi. Knowing her as well as I did, I was sure her methods for retaining her power would have put even Dorothy Draper to shame. Suffice it to say, had the Pepsi executives lived in fifteenth-century Italy, they probably would have hired someone to poison her.

No matter what her role, whether movie star or business tycoon, Joan was a consummate actress. I was never aware of a time when she wasn't role playing. I think she regarded each day as a new scene to play, and every night she checked the *TV Guide* to see if one of her movies was going to be on. "Oh, good—I get the man away from insipid so-and-so tonight," she'd say to Mamacita, like a child who'd just found a cookie. I don't think I ever really knew Joan. I knew all her roles well enough: the coquette, who tittered when she told about the Pinkerton man who slept on the couch when the sound system in her apartment wasn't working; the lady-bountiful role she found more and more appealing as she grew older; the executive who ran her life like a perfectly maintained Rolls. . . . Occasionally she would even play the homey housewife. Whenever I invited her to dinner, she would arrive with her rhinestone bejeweled flask of 100-proof vodka (God forbid she'd be forced to drink 80 proof) and insist on helping my houseman, Yeung, serve dinner and clear the table.

Strangely enough, one of the roles she became increasingly uncomfortable in was Crawford the celebrity. One evening my wife, Suzanne, and I accompanied her to the Merv Griffin show, which was being taped at a Broadway theater. She explained that we would be picked up by her limousine, taken to the taping, and then to dinner. When we stepped into her limousine, we saw that Joan was wearing a gorgeous ensemble with a long pink skirt over pink shorts. Her hands were shaking. She was a nervous wreck. She didn't seem to have been drinking at all, but she had already been accused of being drunk on several television shows and was afraid that, drunk or sober, she'd be accused of it again that night. The last time she had appeared on Merv Griffin's show she had been a bit snockered and had cried about her childhood. When in her cups, Joan got sanctimonious, and these were the only times she would reveal any glimmerings of self-pity.

That night, as the limousine took us across town to the theater district, it was obvious that Joan was terrified of going before the cameras. I felt as if I had an ingenue on my hands. "No matter what I do tonight they're going to say that Joan Crawford was drunk on the Merv Griffin show again," she said grimly. When we arrived at the theater and stepped out of the limousine, we were suddenly surrounded by a mob of star-followers screaming and reaching for her. One pulled her arm, and I ran interference for her all the way to the door. By the time we reached the studio her face was drained of color. Suzanne and I sat in the audience dreading her entrance, for neither of us believed she could pull herself together in time. But she did. She came out in that pink outfit, took off the skirt, and revealed her long, still youthful legs to America. The place went wild. Everybody loves a little showmanship. By the end of the taping she was herself again, bolstered by the audience's enthusiastic response to her artful cheesecake. I marveled at the way she had managed to transform herself from a woman nearly paralyzed with fear into a performer who knew just how to create the right theatrical moment.

When I considered how I had never known Joan for a moment when I didn't think she was acting, I marveled at what a strain that must have been. Because I never felt I knew Joan minus the masks, I never considered her a close friend and was surprised to be told that Joan had listed me in a magazine article as one of her seven best friends. I saw her as a friend but never as an intimate. An intimate is someone you know well. When it came to Joan, I felt all I knew were the roles she played for me.

*   *   *

Suzanne Lickdyke and I were married on Christmas Day, 1968, and we invited Joan to our wedding. She didn't come. I now believe she didn't want me to get married at all. She once told me I would make a good husband for her Tina. Nevertheless, when Suzanne and I arrived in Vail, Colorado, for our honeymoon, there was a congratulatory telegram and flowers awaiting us from Joan. Suzanne and her sister Helene had once operated a boutique on Madison Avenue called Reflections, and Joan had asked them to stop by and show her some small gifts she might buy as Christmas presents for friends. As they showed her some silver items and made suggestions, Suzanne flipped through a large art book on Joan's table called *Four Fabulous Faces*, which featured Dietrich, Swanson, Garbo, and Crawford. Joan gloated when Suzanne commented that she looked that day the same as she did in some of her early films. In fact, Joan was so pleased she lifted up her dress to show them what a nice body she had. Joan was in wonderful shape even at sixty-three, and did not hesitate to show two pretty young women her legs. But she was also her most severe critic. After she saw some pictures of herself at a party she had hosted for her friend Rosalind Russell, she announced to me that she would never be photographed again. And she never was. However, one picture of her was taken unawares by Richard Champion after she went private, and that picture was the last. She was wearing her glasses and mumu, and carrying her dog, Princess Lotus Blossom. Her hair was gray. She may not have approved of it, but I thought the picture conveyed the private Joan in all her humanness.

During those years approaching her retirement from business and social activities, Joan became increasingly estranged from Christina. My last recollection of them together was when Tina underwent surgery at New York's University Hospital. Joan and I visited her there, and Tina was frightened. Joan tried to console her and told her not to worry about losing her role in the television series "Secret Storm" as she herself would step into the role to protect her job. The result was a debacle, but I maintain Joan really thought she was coming to the rescue. She was extremely depressed at the time (it was shortly after the move to 69th Street), and if she bungled her attempt to help Tina, I believe it was done without malice.

After Tina left the hospital, she returned to California and stayed in Joan's small Fountain Avenue place there. Joan disapproved of her daughter's life style as she disapproved of any life she was not allowed to direct. She was fonder of her daughter Cathy, an artist who lived in Pennsylvania. Cathy did some beautiful work with flowers, and I used some of her paintings in my hotel work.

The break in Joan's relationship with Christina came when Joan demanded that Tina leave the apartment on Fountain Avenue and shift for herself. Joan told me she would not let Tina use her contacts any longer. "I'm through trying to help that girl," she said, "and I'm cutting her out of my will just like Christopher." Of all the photo albums of the children that I had seen in her apartment, the one labeled *Christopher* was the least full. Once I asked Joan what had happened to the boy, and she replied that she had totally disowned him. He had caused her embarrassment. He had been rowdy and been picked up by the police, and she didn't come to his aid either. "Christopher was just like my brother," she announced. Christina had told me during our brief friendship that Christopher had married and was living in Riverhead, Long Island. Tina wanted us to drive out to see him, as she liked him a lot and said he was a great person. I was not about to get involved with Joan's private problems with her children, and so I let the matter pass.

I do not think Joan and Christina had much contact in the last ten years of Joan's life. Whenever I brought up her daughter's name or inquired about her, Joan ignored me completely. Joan had no time for understanding. She had time only for order and discipline, and discipline and order made her a star. Motherhood requires a little bending. Kids are notoriously messy, and I don't think Joan's obsession with neatness could allow her to bend even a little. Joan gave as much as she was able, but giving of herself was the most difficult of all. She gave more to the workmen who came to her apartment than she gave to her children. Her generosity was legendary. Over the years she gave me many little presents, one a beautiful velvet-lined box with a burled top that she had had made for Alfred Steele's enormous collection of cuff links. I use the box often. Another gift was the last portrait, the one showing her gray hair. I never accepted that gift, and it was eventually sold at the Plaza Gallery auction.

It's often hard to point to a single event as being the beginning of the end, but with the benefit of hindsight I know what that incident was. *Architectural Digest* wanted to photograph Joan's Imperial House apartment, and Joan had invited me and my good friend, Paige Rense, the magazine's editor-in-chief, for cocktails. I arrived first. Joan was nervous about meeting Paige. She really didn't like journalists. Then she asked me what I'd like to drink, and I told her I'd have some white wine.

"Why the hell didn't you tell me to get that before you came?" she exploded, eyes flashing. I shrugged off the outburst and noticed she wasn't drinking the usual vodka but iced tea, a recent change from her normal pattern. It crossed my mind that she had been a lot easier to get along with when she was hitting the vodka. In fact, she was now being impossible, and I did not look forward to the meeting at all.

Nevertheless, by the time Paige arrived with her escort, Jacques Camus, general manager of the Regency Hotel, Joan had pulled herself together and greeted them as the old familiar Hollywood movie star. She couldn't have been more charming. Gone were the housedress, the ponytail, and the vodka. In their place were the elaborate dressing gown, the perfect makeup and coif, and out came the Dom Perignon. The three of us sat in her austere living room and watched her at her glittering best as she regaled us with some amusing anecdotes about the late Billy Haines, and about her life and her surroundings, which she insisted were modest. She could not understand why anybody would be interested in them. Little did she realize that *Architectural Digest* would have photographed her life style had she lived in one room with a rollaway bed and a catbox in the corner, people were that curious about how La Crawford lived.

That visit with Paige and Jacques Camus was the last time I witnessed the miracle of transformation from Joan the mortal to Joan the movie queen, but it was not the last time I was to witness her Theda Bara side. I had ignored her outburst over my neglect to call in my wine order, but I could not ignore her rudeness to a photographer called in to replace Richard Champion, who had originally been assigned to photograph the apartment and couldn't keep the appointment. The result was the only argument I had with her in twelve years. I had asked Bettina Cirone to pinch-hit when I learned Champion couldn't make the appointment, and she was kind enough to do so. It was a dreadful session. Joan was at her tyrannical worst during what surely must have been one of the most grueling assignments of Bettina's career. When she sat down for a moment, Joan turned to one of my assistants and screamed, "Get that bitch off my sofa!"

"You're the one who acted like a bitch!" I told her after I learned of the episode. She didn't speak to me for weeks. In fact, she probably never would have spoken to me again had I not taken the advice of her West Coast secretary, Betty Barker, and sent her flowers and an apology note. During my exile we conducted business through Betty. Joan insisted the Cirone pictures be destroyed, no matter how great they were, and ordered that the apartment be photographed, as originally planned, by Richard Champion. I was forbidden to be there when it happened.

If Joan never apologized, it simply was not her style. I knew she couldn't say "I'm sorry" because she could never admit she was wrong about anything. Nevertheless, I did think the whole affair had been entirely out of line, even for someone who could be as unreasonable as Joan. What I didn't know was that she had stopped drinking because she was very ill. Having come from a family with a history of alcoholism, and having even supported two relatives who were alcoholics for a time, she knew how liquor could weaken people and made them dependent on others.

Joan had been a heavy drinker for as long as I had known her, but she had always remained in control. Even after her move to Imperial House and the intoxicated public appearances, there were very few times when I felt the alcohol was in control of her. But when she found out she had major health troubles, she cut out the vodka—cold. Her illness had originated in the liver, and I'm sure she hoped that cutting out alcohol would cure the liver problem. It didn't. Joan had cancer. No wonder she was so difficult during those last eighteen months. But, not knowing her secret, I couldn't offer any comfort.

That, apparently, was the point. Joan didn't want sympathy—from anyone. All we knew was that she was retreating more and more from life, first refusing to be photographed, then refusing to leave the apartment. When I did see her, although she continued to look well, she was consistently somewhere between difficult and impossible. It was during these trying years that Mamacita left her and went back to Germany.

Imagine discovering you have cancer. Imagine you don't believe in medical doctors and know you will have to go through all the terrible pain you've heard about by sheer willpower. Then imagine deciding to go through it all without telling anyone. I can't, but Joan did it. Darinka Papich was one of the two or three people who knew. She had been a good friend for many years, and as Joan became increasingly helpless Darinka began visiting her regularly. Another visitor was a Mrs. Campbell, a Christian Scientist who came frequently toward the end to talk to Joan about religious matters. As a Christian Scientist, Joan refused to be treated by a physician, but Mrs. Campbell did arrange for a registered nurse named Maria, also a Christian Scientist, to tend to Joan's needs.

Around Christmas of 1976 Joan started giving things away. She gave Darinka a mink coat in a black and white diamond-shaped pattern. On March 23, Joan's birthday, she gave up smoking the same way she gave up drinking—cold turkey. I don't know why she gave it up. Perhaps inhaling smoke made her feel worse. I last spoke to her on the telephone six days before she died, on May 4, 1977. She wanted to send out two bedside tables to be relaminated and, as usual, was following up on every detail and wondering what was taking the shop so long to get them back to her. She sounded in good spirits. I would have been shocked to discover then how very sick she was.

Two days later Joan was feeling so poorly she made arrangements for Darinka to take her Shih Tzu, Princess Lotus Blossom. The Princess was a true Upper East Side dog with a pedigree longer than that of most of her neighbors. She slept in a little bed with a canopy that matched the draperies in Joan's bedroom. She wore bows in her hair and had never been outside in her life, for Joan was terrified of dog snatchers. Parting with the dog must have been very hard for Joan, because it meant she was acknowledging her imminent death, but she and Darinka made light of the matter. Darinka had a sister who lived in the Village who loved dogs, even bringing home waifs she found on the street. Princess Lotus Blossom, then, was to go live with Zora, and Darinka joked with Crawford about bringing her on Sundays to visit. The lightheartedness was meant to ease the pain. "We knew what was happening," Darinka told me. That Friday, Darinka and her sister took the dog in a station wagon to Zora's apartment, and when her egalitarian collection of dogs met the new addition, Darinka reported they definitely knew they were in the presence of a lady. Nevertheless, by the weekend Princess was a Greenwich Village street dog squatting in the curb with the hoi polloi.

The following Sunday was Mother's Day. Contrary to the stories about Joan's last Mother's Day on earth being spent exiled from all her children, she was not. Darinka had visited that day, and Joan, managerial to the end, had her record all the phone messages. Cindy and Cathy had called, and Christina had sent flowers. According to all reports, Tina had not spoken to her mother since 1972, but she did acknowledge her on holidays, birthdays, and special occasions. Joan was feeling well enough that day to attend to some correspondence, and she dictated three letters to Darinka. One was to an aspiring model who had sent a photograph and a letter asking for advice. Joan signed the letter and instructed Darinka to return the picture with it, then left similar instructions to return a script a man in Staten Island had sent her for her consideration.

Joan was dying in sections. Although she could still sit up and use her upper torso, she no longer had the use of her legs. But her mind was clear and remained so. Late that afternoon,

Darinka saw that she was getting tired and helped the nurse carry her into the bathroom, bathe her, carry her back to bed, dress her, and brush her hair. With Mamacita gone, Joan had no live-in help, but the nurse had been with her constantly for three weeks. On Monday Darinka was back, relieved to find Joan still alive, and the nurse left for a few days. That day, as Darinka was carrying Joan to the toilet, Darinka made the mistake of saying something sympathetic. "I think I said something like, 'I want to pray for you,'" she recalled. Joan said, almost as an aside, "Oh, Darinka, don't do that." Like anyone who has watched a person die, Darinka was plagued by feelings of helplessness and was constantly wondering whether there was anything she might do. Joan, on the other hand, could not tolerate sympathy.

When Darinka later told Christina about the incident, she said she had done so in an effort to explain why her mother had told no one she was dying, to try to convey to her the extent of Joan's refusal to be an object of pity. She was upset when Christina later said in her book that Joan's last words had been, "Goddamn it, don't pray for me." Darinka wished Tina had been with her mother when she lay dying. "It becomes a part of you forever," she said. "If Christina had seen her mother suffer, she could not have written all those horrible things."

Joan spent her last night on earth under Darinka's watchful eyes. The following day, May 10, 1977, was the anniversary of Joan's wedding to Alfred Steele. This was made much of by columnists who persisted in believing that Joan had made elaborate plans to commit suicide, even going so far as to take her life on that special day. Nonsense. For one thing, Joan's religion prohibited suicide; for another, there was no need.

The obituaries read that Crawford died of a heart attack, a minor error in the epidemic of errors that was about to begin. Fans read, then wept, over the reports of how poor Joan's body had been taken down the service elevator and dumped in the back seat of a car. Untrue, of course. Campbell's doesn't do things that way. People read of the elaborate suicide plots. Even Princess Lotus Blossom was incorporated into the richly embroidered stories of Joan's deliberate end. But the scandal had only begun.

On the day of interment, the family went to the mortuary in Westchester, where Joan's ashes were placed next to those of Alfred Steele in what funeral directors call a his-and-her niche. Mrs. Campbell said a prayer, and the family proceeded to the

Drake Hotel for the reading of her will. There Christina and Christopher heard the shocking news that their mother had cut them off without a sou. From beyond the grave came the terrifying phrase fit for an Old Testament patriarch that they were to receive nothing "for reasons well known to them." If there was ever a doomsday pronouncement from the tomb, that was it. Although Joan had been estranged from her two oldest adopted children for many years, no one knew she would go as far as to leave them nothing but bitter memories.

In the months that followed, both Darinka and I got calls from Christina's lawyer asking us to testify in court that Joan was a raving alcoholic and/or out of her mind at her time of death. We both refused, of course. Christina was determined to get her share of her mother's estate, and was suing the charities to which Joan had left the bulk of her fortune. (Cathy and Cindy had received about $77,000 each, and $1 million went to charitable institutions.) Eventually Christina won $55,000 in a settlement, but nearly half of that went to her lawyers and the rest had to be shared with Christopher. She did manage to wrest a legacy out of her mother in the end, for the sales of her book most likely exceeded the amount her mother had left to charity.

I was on a train going from Gstaad to Montreux, Switzerland, when I heard of Joan's death. It was a quiet place for rumination, with some of the most spectacular scenery in the world outside my window. I wrote an article, "Goodbye, Dear Joan," for the *New York Post* and thought back on the twelve years I had known her. The memories flashed through my brain with the speed of the passing scenery: the shockingly tiny woman at the Pepsi fountain; the heartbroken woman leaving her past behind on Fifth Avenue; the tyrant; the persnickety neatnik, Kleenex box and felt pads in hand. The giver. You quickly learned not to admire anything out loud in Joan's apartment because she'd give it to you at once. Most of all, that curious, almost oedipal fascination of sex and motherliness: power and beauty, vitality and fragility, pride and vulnerability. There will never be another like her. Some may be grateful for such a statement. I, for one, miss her and think of her often.

The late Joan Crawford and Carleton Varney.

Here's a picture of Crawford that few have
seen. It was a candid picture that she liked
and wanted me to have.

With Arthur Brody during my halcyon days at
the *New York Post*.

Photographed by Bettina Cirone

With author—Norman Rockwell manages to look as if he had
rendered himself, pipe and all, the Quintessential Yankee at
home.

Photographed by Tom Starling

Chapter 4

Varney the Reporter

When a decorator turns reporter, he has a living-room view of how the people who make news really live. After a while I became fascinated by the relationship between a celebrity's image and his environment. In some cases there was complete compatibility. When I interviewed Norman Rockwell at his home in Stockbridge, Massachusetts, I felt as if I were being invited to walk through the front door into a *Saturday Evening Post* cover. While there were no surprises awaiting me in the Rockwell living room, interviewing Joe Namath at home was somewhat of a shocker. Between the perfect blend and the perfect contrast of image and environment were scores of mind-opening adventures. An insightful interview with Bette Davis taught *me* something about design. A visit to Gloria Swanson, on the other hand, proved to be an Alice-in-Wonderland trip to the Queen of Hearts at her wildest. Contrasting the Swanson debacle was an interview with then soon-to-be First Lady Rosalynn Carter that revealed a soft and homey woman who was planning to bring her sewing machine to the White House.

Omar Sharif provided me with an interview with the accent on the view. A chance interview with Emilio Pucci on a transatlantic flight resulted not only in a column but also a friendship. An "interview" with Princess Margaret surrounded by hoards of Beautiful People on the island of Sardinia was one of my better examples of turning a bit of *haut monde* diversion into a design statement, but my best noninterview was with Richard Burton's stateroom aboard the *France*.

People told me the craziest things. They also provided me with information I didn't know what to do about. Martha Mitchell informed me that she wished her entire world was pink. Mrs.

Franklin D. Roosevelt, Jr., announced that she had never done a room in blue. A more bellicose point of view came from fellow designer Oleg Cassini, who stood amid his collection of Renaissance armor and weaponry and said darkly, "I'm from a warrior class. In the fashion field you have to be a fighter—for survival." Into the tape recorder went conversations with superstars, politicians, sports heroes, industrialists, crowned heads, jet-setters, and hard-working people who had made it to the top; out came a column about life styles and design that I hoped would be useful and interesting to my readers.

The pursuit of a story sometimes took me places I would rather not have gone to see things I didn't intend or expect to see. On these occasions I was caught in that eternal reporter's dilemma of how much of someone's private life should be revealed for the sake of a good article. I formulated a rule during those years of writing for newspapers that although I would often describe the life styles of people about whom the public seems to have an insatiable curiosity, I would not create sensational copy that had nothing to do with the topic—which was always how people lived. *But.* Writing a book is different from writing a column. As I paid visits to my files in preparation for writing a chapter about my visits to the shrines of newsmakers, I began reliving some of those private moments with public figures and decided to tell more, if not all. I must continue to walk the streets with the typical New Yorker's wary attitude toward chance disaster. Muggers, falling lintels, and careening taxis are one thing, but being attacked by an outraged celebrity is not my idea of how to make the front page. These stories, then, are outtakes, the ones I left out of my columns.

*   *   *

My writing career began in my youth. In high school I was editor-in-chief of the yearbook and school magazine. I also won several essay contests on subjects familiar to anyone of my generation who had writing aspirations: brotherhood, peace, democracy, and other oratorical topics. Nothing page-turning, but it taught me how to string cogent thoughts together. At Oberlin I was on the newspaper staff and a yearbook editor.

Everyone knows, of course, that such a list of credits won't get you far in the Concrete Apple, but being a decorator was never enough for me. I was inspired by Dorothy Draper's success as "Ask Dorothy Draper," the first decorator/columnist. I decided to try my hand at it. Of course, Dorothy's famous name sold her column, even though someone else actually transcribed her thoughts into words (not at all uncommon in the syndicated column business), but I decided to try another approach.

In 1962 I began writing *You and Your Apartment*, my first book. It was not written for people who live and breathe interior design, the kind who spend an entire afternoon chatting about Chippendale and the future of minimal decor. At the time I wrote the book, most decorating books were written for this select group, and I have always been bored to death by them. People who fill up their lives placing just the right bibelot on the perfect table, being seen at the right parties and getting to know the right people who will come to theirs are the very people I spend a lot of time avoiding. Being right has never had much appeal for me. I prefer the company of people who are occasionally wrong, who do unexpected things and live in less-than-perfect rooms. Perfect rooms, like perfect people, are not only intimidating but they leave little room for growth. My first book was for these less-than-perfect people who no longer lived in houses with lawns, garages, basements, and attics, but in apartments that were always, it seemed, one room too small. *You and Your Apartment* was the first book devoted to apartment living, in spite of the fact that millions of people all over the country were living in them.

Robert Amussen, my editor at Bobbs-Merrill, told me while the book was still in the works that it looked as if we had a winner; encouraged by my success, I decided that next I'd like to try column writing. I was renting a house that summer in Southampton, New York, and used some extra energy writing a kind of at-home column for the local shiny-sheet weekly. For my on-the-job training I received about $25 a week for serving up news of Southampton socialites and how they lived and entertained and otherwise spent their money. It wasn't my cup of Djarleeng, but it was good experience.

You and Your Apartment did so well I decided to write another book, *The Family Decorates a Home*, which outsold my first. By then it was 1964, and Dorothy Draper was living in a nursing home in Cleveland while her writer continued to turn out "Ask Dorothy Draper" columns. After Dorothy died, newspapers all over the country sent in cancellation notices to the syndicate, correctly assuming that readers would not relish getting their decorating hints from beyond the grave. The column died with Dorothy, and unlike the advice columnists, she had had a monopoly on the subject.

I had an idea to recapture the papers that had canceled and called Glen Adcox of Adcox Associates who, along with his wife, Gertrude, were the best news syndicate people in the business and I said, "You don't know me but—" Glen did know me, and my books, and straightaway gave me a crack at my own decorating column. He said he was counting on my position as the young president of a time-honored firm and the author of two successful decorating books. It was the latter, I think, that caused him to accept my offer.

The column's name was a problem. In keeping with the title of my second book, I settled on "Your Family Decorator," a name that has stuck right up to the present.

I then began a campaign of persuasion, with the help of Adcox, that I was the rightful heir to the Draper column. It wasn't easy. A decorating column is not of such earth-shaking importance that every newspaper has to have one, but my selling idea was to increase readership by being useful in ways that ordinary people could relate to. The great majority of people in this country can't afford a decorator yet really need some professional ideas when it comes time for a change. Change is risky and expensive, and many find it brings out all their insecurities. The persuasion campaign worked; many papers that had canceled Dorothy Draper's column agreed to carry mine. I was gratified in getting as many as I did, for in spite of my books, I was still very much an unknown within the industry.

The only paper that gave me any trouble was the now defunct *Boston Record American*. When they took my column I felt a flush of pride, having grown up in the suburbs of Boston, but before it even appeared the paper canceled my contract. When I heard why, I didn't know whether to laugh or have a small tantrum. It seemed I had written an article in which I had suggested that end tables should be the same height as the sofa arms and that coffee tables should be two inches lower than the sofa seat. My syndicate, Adcox Associates, told me that this advice had apparently deeply upset the publisher's wife. "How *could* anyone suggest such a thing?" she had allegedly told her husband. "This man knows nothing about decorating and he should not be allowed to appear in the *Boston Record American!*" Boston, as everyone knows, is tradition bound, and one tradition, apparently, is that one's sofa must not look down on one's coffee table. I was relieved to discover my column was not too far out for another dignified Boston paper, the *Boston Globe*.

My career took a big leap five years later when my column was bought by Dorothy Schiff's *New York Post*. At that time New York was rapidly becoming newspaper poor. Gone were the days when people could choose among the *Journal-American*, the *World Telegram and Sun*, the wonderful *Herald Tribune*, and the *Daily News* and *Daily Mirror*. Aside from the monumentlike *Times* the only likely survivor of the demise of the New York dailies was the *New York Post*. Although I knew Mr. and Mrs. Donald Stralem, distant relatives of the formidable Mrs. Schiff, I decided I would try to get into the *Post* on my own merits. No connections—just phone to phone.

I called Mrs. Schiff. She said, "Send me some material." I did. She bought it and locked me into position, journalese for appearing on the same page in every issue. Those were the halcyon days for columnists at the *Post*: Pete Hamill, Jimmy Breslin, James Weschler, William Buckley, Max Lerner, Harriet Van Horne . . . top-flight writers with widely varying points of view all wrote for the *Post*. Dorothy Schiff really knew how ro run a newspaper.

Most people read the *New York Times* in the morning and bought the *Post* for the commute home, so home was on their minds when they read my column. It was an instant success. My cup was running over. I loved writing "Your Family Decorator" and my other features. And there was yet another bonus: as a columnist I met more celebrities than a dozen clones of myself would have had for clients in a lifetime.

As soon as my column appeared in the *Post* I became a very popular fellow. Calls for invitations to social events began pouring in. Even people I had known when I was young started calling me. I think I received more invitations to events than John and Mary Lindsay. It didn't take me long to discover that in New York the name of the fame game is getting yourself mentioned in the papers as often as you can. Everybody who is anybody or wants to be, from football players to society matrons, hires publicists and press agents to see that they get their names done up in that favorite color scheme of the status seeker: black on white. I started getting calls at two and three in the morning, much to my wife's chagrin. "Hello, Carleton? At last I've caught you at home. Listen, we're having a little get-together on Saturday evening to celebrate the opening of our darling little Provençal restaurant. . . ." There was no escaping them, even in the stratosphere. Airline hostesses would lean over Suzanne and coo, "Carleton Varney? You're just the person I want to talk to. When I'm in New York, where's the best place to get a room divider?"

I loved it.

*   *   *

One of the great advantages of my combined role of celebrity interviewer and decorator was the opportunity to find out whether personalities matched their homes. Sometimes the answer was a resounding yes. Flamboyant Ethel Merman's love for strong color is an obvious example. When I interviewed Hermione Gingold before she stepped into the leading role in Stephen Sondheim's *Side by Side,* I anticipated a whimsical woman out of a Colette novel, for my fondest memory of her was her role of the retired courtesan in *Gigi.* I was not disappointed. Hermione lived in a nineteenth-century atmosphere of old white wicker, eyelet, ruffles and—whimsy. Like Hermione. When it was time to take her picture, she knew exactly how to convey the image she wanted. She curled up on her bed, arranged the eyelet counterpane around her, and gazed knowingly at the camera from behind an enormous fan. The coquette at home, but done with an amusing lightheartedness that told me she really was what she seemed, knew it and loved it.

The same was true for Norman Rockwell. He sat in his living room in an open shirt, pipe in hand, and exuded simplicity and ease. All around him was old New England—rockers, oil lamps, rag rugs, pieces right off the cover of the *Saturday Evening Post.* He was perfectly candid about his art. Yet, it was calendar, he admitted, straight from life. Just like himself. I'm sure he would be amused to know that shortly after his death, the price of his art went sky high and keeps going higher.

Not all people are so sure about who they are and what they want. I had some interviews with personalities in which an attitude of discomfort pervaded the room because the ambience of their surroundings reflected someone else's character, not their own. Believe me, the culprit is almost always an egotistical member of my profession, the kind of decorator who must leave a signature behind, like fashion designers who have a penchant for splashing their names on scarves and luggage and jeans.

Of all the mismatches I encountered, the most startling was the East Side New York brownstone duplex apartment of Joe Namath. As usual, I went to the interview conjuring up Broadway Joe at home. Now, if I were a football hero from Beaver Falls, Pennsylvania, I would probably call a decorator and say, "Give me something plush, ritzy, manly, sexy, and above all comfortable because I'm a big man and I get hurt a lot. Do it up in browns, plaids, leather, thick carpets, and give me a game room and a *Playboy* bedroom." That's how I pictured Joe Namath would fulfill his heart's desire. I was in for one of the big surprises of my journalistic career.

First a little suspense. The photographer and I arrived at the scheduled time, but Joe did not. Finally, after we had spent about an hour sitting on a hard brownstone stoop, Joe ambled up 82nd Street. "You're early," he said.

I for one was not about to argue about who was early and who was late.

"Well, come on in anyway," he said with an amiable grin.

The first thing that fell upon my eyes was an enormous bar in a rather small foyer. It was of a scale one might find in a men's club in England, about 10 to 12 feet long, big enough to accommodate the entire first string of the New York Jets. Well, so far there were no big surprises. The bar was a bit big for the room, but so what. From my bar stool I caught a glimpse of Joe's game room. It had the typical brownstone bay window, and the room was painted a baby blue and white with heavy emphasis on the molding, which was trimmed with a gold appliqué. The ceilings were encrusted with gold gilt. The juxtaposition of all that ormolu with the pool table and the one-armed bandit struck me as a bit like playing poker in the palace at Versailles. But the surprises had only begun.

Joe's living room was painted a soft white of a mauve tint. A materalaisse fabric in the same color as the walls graced the sofa. Some smallish gold gilt chairs were scattered about, and when I visualized Joe's beefy football-playing friends lowering themselves gingerly into those spindly chairs, I wondered what on earth had compelled him to go in for that style. The windows were treated with red velvet swags and Austrian puff shades. Everywhere I looked were bronze Victorian fixtures and Baroque figurines in extravagantly heroic poses. One living-room wall was filled with little white and gold pedestals on which sat dainty arrangements of porcelain flower clusters.

The kitchenette walls were covered with hot-colored flowers. I looked everywhere on that first floor but could not find the occupant. Then Joe mentioned he had put the apartment together with the help of a decorator, and my mind was completely blown. I couldn't imagine how a decorator could have designed a house with such complete disregard for the person who was to live in it. Did he really think Joe would enjoy coming home from a grueling football game with his leg wound in tape and sit carefully on the edge of one of those gilt chairs? Either Joe had found himself a decorator who had intimidated his client into living with ormolu, gilt, and flowers, or Joe really wanted them. It is always possible that a client, particularly one whose childhood was not affluent, secretly yearns for whatever the most elegant house in his home town looked like. Once he becomes wealthy and can have anything he wants, that's what he goes for, no matter how far removed it is from his own style. I found it hard to believe Joe could be intimidated into accepting something he didn't really want, and decided that what I was looking at was a re-creation of the finest house in Beaver Falls through the memory of a home-town boy who had made it big.

Life photographer Harry Benson dropped by, and we all sat at Joe's big bar for a drink. I found Joe altogether pleasant but not easy to talk to. He is apparently quite reserved with people he doesn't know, and it was obvious to me he would much rather have talked about football than about his life style.

"Can we see the second floor?" I asked, and at once he got up and we bounded upstairs. I found myself at the threshold of the bedroom of Joe Namath, a fantasy place if there ever was one for the admirers of this phenomenal man. Two enormous lanterns aglow with amber lights hung at either side of the bed. The color scheme was a pleasant rust and brown, and a brown velvet spread covered the bed over which hung a small tented canopy. The furnishings were the same French ormolu of the downstairs, and I regret to report that there were no mirrors on the headboard and ceiling. No Jacuzzi. No Hugh Hefner influence anywhere to be seen. Nevertheless, Joe would not permit the photographer to take a picture of that room. As we walked around the bedroom Joe suddenly said, "I'd like to make some changes around here. I'm not so happy with the way it turned out."

"Have you talked to your decorator?" I asked. There is, be

lieve it or not, some honor among members of my profession and I always try to avoid intruding on an unhappy decorator client relationship unless I'm sure it's fair to do so.

"I don't want to talk to him about it," he said, "What do you think we could do to the bedroom? I need a soft bedspread— something that feels good."

It was obvious to me by then that Joe realized the apartment needed to be pulled together, and I admired his candor and willingness to have it redone. It's hard to admit a mistake about something as personal (and expensive) as one's dream of the perfect living space gone awry.

"I'll draw up some schemes if you like," I said. "You can drop by the office later and see them."

"Fine," he said, and we trotted downstairs for some picture taking. We ran one of Joe slouched in one of his richly ornamented armchairs in the living room, his sneakered foot resting on the back of the matelassé sofa.

I was proud of my staff the day Joe came to the office to look over the decorating plans I'd prepared for his bedroom. The women who work with me are exceptionally discriminating and unflappable, but the day Namath was to arrive they were in a tizzy. However, when he walked in the door they were cool. No one swooned. They treated him with warm but professional courtesy and a certain deference I hadn't noticed before. There's definitely an aura around men like Namath. Like Gable, Brando, Dean, and Mick Jagger, they all manage to turn sophisticated grown-up women into sixteen-year-olds while other men look on with (I admit it) envy. What's so special about this guy, we ordinary males are prone to ask, that sends the hearts of normally blasé women into palpitations? Some men's sexiness seems to awaken the primitive "Me Tarzan, You Jane" impulse. Nevertheless, Joe left the office without so much as one squeal having escaped from my staff into the electrified atmosphere. Even after the guy had gone, the place was charged. I admit I was a tiny bit jealous. They'd hung on his every word, for God's sake.

He had taken my plans, sketches, and estimates with him and said he would get back to me soon about the work. A week went by, and then another. One morning around ten I finally called his private number and heard a muffled and befogged, "Who is this?" at the other end of the line. When I told him it was Carleton Varney calling about the plans, he said, "Call me back around four." I hung up, feeling a little chagrined, as if I had committed a *faux pas* getting someone out of bed in the middle of the morning.

When I called him later that afternoon he politely told me never to call him before noon, as he liked to sleep late. I agreed to conduct business in this fashion, but I could predict a scheduling problem that might further compound the communication problem. Workmen like to get started early and finish before five P.M., which seemed to be when the Namath day got going. Finally, after many unreturned phone calls, I realized something had to be done.

From the beginning of the Namath project I knew that any money Joe spent had first to be cleared by his lawyer, Jimmy Walsh. I had a feeling Jimmy wouldn't let his client spend one more cent on decorating, and he also knew that Joe was a man on the move, not remaining in one place long enough to enjoy any decor. One night I met Jimmy Walsh at a party and told him I didn't appreciate the way he had disallowed any more decorating funds after all the work the office had done—gratis—for his client. In the end, we provided Joe Namath with one brown velvet bedspread, and even that was a total debit. He had taken one look at it and demanded a softer one. It was sent back to the workroom, and a second bedspread was made of softer velvet. The bill was for $295 and change, and we ended up eating the first bill. I later read in the *New York Times* that Joe and his decorator were involved in a lawsuit. I didn't know who was suing whom, nor did I know by that point where my sympathies would lie if I did. One good thing did come of the Namath affair: when it was time for Joe's lawyer to hire a designer for his Park Avenue law firm, Bushkin, Koppelson and Walsh, he hired my firm to do the job.

Another interview with a popular heartthrob took place in a hotel suite at the famous Westbury Hotel on London's Bond Street. The top-floor suite had been originally designed by Norman Hartnell, Queen Elizabeth's dress designer, and he had turned the rooms into an aviary. Birds were everywhere: porcelain birds perched on the chandeliers, light fixtures, and sconces. One even sat on birds: each print-upholstered piece of furniture featured birds of every kind. Every time I opened a closet I expected a bird to fly out. It was all too much—too many birds is the making of Hitchcock horror films, not havens of comfort to the weary traveler. When I took on the redecorating of the hotel I took one look at the Hartnell Suite and said, "Less birds." I loved the idea, but the execution had gone beyond whimsy. It was time to depopulate the aviary.

One year, the guest in the newly redecorated Hartnell suite during my six-week maintenance visit to the hotel was Omar Sharif, who was staying there while making the movie *The Tamarind Seed* with Julie Andrews. Suzanne and our son Nicholas had come to London with me, and we had run into Omar several times since our arrival. Each time I had noticed he couldn't take his eyes off my wife.

Elsie Lumsden, the Westbury's housekeeper, with whom I had a good relationship, had told me, "If you want to interview Mr. Sharif, I can arrange it." She did, and crafty lady that she is, she came with me. We were shown into Omar's living room in the Hartnell suite and told that Mr. Sharif was in the shower and would be out directly. A few minutes later I looked up from a magazine to see Omar stepping into the room in all his splendour: black curly hair, expressive spaniel eyes, white flashing teeth, bare chest, and a white terry robe that was a few inches short of modesty. Omar had, for some reason, decided to wear to the interview the shortie bathrobe supplied by the hotel. One like it hung on the bathroom door of every room. Omar sat down on a bird-print sofa I later covered in green velvet and proceeded without ado to tell me how he lived. "I'll tell you anything you want to know about how I live in Paris," he said. And he did—with enthusiasm, wit, and excellent detail. It was one of those blessed interviews that practically write themselves.

A good interview can happen anywhere. Recently I was flying from Paris to New York when I recognized Emilio Pucci sitting across the aisle. Noticing the seat adjoining him was empty, I decided it was silly to spend the next six or seven hours in the air doing nothing when I could be learning something. I introduced myself, and we had a stimulating conversation all the way back to New York. One of the things he told me was to always have a black velvet jacket hanging in your closet ready for use with a bow tie in the pocket. If you're invited to an affair and don't know how you should dress, wear the velvet jacket. If it's formal, clip on your tie. If it's not, you'll look good anyway.

The most disastrous interview I ever had came out of an idea that originated with a photographer friend from California, Ellen Graham. I wanted to do a story on how to use photos in the home, and she said, "Let's do it with Gloria Swanson. She's a good friend and I have a lot of pictures of her." I agreed, knowing the Swanson connection would enhance the article. After all, she was one of the Four Fabulous Faces, along with Dietrich, Garbo, and Crawford, and for an entire generation of people, when it comes to glamour, Gloria Swanson is the *dernier cri*.

She lived in a Fifth Avenue maisonette with her husband, Bill Dufty. It was a rather dark apartment that had an entrance into a large drawing room with what looked like a garden in the back. Her husband greeted me warmly and was most helpful during the interview. Swanson, alas, was not. She entered the room; instead of a vision, I beheld a specter. It wasn't that the Fabulous Face had grown old—not at all. A beautiful face in old age often radiates a new kind of softness and wisdom, but in Swanson's case the face had set into lines of downright meanness. What the visage foretold was about to happen.

As she came into the room, I had been arranging a group of Ellen's photographs on a table for the photographer. Swanson came rushing over and said, "Why did you move these things around? I don't want people to think I have pictures of myself around here. I'm not *that* vain!" I looked around the room and everywhere my gaze fell there seemed to be pictures of Gloria Swanson in all her youthful splendour. Staring up at me from a nearby table was a copy of *Four Fabulous Faces*. Her reaction was so strong I decided at once to change the focus of the story. I recalled that Joan Crawford, who did not have many pictures of herself around, had once become very upset when *Architectural Digest* published a photo taken in her dressing room in which a small, unobtrusive picture of her had been blown up, giving the reader the impression that Crawford lived with an enormous picture of herself in plain sight. It nearly drove her crazy. "You *know* I don't have a lot of pictures of myself around," she railed.

I could understand Crawford's attitude, but catering to Swanson's sensitivities as I stood in the middle of a room with Gloria Swanson photos all about was a little more difficult. Then she said, "I'm not even ready for pictures." And, "No," she said, "you cannot photograph me in my home." This was the first I had heard about photographing Gloria alone. The plan had been to photograph Gloria with Ellen's collection of photos, as the story concerned how to use photography in the home. I recovered in time to say, "You look great," to which she turned her backside to me, kicked up her foot until I could see the sole of her shoe, and said, "Merde." She delayed her exit for a moment with a shrill, "If you *ever* use any of those photographs of my home in your newspaper, I will *sue.*" Gloria left the room in a puff of smoke.

Her husband salvaged the interview by suggesting we use one of his pieces of sculpture as a background for some of Ellen's photos. The afternoon had been a fiasco for me and for young *New York Post* photographer Mary McLaughlan. From the start Swanson had regarded us as intruders into her private world. As for me, I had seen the somewhat dark ambience of her surroundings and was not surprised to find some of it reflected in her face that afternoon. Sometimes being a reporter takes you inside places you wish you had not seen.

One of the great challenges of writing a regular column is always having something to say. Usually turning a few bits of information gathered during an interview into an article was not a big problem, but there were times when, like the Swanson interview, there was no story (at least not one I could write in "Your Family Decorator") or the celebrity turned out to be hopelessly dull, or like my column on Princess Margaret on the Costa Smeralda, I ended up creating a story out of a bit of cloth. Patchwork at that.

Ah, the Costa Smeralda! At the time of my story the Aga Kahn was turning this coast of Sardinia into a new, ultra-chic Riviera, building hotels and selling lots to vacationers. The English love a seaport, and the presence of Princess Margaret and Tony Armstrong-Jones was very important to the Aga Kahn's development plans because they helped attract English money. I had at one time hoped to do some hotel design for the Aga Kahn's consortium account and had gone to Puerto Cervo, the principal town on the Costa Smeralda, to make inquiries with Peter Hengel, one of the Aga Kahn's right hands. I deduced they really wanted an Italian for the job, but by the time I realized I wouldn't be winning the Aga Kahn for a client I had made several friends in Sardinia and had fallen in love with the place. As I make it a rule never to vacation where I have done work because I'm too available for consultation, I was glad I was going to come to Sardinia as a vacationer and not a decorator.

For three years I took a house on the Costa Smeralda. One year I rented a white sculptured Moroccan-style home that looked somewhat like the villa Elizabeth Taylor lived in in the film *Boom!* Tony Curtis had rented the house the summer before, and I found that if I puttered around in the front yard the cars would slow down at the Romanzino turn on the other side of my big wooden gate and voices would call out, "There he is! There he is!" I had a lot of fun flashing my best Tony Curtis grin as they drove by.

The big event of every year in Sardinia was Puerto Cervo Day, a benefit regatta for yachts and sailing boats sponsored by the Aga Kahn. Suzanne and I always accepted our invitation, and we often went to the porto early to watch the people. As the Tony Armstrong-Joneses always presented the awards, the Beautiful People never failed to congregate, like pilgrims to Mecca. Henry and Christina Ford were there, the auto heir looking a bit pudgy; and Bettina, Ali Kahn's beautiful model friend, glided between the tables collecting glances. We also saw many of the lesser-known faces of the European industrial magnates, people much more powerful than your average celebrity, with names like Krupp and Agnelli. They were all there, it seemed, and it struck us that the atmosphere was a bit like Palm Beach: everybody had made it to the party, but no one was exactly sure why.

Rumors flew that Margaret and Tony were fighting like hell. They both looked a little out of place, as if they had just flown in from a higher latitude and hadn't adjusted to the sea change. Tony's face was impossibly tan, and Margaret was wearing a heavy patchwork-quilted skirt, a stifling contrast to the light-weight cotton midsummer garb everyone else was wearing. As I watched her make the presentations I got a brilliant idea. I'd write a column on patchwork and the quilted look, inspired by a princess! I did, and it got to the top of the women's page. Quilting was big that fall, and I like to tell myself it was all because of me and Princess Meg and the dinner we attended together at the Puerto Cervo Yacht Club. With about a thousand others.

Eventually Sardinia proved to be less than paradise. Even though I had gone as far as to buy property in Piccolo Pevero and had drawn up architectural plans for a house from which on a clear day one could see all the way to Corsica, I was beginning to have second thoughts. There was a handsome-looking Moroccan-style club on Puerto Cervo where jet-set people went to smoke all sorts of things; it was raided like clockwork by the Sardinia police—but never when royalty was on the premises. As the island is a long plane ride from New York, we decided the place wasn't the best for vacationing with small children. However, vacations in Sardinia had offered us some wonderful times—and me about sixteen inches of column.

My story on Martha Mitchell was another interview that

arose out of a social occasion. I had been invited by my friend Dick Ridge to a cocktail party at his Park Avenue apartment. It was one of my former addresses; in fact, I had occupied the same apartment on another floor. Walking into his apartment under those circumstances, I got a jolt of *déjà vu*, a weird feeling that everything looked familiar and yet wasn't. Sitting on the sofa was someone also familiar and from the recent past, Martha Mitchell. I had never thought of her as a person with her own identity, always associating her with the Fall of the House of Nixon in which her role was that of a slightly crazy and possibly drunken Southern Belle who called up reporters in the dead of night and told them she knew of terrible deeds that had been done. I tried hard to connect the rather frail-looking woman sitting alone on the couch with the person she had played in history, and found it hard to do so.

I was also curious about her for another reason. The pleasant woman with the wan smile was supposed to be—what? Out of control, mentally unbalanced, alcoholic, or just a loud talker? Whatever she was, she stepped off history's stage in a very ignominious scene: injected in the derrière with a needle full of tranquilizers by the plumber's medical squad. Then tragedy and more tragedy. Her husband was disgraced. She divorced him. They fought in court over their daughter. Her ex-husband was convicted. And the most recent blow: doctors had told her she had a disease that seemed to be dissolving her bones.

In spite of all the bad times, she looked very well that afternoon. She was dressed in shell pink, and, like Crawford, everything matched. I had been talking to Pat Loud, another woman everyone found intriguing, when I saw Martha Mitchell was alone. I went over and introduced myself. We talked for half an hour about a subject she seemed to be very interested in, interior decorating. Her tastes were definitely on the delicate side: she loved pink and white and liked to use the colors of her china as the basis of a color scheme for a room. There was something of the powder puff about her, very much the Southern Belle, although Little Rock and not Atlanta. She was charming and voluble but never lost a faint hostility in her manner, as if she expected to be attacked.

Martha Mitchell was living alone in New York, and I asked her whether she liked it better than Washington. "Oh my, yes," she said. "I wish I'd never been to Washington. I'm a real New Yorker. I like the chance it offers me to be a private person." As

Martha was obviously trying to put the past behind her and wanted anonymity, I was not going to ask her any personal or political questions.

I never saw Martha Mitchell again. The next time I heard of her, she was dead. Had Martha not lost her anonymity for a few terrible years, most likely she would have lived an uneventful but happy life, her name appearing in the papers only when her daughter came out and got married or she was involved in social affairs as the wife of a prominent lawyer. Surely she would never have exhibited herself to the country as a loud, shrill, sassy lady who couldn't keep her mouth shut if she hadn't found herself in a situation she couldn't handle. That Martha was a fire-eater and no lover of china pastels—or so it seemed. Who knows how much she knew and how it made her suffer? I hope someday someone tells us what really happened to Martha Mitchell.

My most memorable noninterview was with Richard Burton, or rather with his stateroom. I like to write about temporary living arrangements and how people turn them into homes, and finding myself on the last voyage of the *France* with Burton as a fellow passenger, I thought I could get a good story about him. He had just broken up with Taylor on one of those many separations before the final split, and was on his way to England to make a film about Winston Churchill. Although he had been looking particularly morose every night when I saw him walking on deck accompanied by his female secretary, I decided to try for an interview. I sent him a note asking for one. No answer. The *France* churned its way across the Atlantic, and Burton became more sullen-looking each day. It was obvious he was not about to grant me an interview. I knew his stateroom number, however, and convinced my deck steward to let me see the stateroom. Result: a piece on a famous Welshman on a floating French palace, the decor of his stateroom an equally stately burgundy, light blue, and gray. Interviewing Burton's ultra-French stateroom was, I must say, a piece of marzipan compared with some of the interviews I had been having of late, and it did create what I had intended: a description of how people live, whether at home or en route.

Another fascinating insight into how people create their own environments in temporary situations was a story I did on hospital decor. I had decorated Carolton Chronic and Convalescent Hospital in Connecticut, and had gone to give the place a little checkup when Carmen Tortora, the director and a good friend, informed me he had a famous patient there who had just done a little rearranging of her room. "Who?" I asked. "Bette Davis," he said. "She's moved the bed to the center of the room."

I was intrigued. Whenever I have finished a decorating project and return to find changes have been made in the furniture arrangements, I am always eager to pursue why. Humans, after all, do not live in rooms the way actors do on a stage set, following predetermined blocking patterns drawn up for a pleasing tableau effect from the audience's viewpoint. Every time someone starts rearranging furniture in a room I have designed I learn something about the focus of those rooms in terms of how they are being used.

Hospitals are a real challenge to an interior designer. The first consideration, of course, has to be meeting reams of medical requirements, and after a design has passed muster with the hospital officials and medical personnel, a designer hopes there will be a little room left for considering the needs of the patient too. Unfortunately, this is not always the case. Too often, by the time everyone else's demands have been met, the poor patient is left surrounded by murky hospital beige and green, cold tile, and an ambience that makes only one statement: antiseptic. No wonder people dread spending time in institutions, whether as patient or visitor.

When I designed Carolton I had the complete cooperation of the director in considering the emotional needs of the patients. He didn't even flinch when I papered the ceilings with bright flowered wallpaper. After all, the ceiling is what patients see most while lying on their backs, and rather than study the cracks, why not let them look at something beautiful? Flowers bloom on some of the ceilings at Carolton. Scientists have determined that certain colors like melon, lemon, and other citrus colors stimulate the appetite, and as most hospital food needs all the help it can get, I painted the walls at Carolton in shades that would please the eye while they stimulated the salivary glands. I was delighted to be able to incorporate many of the ideas I had dreamed about for turning a hospital into a cheerful temporary living environment, and was very pleased with the results. Consequently, when I heard Bette Davis had tried to improve on it, I was curious to hear how and why.

I called her room and introduced myself as the decorator of the hospital. "I hear you've made some changes," I said. "Yes," came the reply in that unmistakable voice. "I moved the bed to the center of the room so that it looks out on the garden." Instinctively, Bette Davis must have known that the focus of a room is determined by how the furniture is placed to the left or to the right. By placing her bed dead center, the focus zoomed right out of the window and into the garden. I complimented her on her insight, and she complimented me on my flowery wallcoverings. Since then I have tried to incorporate Bette's concept in other projects.

My years at the *Post* were happy and fairly uncomplicated. I got along well with my boss, and it crossed my mind on occasion that a woman with a strong personality whose name happens to be Dorothy does not have to be difficult to work for. Like Dorothy Draper, Dorothy Schiff had learned the hard way how to be a successful executive in what was still very much a man's world. I marveled at how well they had learned how to employ the universal executive techniques of intimidation, withholding praise, and other clever forms of manipulation; and when they were both at the top of their form, they played the corporate power game in a manner worthy of Daddy Warbucks.

One day Dorothy Schiff called me into her office. One of the techniques of the game, of course, is summoning one's staff without letting them know why, and I approached her office without the slightest idea of what I had done, didn't do, or might do that Dorothy wished to discuss. Only once had word come from on high that the boss was displeased, and that was over a photograph I had run in the *Post* that had also been run in an advertisement in *House Beautiful*. Mrs. Schiff had sent me a memo, citing the exact pages where the offending photo had appeared, both in her paper and in the magazine, and requested I never repeat the mistake in the future. I did not.

Her office was vast and oval shaped, the egg being, I guess, the conformation of ultimate power in our society if the shape of the chief executive's office is of any symbolic importance. It was furnished well with an enormous English desk, camelback sofa, and other impressive period pieces, some of them covered in Crawfordesque clear plastic.

Mrs. Schiff was sitting behind several acres of burnished wood as her secretary ushered me in. I set out on the journey to her desk, but just short of my destination she got up and crossed over to the camelback couch, curling her feet under her rather seductively. I thought she was an attractive woman. She had a certain majesty about her that may have been innate or may have been learned, the result of her eminence as a publisher of one of the country's big-city newspapers. I also noticed a reserve that bordered at times on shyness. She smoked constantly and was startled when someone opened the office door without knocking, but when she looked at me with those clear eyes, her gaze was so steady and piercing it was downright unnerving, as if she were looking right through me to the green and white palm tree patterned draperies behind me.

After some light conversation about my books, my life, and my ambitions, she revealed the purpose of the meeting. She wanted to pick my brains about office lighting before calling in some consultants to do an overhaul. I was to enlighten her about some of the more technical aspects of lighting in order to prepare her for dealing with experts. We drew up some tentative plans, identified some of the existing problems, and when she felt she knew enough, she said to me, "You know, you're a bit of an egghead." If her comment was meant to flatter me, it succeeded.

The lighting consultants arrived one afternoon for a meeting with Mrs. Schiff and me, and with that overbearing, take-charge manner affected by many experts as a method of intimidating their ignorant clients, they began to lord it over Dorothy Schiff. But they were playing power games with an expert, and she was not about to be intimidated. Mrs. Schiff directed the experts to leave, and they did! She never requested help with her lighting problems again.

On another occasion she approached me about a personal decorating matter. Normally I would not risk taking on a client who was also my employer. Too many things can go wrong in a residential job, and the rule is, the more a person worries the more things *do* go wrong. In this case, not only could I lose a client's good will but a column as well. Dorothy had been at a dinner party at her daughter's home in East Hampton where her decorator, Renny Saltzman, had also been a guest. She had told him she wanted to redo her bedroom. Renny had replied, "Carleton Varney is the decorator in your paper. Why don't you get him to do the job?" "Renny," Mrs. Schiff had said graciously, "what a wonderful idea."

And so it came to pass that I became the decorator of the boss's bedroom. Her walls were painted in a pink and white cross-thatch strie of my own invention, and the draperies were to be French chintz, pinks and greens on white. In spite of all the worry, things were going well. The needlepoint rug had been laid, and the draperies had arrived. On the day of installation Mrs. Schiff was due home at six-thirty, at which time the job was supposed to be done. The installation man inserted toggle bolts into the plaster and hung the valence rod, and then we watched in horror as the wall around the toggle bolts began to crumble, the rod crashed to the floor, and the French chintz draperies set-tled over it in a heap of crumpled flowers. As I stood over the mess I heard the voice of Dorothy Schiff calling out "Varney, you're fired" in my mind. My boss cum client would arrive in an hour. We worked frantically, and by the time she came in the door we had managed to get the draperies back up, hiding the carnage of the cracked wall. Fortunately, she thought the room looked wonderful, and when I explained about the cracked plas-ter, she took it all in stride. New Yorkers are accustomed to the hazards of living in elderly buildings, and Dorothy's was an ele-gant old duplex with a long history.

The plasterers and painters repaired the damage the follow-ing day, and "Your Family Decorator" continued to appear on page 21, but my journalistic career was in for some changes. Shortly after the decorating project for Mrs. Schiff, I wrote the first "Home" section for the *Post*, 25 pages long and a first in the city. I like to think I influenced the *New York Times* in their deci-sion to run a design feature in the "Home" section that appeared in their paper every Thursday.

I was riding high at the *Post*, too busy with new ideas to notice that the winds of change were sweeping the place. Then one day came an official announcement: Dorothy Schiff had sold her paper to an Australian millionaire I had never heard of. His name was Rupert Murdoch, and I was led to believe that the first thing he told his staff on the day he took over was that there was to be no change in the general tone and format of the *Post*. Everyone was to stay put and keep on writing. There were to be immediate changes in personnel—many, many changes. A new woman editor was hired to supervise my "Inside Design" col-umn, a woman of whom I was not particularly fond. In the be-ginning I had worked with Arnold Earnshaw and I enjoyed work-ing with him. Unfortunately, the *Post's* editor moved Arnold to another position on the paper, and I was left in the clutches of the lady editor. Like minor clerics at the Vatican, we columnists watched head Pooh Bahs come and go, and kept turning out words in hopes that the new regime would continue to allow us our allotted column inches.

About a year after the Murdoch takeover, I couldn't help but notice that the paper had begun to change drastically. The new *Post* was different all right. Dorothy Schiff's sedate black masthead was changed to fire-engine red. Headline writers were apparently under orders that every front-page head was to be in ten-point type, or Second Coming as it is known in the trade. The headlines had to include one or more of the following words: *shocker, bombshell, grisly,* or *horror.* Every day a new Armageddon hit the newsstands. The stories themselves tended to be very brief pieces served up raw and juicy.

By the time Murdoch had completed redecorating the *Post* to his taste, its style was just short of the "Mother Eats Baby" sensationalism of the *National Star,* which Murdoch also owned. The *Star* had gone full color and was soon making its rival, the *National Enquirer,* which for years had been the yellow sinkhole of the newspaper business, look like the *Wall Street Journal.* Meanwhile, in New York the daily high-pitched screams of the *Post's* front page was beginning to make the feisty *Daily News* look as sedate as the *New York Review of Books.* For sure, things were changing fast in the newspaper business, and I was beginning to feel somewhat uncomfortable. No one ever got murdered in my column. I was increasingly aware that there was nothing sexy or violent about refinishing wicker or changing color schemes, and I had a feeling the handwriting was already on the wall in letters that were a dripping red.

My premonition proved accurate. The lady editor decided she could write my copy better than I could. I left the *Post* with great sadness. Once you've played New York, you're never satisfied with out of town, no matter how well you do out there, and I began looking around for another New York paper to carry "Your Family Decorator." In this state of near depression my spirits picked up a little one night while watching television and seeing a highly polished commercial for a *new* New York daily. It called itself *News World,* and it was so family oriented it didn't even carry cigarette or X-rated movie ads. What a stroke of timely fortune! Surely a paper as wholesome as this would be interested in a family decorating column. Little did I know when I picked up the telephone the following morning and asked to speak to the features editor of the *News World* that I was about to go from Murdoch to Moon.

I met with the publisher, a young, intelligent, well-bred, well-educated, and altogether nice person, and was told that the *News World* would be delighted to run my column—plus a once-a-week design page. For the column I would receive $200 a month, and for the weekly design page $400, making my total monthly income from their paper five times the amount I had made at the *Post*. The paper, he informed me, was owned by the News World Communications Company; the circulation was about 90,000, far less than the *Post*, certainly, but at least those 90,000 were New Yorkers.

I couldn't help noticing that over the publisher's desk loomed an enormous portrait of the Reverend Sun Yung Moon, head of the Unification Church. Was the *News World*, I asked, owned by Reverend Moon's church? Yes, was the answer. Well, I thought, so what? The marriage of religion and journalism did not always spell trouble. Look at the *Christian Science Monitor*—a fine paper. . . .

My space in the *News World* was great. My appearance was heralded by a first-class promotion campaign. "Carleton Varney comes to *News World!*" ran the full-page ads. The editorial offices were in the old Tiffany building, another undeniable touch of class. The staff seemed to be ecumenical. None of the Moonies I worked with tried to convert me. The quality of the paper itself was excellent; I had read it several times from cover to cover and had failed to find so much as a sentence, a phrase, even a word that might convey a subliminal message to induce readers to turn their money and talents over to Reverend Moon.

My first introduction to the strange and secret world of the Moonies was through a staff photographer who had been assigned to me. He was a handsome fellow, a native of Florence, and he had lived all over the world. As a professional photographer he had seen his share of *la dolce vita*. Yet he had been a Moonie since 1973. One day he came into the office to work with Carol St. John, my coordinator for the weekly "Home Design" column, in a state of bliss and told her he had just become engaged. Carol congratulated him and asked, "How long have you been dating her? You never mentioned you had a girl friend."

"I just met her on Friday," he replied. "Did you see the picture in the paper?'' (''The paper'' to a Moonie is *News World*.) He then showed her a photograph of 1,500 smiling faces, alternately male and female, that Reverend Moon had united in a two-day engagement ceremony at the grand ballroom of the New Yorker Hotel.

I was tending to some business that morning at the Greenbrier when I received word of an urgent telephone call from my office. It was Carol. She told me about her bizarre conversation. ''Do you know what you're getting into?'' she said darkly. She had spent over an hour arguing with the newly affianced photographer and was shaken by her inability to reason with him. ''He told us Reverend Moon makes the selection of mates because romance ruins a marriage,'' she said in alarm.

''That's not so shocking,'' I said. ''Getting married for love is a pretty new idea.''

''Carleton,'' she protested. ''This *News World* thing is getting spooky. It's not good for your image either.''

At the time I disagreed. The *News World* was a respectable paper, I said. In fact, it was the most sedate paper in town, more family oriented than the *New York Times,* and the best New York vehicle for a column on home decorating. My reaction must have been a little defensive, for I was beginning to look askance at the entire Moonie business. I too had been having discussions with my Moonie photographer. As I listened to him I kept saying to myself, ''He's so intelligent, so urbane. . . .'' His answers to my arguments baffled me and left me sputtering.

> *Question:* Why did Reverend Moon pick you and Marilyn?
>
> *Answer: Because I am a man and she is a woman. Reverend Moon's perception is spiritual, not external.*
>
> *Question:* How about all that real estate? Don't you think it's a little bizarre that he's buying up every vacant hotel and mansion in New York State?
>
> *Answer: The Catholic church holds a lot more real estate, and no one complains.*
>
> *Question:* Isn't it strange, living a celibate life after the kind of adventures you've had?
>
> *Answer: In the Orient you don't use forks. It's not strange from the inside, only from the outside.*
>
> *Question:* But how about all those stories of brainwashing and people being held captive, the books, the articles—

Answer: That's silly. We have free will. People can come and go as they please.

Question: You turn most of your salary over to the Reverend. Don't you think he should live as frugally as you?

Answer: I wish he were living in an even more opulent style than he is.

Slowly, in tantalizing glimpses, I began to put together the Moonie life style. Sometimes it sounded like school; other times it sounded like the army. Men lived on one floor in the Manhattan Center, women on another. They lived in single and double rooms and ate in a communal dining hall. Each floor had floor captains appointed by Reverend Moon's hierarchy that took charge of cleaning duties. Clothing and linen were laundered in a communal laundry. I had seen the Moonies working from across the street, happy faces folding clothes. During the day most of them went to work. And gone were the days when just about every Moonie you ran into was selling candles or incense. From architects to day laborers, everyone was "given the option" of turning his paycheck over to the church, and it seemed everyone did so under penalty of appearing less than zealous. I knew the several Moonies who worked for me all turned their checks over to the Reverend (they were skilled artists; I paid them well, and they were worth it), and they were always very anxious to get their money.

Everything was taken care of by Reverend Moon. Even medical care was paid for by the church if a Moonie was destitute. Children were cared for in a Moonie nursery and, although they later went to public school, Reverend Moon was hoping soon that the church would have its own schools as it had its own newspaper, communication network, ballet companies (complete with dancing school for "Little Angels") and even its own rock group. Yes, Reverend Moon's rock group, Sunburst, played at a local coffee house and at the cultural center in the New Yorker Hotel.

The hotel was about to be turned into a monument to Reverend Moon that would rival the temple of Abu Simbel. I had been to the New Yorker. The publisher of *News World* had invited me down to see the transformation. I have done so many hotels I'm accustomed to seeing them in a state of chaos, but what was going on at the New Yorker wasn't renovating as much as gutting out and rebuilding. It was an eerie sight, that huge, empty lobby with only the chandeliers left as a reminder that once it had been a hotel. Workers wearing overalls scurried back and forth with wheelbarrows of cement. I seriously questioned whether they had the proper permits for the extensive work they were doing.

As usual, all the Moonies were smiling as they went about their labors. I had to hand it to Reverend Moon. He was much more shrewd than your average Ramses. The workers who built the pyramids had to be beaten and threatened with death in order to get them to build those great temples of immortality for their leader-gods in time for their deaths. Reverend Moon had found that a willing volunteer was far more economical and easier to manage than a slave. (Although I never could figure out how much freedom the converts actually had. People at *News World* had an alarming tendency to suddenly vanish, and when I'd ask what became of them I'd be told, "He's in Seattle now," or, "She's working in Boston," or simply "assignment change." When the paper's publisher, his wife, and three kids disappeared, I became alarmed. All I could glean was that they were somewhere on the West Coast. I really liked the publisher, and he loved his job. Why was his whole family suddenly spirited away to the other coast?).

That trip to the New Yorker Hotel was a real eye opener. Right in the middle of the most urbane city in the country, maybe even on earth, a secret feifdom was being built, a center for the Unification Church of America. Aside from worship purposes, the building was to house an entire, elaborate counter-system, a walled castle behind which everything a Moonie could possibly want would be available, from a rock group to the ballet. There was a conference center, a theater, a dance hall, radio and TV communication center, even an opera house—all in tribute to a man who would neither confirm nor deny that he was the Messiah. The decor was heavy into gold and red. The only thing missing were the Laotian bells. On the upper floors the walls were gold flocked, and everywhere were those enormous portraits of the Reverend with that little Mona Lisa smile. Why is that man smiling? I used to ask myself. Now I knew.

His converts had the same smile, but they were also bafflingly in touch with the times. They had a sense of humor like the rest of us. Beyond the veneer of the automaton were human beings who functioned well, were in touch with the world, and even found it amusing. The best example of Moonie wit was *Not the New York Post,* a hilarious spoof of that by then thoroughly Murdoched paper, which I read as it came off the church-owned press in New Jersey. On the whole, I found the Moonies mystifying, like people I thought seemed familiar but spoke in different tongues.

While Reverend Moon was busy rekindling the spirit of Christian sacrifice and love in the country, something happened at the executive offices at *News World* that resulted in my receiving a letter that read "We have recently undergone a fundamental reorganization. . . ." New names appeared above the signature titles, new people to contact should I ever have any future story ideas. My removal was as swift as that of the Moonies I worked with who were sent elsewhere to fulfill their master's purpose. But as Reverend Moon didn't have the power to transfer me and my family to Seattle or parts unknown, he merely terminated my services.

So here I am without a New York paper, but who knows what the future will bring? In the meantime, I still write my syndicated "Your Family Decorator":

"Dear Mr. Varney. My room looks dead! Please help!"

"We have a navy blue velvet davenport and two dark red chairs . . ."

"Your being in New York where access to fabrics is more available brings me to write this letter in desperate hopes . . ."

"My husband and I are remodeling the bathroom ourselves and we would appreciate . . ."

"I can no longer care for my Terrazo floors. What kind of vinyl . . ."

"We have an aquarium that can't be removed without ripping the wall apart. How do you decorate around a fish tank?"

It's questions like these that keep me thinking, keep me writing, keep me in touch with what goes on in the real world far removed from the chi-chi salons and the soigné showrooms of the Manhattan decorating scene. I'd much prefer applying my creative thinking to that permanent fish tank in Cleveland. I thrive on sending out ideas to people who often need only a litle nudge of inspiration to change their rooms in ways that truly bring them pleasure. I find the column satisfying, but you know the old song about the bright lights of Gotham. Someday I hope to be back on the newsstands of New York.

Chapter 5

From Hell to Heaven
with a Few Stops in Between

Every profession has its ups and downs, its pussycats and ayatollahs. My successes in the decorating business have come about both with and without the help of my clients, and their satisfaction, I have discovered, has nearly always been determined by their own expectations. What do people want from a decorator anyway? I have had clients who wanted a technician/ expeditor; and I have had others who wanted a Pygmalion, a role I don't like at all. I have had people who wanted a facade of culture. "Make me a collection," they are apt to say. Like buying books by the yard, this request usually means "Gimme some culture." When I suspect that people have come to me to demand that I create rooms which will make them hip or cultured or grand, I know I'm in for some rocky times. Being asked to play Pygmalion always ends in trouble because when the play is over for the decorator, the clients are left on stage alone, uncomfortable in a setting that does not reflect who they really are.

It all boils down to a matter of ego. The easiest jobs are invariably those for people who have a secure and well-defined sense of identity and tend to look on the decorator as an expert who takes charge of the details. One such client was Pauline Trigère. When I first met her socially, she said, "I don't know why anybody would want to hire a decorator. I wouldn't want anybody helping me with my own rooms." Nevertheless, I told her if my office could ever be of help to her, she should feel free to call.

Author's note: *Each of the characters depicted here is not only fictitious, but a composite of several people. Any similarity between an actual person and the character as depicted is purely coincidental.*

When she did, it was strictly a matter of efficiency: she'd plan the change, I'd make suggestions and then make it all happen.

Her Park Avenue apartment was done in black and beige, reflecting her special brand of understated elegance. She had delayed refurbishing because of her busy schedule, and wanted a great deal of reupholstering and painting done. "I just couldn't get to it," she said a little apologetically as we walked around her apartment taking notes. "Sometimes people never 'get to it,'" I told her. "In your case, that's all you need me for—to pull everything together." I noticed her furniture was too large to be taken out of the apartment, and I'd have to have my upholsterers do the job in place. Other than that, her requirements were simple.

After she decided on a color scheme, she planned to go out of town on business while the apartment was painted. I was also going to be out of town, and the paint job would be done while we were both gone. I told her not to worry about a thing, and put one of my women decorators in charge of giving her walls a strie treatment, which is a combed wall texture. When Pauline returned, she took one look at that $6,000 paint job and hated it. Lesson learned: for those who really know who they are, make no assumptions. Someone as design-conscious as Pauline should always be around while work is in progress. In other cases I prefer having a client away, sometimes far away, while the workmen are disrupting their little castle.

Other than the lost paint job, doing Pauline's apartment was a sheer pleasure. Her own touch, not mine, was everywhere. Tables held large glass bowls in which she dropped her costume jewelry, a couch sported pillows in a fabric she had once bought for a dress and never made. Everywhere were personal, meaningful touches, and her apartment had not been restyled as much as spruced up. We've been friends ever since. My signature is a scarf instead of a necktie, and many of them are from Pauline; they sometimes arrive in a gift box with a little note that reads, "Here's a little Trigère to wear around your neck."

In such cases the client takes much of the credit for the success—not that I don't have an ego too. I once decorated Copley's Restaurant at The Copley Plaza in Boston and later read in a magazine that the hotel manager's wife had done the job. I saw red. In other cases, a client may have been so utterly uninvolved that taking credit for a job gives little satisfaction. I once had a man give me instructions to do his entire New York apartment in red, white, and blue. Then he left town. I didn't see him for the seven months it took to do his nine-room apartment. It turned out the place was merely going to be an alternative to staying in a hotel when he and his wife came to New York, a sort of patriotic *pied-à-terre*. The couple had as little connection with the decor as they would have had with a hotel room. My attempt was to give them something pleasant, but there was no individual personality around which I could make my plans. That's no fun either.

What is a challenge is working with people who don't quite know what they want but would like to define it. If they come to me and say, "I need some help redoing my house," I feel hopeful; but if they say, "Can I see some examples of your work?" I don't bother with them. I don't want to decorate apartments in my style, and any residential job I have done before is not an example of my work but someone else's style as defined and custom-designed by both of us. Of course my commercial work has a particular look, because the job is less a personal statement of life style. My residential work does not, and if it ever does, I'll stop doing it.

I am always fascinated visiting places where cetain decorators reign supreme, leaving their stamp all over the best houses in town. I can actually walk into some of them and say to myself, "So-and-so has been here." This one-look supermarket approach to style often results in a lot of unhappy people being stuck for years with a decorator's momentary whim. The decorator moves on from scenic wallpaper or collages of baptismal gowns on the wall or soft sculptured furniture or chrome-and-glass or white-on-white or batik, minimal, high tech, or whatever the latest rage decorators are getting together, but thousands of people walk around in rooms full of someone else's passing fancy and wonder why they're dissatisfied.

Gatherings of decorators sometimes give me a good laugh or two and then a chill. Any decorator who swoons over the curve of a Queen Anne chair, trails chintzes from room to room expounding designer theory and philosophy, or sits in an empty room and ponders, turns me off. Decorating is not just about concepts. It's also about people who live in rooms. Whether it's for a single room with a kitchenette or a ninety-room mansion, if an occupant has hired a too much, too fancy decorator, he had better be ready to put his foot down unless he wants to live with a bronze cuspidor his decorator found on lower Broadway and nearly fainted over—for two days.

I have to confess that when it comes to my fellow decorators,

I'm pretty much of a loner. I have a few decorating friends I
enjoy—Lola Marshall, Dick Ridge, Richard Himmel, Tom Harai,
Robert Metzger, Georgina Fairholme, Angelo Donghia, to name a
few. Plus my own staff designers—Ernie Fox, Nancy Miller, Ron
Troy, Carol St. John, David Laurance, Don Phillips, and Christy
Bassett. Over the years I've found that many decorators envy one
another. They generally do not like to share, and I never ask another designer where he acquired this or that. I once talked to a
decorator in my own office about her design ideas. I wanted to
write a column about her favorite color scheme. She was appalled.

"I can't tell you that," she said.

"Why not?" I asked.

"Why should I give away valuable ideas for free?" was her
reply.

Some decorators tend to be envious and afraid; like little
Midases, they hoard their ideas. I don't like their attitude but I
have learned, with the help of a lot of psychoanalysis, that I don't
wish them any harm. There's enough work to go around, and
good designers are always busy.

Another occupational hazard is snobbism, if the decorator
takes himself too seriously. I know I have become more tolerant
as the years go by. A decorator is supposed to be a tastemaker,
but that doesn't mean everyone else's taste is bad—even if I
happen to hate it. A few years after I joined Dorothy Draper I was
asked to judge a coloring contest held by a well-known furniture
tycoon. The judging was to take place on the family yacht, an
enormous floating palace with a rather sinister history, as the
previous owner had been murdered on it. The furniture tycoon
had had the yacht decorated to his taste. The stateroom walls
were done in red velvet and gold sequins. The quilted vinyl sofas
were trimmed with mink tails. The lounge chairs were upholstered in all manner of imitation zebra, tiger, lion, and
leopard.

When the hostess demonstrated her newly designed lounge
chair (also upholstered in fake fur) which opened out into an
ironing board, my then fiancée Suzanne could control herself no
longer. Our faces were red with swallowed laughter, and when
we hit the buffet and were served whole veal cutlet hors
d'oeuvres the size of salad plates—and given no cutlery—we
knew we had to get out of there. Looking back on the incident,
I'm a little unhappy about the way I acted. I've discovered there

are a lot worse things in this world than bad taste. Besides, that yacht's decor today could be considered fabulous punk! Who's to say that today's so-called bad taste won't become tomorrow's rage? Though I hope not! Remember the silly lamp in uncle's garage that turned out to be a Tiffany?

If a decorator suffers from a severe case of snobbism, it makes him mean, and watch out if you're the victim! I was once having a drink in a bar on 57th Street and couldn't help but hear two decorators talking shop next to me. I didn't know who they were, and they didn't know who I was. At the time I had just done an interior for the New York City cab, and *Time* had a story on it with the unforgettable headline *Drab Cab Goes Fab*. My model had a checkered vinyl seat and racing-green vinyl floor. As I was absorbing stray bits of conversation from the two men next to me, I suddenly realized that the subject of their conversation was me. "He has no taste," hissed one. "He grabs everything," said the other.

That bit of sniping was child's play compared with another decorator's feelings. I had endorsed a fragrance for Claire Burke, and a feature of the campaign was an ad showing me holding a bottle of their room spray and saying, "Fragrance is as important a part of decoration as color." The ad appeared in *Vogue* and other trendy magazines.

One day I opened my mail and found a note from Mary Kay Young, president of Claire Burke, who had received a tearsheet of the ad anonymously in the mail. She sent the tearsheet to me with this message attached: "And here's a note from one of your fans." At the bottom of the ad someone had neatly typed the words "In New York we think of Carleton Varney as somewhat of an asshole." The president of Claire Burke had taken the matter lightly, but at the time I saw little humor in it. Who could have been so malicious? How sneaky to send it typewritten, how cowardly! Today, having mellowed over the years, I'd probably hang it on the bulletin board for a few office chuckles.

I have also taken measures to keep the hassle of being a decorator at a minimum. Although Carleton V Ltd., the fabric and wallcovering house, is an affiliate member of the American Institute of Interior Designers, I don't actively attend committee meetings. And while we entertain a few decorators in our home, I save my social entertaining for a few friends in diversified fields. I hear decorating craziness in my office all day long.

Now that I have thoroughly terrified the reader about hiring a decorator, let me assure you that there are hundreds of easygoing, kindhearted, and thoroughly professional decorators all over America. How should the relationship begin? This is how I try to establish it: I ask a few simple questions, starting out with "What's your favorite color?" Then I ask a few more. Then I stop. A client may say, "Don't you think you should ask me what I want?" And I can answer, "You've told me you like earth colors and can't live with red. You've told me you don't like draperies at the windows. You'd really like to throw out your carpets and go with bare floors. You sleep in a double bed, you want a TV in the bedroom, you dislike big prints and about fifty other things. I know enough to get us started." And then we're off, making changes my clients, not their decorator, really want.

That's not to say I always agree. Over the years my own tastes have evolved to a point where I want less and less, and if a client wants more and more, so be it. If I ever start insisting clients live the way I like to live, I'll retire. If they want the South of France on Lexington Avenue, they get it: baskets hanging from the ceiling, strands of onions, wooden spice jars all in a row, bouquets of copper kettles—the works. Some people dream of the islands and want their living rooms to feel like Tahiti. So be it: bamboo, tropical plants, Pacific blue walls, Gauguin colors in the upholstery. If they dream of New Hampshire, I give them wide brick fireplaces, wide plank floorboards, wooden beams, and gingham. If the new look makes them feel warm and cozy and good about opening their front door every night, then I'm happy, for it means I've put enough of their own personalities and needs into their new decor to make them feel serene in their new environment.

Into every career comes a few catastrophes, and my number-one nemesis was a client who didn't know what she wanted. She wanted everything, and she wanted nothing. She wanted the same look, she wanted an utterly different look. She wanted order, but when she got it she nearly flipped out. I never did figure out what she wanted, except to make trouble. Decorating her apartment was my most miserable residential job, and it grew out of my inability to define what would really make her happy.

"Lillie" was a best-selling songwriter. Unfortunately, I must disguise her identity because she's definitely the kind who would sue. She was referred to me by her agent. "Lillie is a bit difficult, but I'm sure you can handle her," the agent said, a little too breezily I thought. I first met the famous songwriter in my office. She had sold her latest sounds and lyrics to a movie studio and had changed her image to match: good-bye social worker, hello Harlow. Her hair was impossibly platinum, and she wore huge dark glasses and a full-length sable. Within five minutes I knew how many languages her songs had been translated into, how long her latest disc had been on the top of the charts, who had bought the new tunes and for how much, and who was going to sing her new songs in a forthcoming movie. I even found out how many famous people she was related to. In other words, I knew a lot about my new client—but I knew nothing about what she wanted me to do for her. What did she want her apartment to look like? What did she like? What didn't she like? I hadn't a clue.

We went to see her apartment. Her ex-husband, an insurance man, had left her for a younger woman after a twenty-year marriage, and as I looked around the apartment I saw how the turn of events had devastated her. The place was in chaos. Water-streaked window shades had come loose from their rollers and hung in tatters. Papers, books, magazines, clothing, old containers of Chinese take-out, overflowing ash trays, dead plants, cat-tattered slipcovers, cardboard boxes full of broken lamps and other discarded objects—the place seemed to overflow with the detritus of a marriage. Only the rolltop desk in the corner where she had written her hit songs was in any semblance of order.

Lillie stood in the middle of her apartment, flung her sable on a chair heaped high with dirty laundry, and declared, "I must have order. In my new apartment I want everything new, and I want everything in its place. Most of all I must have an office in my apartment where I can compose. Writing here is impossible, and I've got to get going. I want to write a Broadway musical."

Now that I knew what she wanted, I got to work. Order is what she got. Jane Austen should have had such a place to write. Tolstoy should have written *War and Peace* in such a streamlined setting. The office, complete with baby grand piano, we made for her to write was a songwriter's dream. The desk area had ample space for books and papers, recording devices, a typewriter lift, a pegboard on the wall above it, and drawers for everything beneath it. Paper clips, rubber bands, stamps, tape—everything had a nook, a cranny, or a niche. That writing area, we told ourselves with pride, gave no one, certainly not a famous lyricist and composer, an excuse for not writing the new "Oklahoma" or "My

Fair Lady." Lighting came over the left shoulder, and lights beamed inside the cabinets every time a door was opened.

She instructed me to send her old desk to the Salvation Army.

Throughout the apartment everything was to be brand new. She chose a color scheme of cantaloupe, beige, and brown, then selected fabrics for all her new furniture. Everything would be installed new, clean, and shiny in her modern penthouse apartment. During this phase a voluminous one-sided correspondence began to fill my files. Each letter was typed, single space and never less than two pages long. Every detail of the work we had discussed was put to writing where it was restated, debated and resolved. Having never had a famous songwriter for a client, I attributed her letter writing to a writer's necessity to make things real via the printed page or printed song sheet. Nevertheless, there was a note of hysteria in the correspondence, which bothered me.

When everything was ready to be installed, her agent called and advised me to get Lillie out of town. "I think it would be best for her to walk into a finished apartment," she said. I agreed wholeheartedly, and a great sigh of relief was emitted by my office staff and workmen when the lady left for Europe for two weeks. We finished the job in quick time. The apartment looked—like what she wanted. Everything had been done according to her specifications, from the carpet to the molding along the ceiling. She came back. I heard nothing. Two weeks went by.

Her agent called. "You know, Lillie's very unhappy about the apartment. She says she can't function in it."

"But it's everything she asked for," I said.

"I know, but she says she just can't write in it."

I realized I would have to visit Lillie to avoid any potential legal problems.

She greeted me with fire in her eyes. "I hate it," she said. "How could you do this to me?"

Everything, it seemed, was wrong. The rugs were wrong; the window-shade installation was wrong; the furniture, color, lighting, kitchen sink, bathroom shower, bed cover—there wasn't a single thing that was right. And the worst of it was she had writer's block.

"You've got to find my rolltop desk," she said desperately. "Call the Salvation Army. If somebody's bought it, God forbid, find out who bought it. I've got to buy it back. Your desk thing is just wretched."

I told her that retrieving desks from the Salvation Army was not part of my job. Really steaming now, she led me through the living room and out the front door. As I walked through at a fast clip I noticed that the superneat, everything in its place apartment already looked just like its predecessor. In the course of three weeks a section of the window curtain had been pulled down and left hanging; nail polish had been spilled on the beige sofa; and food, clothing, and bottles were strewn everywhere.

"Look at this place," she yelled, gesturing wide. "I hate it. It's not at all what I wanted, and *you* know it."

She did not sue. She did not dare. Her habit of always reaching for immortality through the song sheet had done her in. I had a bulging file folder full of her voluminous letters in which she had spelled out everything she wanted, from the length of fringe on the draperies to the circumference of her drawer pulls. When she wrote me a letter accusing my workmen of drinking up all her liquor, I ignored it. Lillie dropped from sight. As the years went by I would indulge myself every now and then in a few mean thoughts about her. Like, "Hmmm, it's been five years now since Lillie's songs have been on the charts. Wonder if my desk's still giving her writer's block." The usual fairy-tale curse is seven years. By year eight I was sure any Sunday I'd be reading in the *New York Times* about Lillie's latest records. But my desk had apparently delivered a double whammy; it was fourteen years before Lillie broke into song writing again.

Less than a year ago, I got a call from her. It had been so long I didn't connect her first name with who she was, but I recognized the imperious tone at once. "I need your help," she announced. "A hinge is off one of the cabinets your woodworking man put in. Who is he? I want to hire him to repair it."

With great glee I told her never to dial my number again.

In attempting to analyze why this particular client was so ill-suited to having a decorator come in and help her change her life, I see that a combination of circumstances worked against the relationship, events that caused her ego first to expand and then to shatter. First the raging best-selling records, then the desertion. And to make things a little more painful, she was discarded in preference for a younger woman. There she was, age forty-eight, but who was she, what did she want, and what was she worth? Of all the times to ask herself what she wanted, she couldn't have been in a worse frame of mind.

She thought she knew: she wanted order. After all, her life had just fallen apart. But she didn't really want order, and her error, she thought, could be blamed on her decorator. When that didn't work, we were through. I am always sad when the client-decorator relationship doesn't work out, and since my experience with the famous Lillie I have learned to watch for the potential situation of being made a scapegoat. I have learned the hard way to watch for the ego. If it's secure—even oversized—I can manage to form an alliance that will turn out happy. If the ego is shaky, I'm in trouble. As for Lillie, fame came to the deserted middle-aged wife who then tried to get me to put her life back together with surface order. With such expectations, the relationship didn't have a chance.

In contrast to Lillie is an experience I had with a big hotel chain and a man who was about to buy it. Harold Geneen was chairman of the board of ITT. His company had called me in to evaluate the Sheraton Hotel chain, which ITT was considering buying. I was to visit Sheraton hotels across the country and do a survey to evaluate their interior design. I wrote a report in which I told Geneen's company that the chain's hotels looked alike. Sheraton bedrooms and suites were designed around a system called the "Redbook" in which fabrics, carpets, furniture, pictures on the wall—everything from lamps in the suites to bedspreads on the beds—was chosen from numbered styles in the Redbook. I told him I didn't think people wanted to go to Hawaii to stay at a hotel that looked like the one they had stayed at in Detroit, and recommended dispensing with the look-alike style and allowing the design of the hotels to reflect their locales.

I don't know what Geneen thought of my report, but he trusted my judgment enough to meet me in Key Biscayne to discuss redecorating the Royal Biscayne Beach and Racquet Club there. Key Biscayne at the time was heavy Nixon country. The look was sedate conservative Republican, safe understated elegance, the kind you know is expensive but can't remember afterward what it looked like. I met him on the grounds, and we walked around the buildings. There was only one word to describe them: ugly. The main building was just concrete blocks cemented one on top of the other, a real eyesore in a beautiful environment. Other outlying bath-changing houses had cedar siding; they were relatively well built, and relatively pleasing.

"Well, what would you do with this property?" Geneen asked me. We stopped, and the entourage formed a respectful semicircle around us, all ears. "I'd paint all the buildings pink," I said. "I'd paint the concrete block hotel pink, and I'd use lime green louver shutters on either side of the windows with white window frames. I'd move in as many palm trees and as much foliage as I could get and paint the front of the main building pink with white stripes." I also recommended the pink and white stripe treatment for the bathhouses.

Silence ensued. Geneen resumed walking. I walked beside him, and the entourage walked behind. The atmosphere back there was definitely funereal. Several very long minutes went by. Finally Geneen turned to me and said, "If that's what you want, that's what we'll do." And we did. Geneen was the kind of executive who chose his experts carefully and then trusted them. For someone in a position of power I found him remarkably soft-spoken and almost gentle in his manner. Philip Lowe, first president of ITT-Sheraton, under Harold Geneen's chairmanship, later gave me carte blanche to do the Sheraton Waikiki in Honolulu, one of the largest convention hotels ever built, and I loved doing it.

Geneen later confided he had been momentarily stunned over the prospect of painting all that cement pink and white, but he gave me his consent because he had to assume I knew what I was doing. As it turned out, the Royal Biscayne Beach and Racquet Club was a real Cinderella case, one of my most successful transformations.

Over the years I have kept in contact with Harold and June Geneen. They send me kind notes and maple syrup from their New Hampshire farm, and whenever I need the ultimate reference he sends me a nice letter about how pleased he has always been with my work. Basically, I think we clicked because he agreed with my general design concepts, which is that rooms should be light, airy, and uncluttered, and then left the details to me. The Geneens have also frequented my Greenbrier Hotel, which they loved, and have lived in a suite at the Westbury Bruxelles, a Belgian hotel I decorated in 1963.

But a decorator is trained to think in terms of personal statement, the more intimate the better, and when he takes on a monolithic corporation he finds that what he does best is a threat to some people. He quickly discovers that innovation terrifies the occupants of executive suites. The machinations there are so complex, the fear so intense, the cutthroat corporate climbing so all-pervasive, that a simple decision like changing the style of a headboard is debated as if everyone's job were on the line.

The highly volatile client-decorator relationship is also sometimes manipulated by the client to fill other needs besides getting the pictures hung just so on the wall. My experiences with a Western belle on the make was one vivid example of my being forced into a role I particularly hate, Pygmalion. I hate it because too often the relationship ends in sadness, if not disaster.

In 1963 I was decorating the Westbury-Bruxelles and practically lived in the air. My working week was an interminable shuttle across an ocean and part of a continent to and from my New York office and the Belgium hotel. Week after week, I took Thursday evening flights from Kennedy Airport for the seven-hour plane ride, then back again on a Sunday flight to drag myself in to work by Monday morning. I had just become engaged to my wife, and my enthusiasm for the hotel competed with my desire to be at home with her.

I was relieved when the hotel was nearly finished. Management had planned a gala opening in the handsome Panorama room featuring good entertainment and a cast of foreign dignitaries. We were working right down to opening day to get the finishing touches in place, and just as the top Knott Hotels brass arrived, I was finishing an adjustment of the crystal lighting fixtures, which needed some extra battening down. Once they were secured, as the wind blew through the crystals the lobby gently reverberated with sounds reminiscent of Oriental wind chimes. One last touch: some handsome and delicate Chinese screens painted by an elderly Chinese named Mr. Mui whom I had discovered in Paris. I hoped his screens would be a wedge in the door for the approval by the Knott Hotels main office of more Oriental art. Then we hung the final touch, which were baskets of live plants suspended from the lobby ceiling. With a few minutes to spare, just enough time to get changed for the gala, we finished the job.

One of the uninvited paying hotel guests who happened upon the opening was attracting a great deal of attention; in a room full of knockouts, she stood out like Dolly Parton in a room full of Girl Scouts. She was in her late twenties, a real Colorado cowgirl type, a Betty Hutton with a Jayne Mansfield body, and she displayed her enormous breasts with great pride. She painted herself up with lots of cosmetics and lipsticked her mouth into a perpetual kewpie-doll pucker. This was, remember, 1963, and the sexual revolution was about to storm the Bastille. Dotty, as I'll call her, was part of the action. Her eyes were bright, her hair tinsel silver: she was absolutely electric. Her miniskirted legs or her Venus de Milo breasts—where to look? Dotty's eyes said, why just look?

Not only was she a knockout, she came out sparring. Dotty, I found, had just been divorced and had flown from Denver to Europe to trade up. She was aggressive all right. She had been in Bruxelles only a few days before she had found out about the opening of the Westbury. Somehow, she got herself invited to the gala, and in a couple more days got invited to sit at one of the executives' tables. I can't say he seemed to mind. Dotty's ex-husband, I was told, had forsaken the stock brokerage firm he belonged to, a very respectable one at that, to go into the fertilizer business. That was bad enough, but things got even worse when his un-chic line of work didn't bring in as much money as Dotty would have liked. She had left him in Denver with her young twin sons, whom she had named, with characteristic restraint, Rodney and Derek. There had been enough money from the divorce settlement to pay for a trip to Europe. From there she was out to meet a man who would fulfill all her dreams and satisfy all her hungers.

When one of the Knott Hotels executives and a group of other people went on an all-night party to take in the Bruxelles nightlife, Dotty managed to get herself included. She also made it clear to me that she would like to get me between the percales, but I told her my intended, Suzanne, in New York had an exclusive on me, and I'd be taking the New York flight home soon. Female amazons, even in red sequins, have never held much power over me. I'm sure she found many others who were willing.

One day, back in New York with the Bruxelles-Westbury just a distant memory of wind in the bell chimes and a rush to meet deadlines, I picked up the telephone and heard a vaguely familiar voice. "Hello, Carleton," she said in her most seductive drawl. "This is Dotty, from Denver. 'Member me?"

"Yes," I murmured.

"I'm just watching you on Dinah Shore's show. Isn't that a

gas? I'm watching her talk to you while you talk to me. It's a real trip." And that was that. Apparently she found me more interesting on TV than on long-distance telephone, for after her abrupt call I didn't hear from her for a while.

Then, in the mid-1970s, I was in Denver doing promotion for a home sewing company. I had been demonstrating the many uses of ribbons in the home in a Denver department store. I showed how ribbon could be used for valance trimming, for bedspread trimming, and how to use ribbon as welting on chair backs. I was busy talking ribbons when I heard a voice in the front row of the circle that had gathered around me. "'Member me?" I looked into two heavily shadowed and mascaraed eyes, a cascade of blond hair, a pair of kewpie-doll lips, and a voluptuous body dressed in a bright yellow polyester pant suit. Dotty had gained a lot of weight. Her figure was now more Rubens flesh than Hollywood starlet, but she hadn't changed her demeanor by one wiggle. "I saw the ad in the paper that you were going to be here," she said breathlessly, "and I just had to get together with you—for old times' sake."

The crowd dispersed, but Dotty remained. She said she had many exciting things to tell me. She had remarried, a man named Bennie, who was in the cattle business making millions—and she now had everything she had ever wanted. Except a truly wonderful and socially acceptable house. Rodney and Derek were now fourteen, and the four of them had moved into a huge house in an exclusive section of Denver close by the country club. She insisted I come out to see it, and I found I could not refuse. Basically she was a kind person, and I wanted to be nice to her.

She picked me up at my hotel (The Brown Palace) in an enormous baby blue Lincoln convertible with the top down, and we were soon on the way to utter disaster. But, I didn't have an inkling of it at the time. This was the West, I told myself, where everything is done in a loud voice and with a big gesture, and I rather liked the lack of restraint. Besides, it wasn't every day I got to ride through town in an open Lincoln with a platinum blond. It was like being in the homecoming parade, a thrill from high school that had somehow passed me by, and Dotty's enthusiasm for her new life was contagious.

The new home was huge, and it was also quite beautiful. "Just look at it, Carleton!" Dotty cried. "You have to help me with it. You've got to make it *me*."

I already had a strong feeling she didn't want the house to

look like her at all. She wanted me to do it up in a way that would be sure to receive the social approval of the Beautiful People of Denver.

I met her husband, Bennie. He too seemed eager to have the house transformed into something the whole town could be proud of. I told her I would do her house, using my own Carleton V fabrics and wallpaper designs and all the design work on a 25 percent fee (a figure so low it was practically a giveaway, even then), if she would use local contractors for painting, carpenter work, and upholstering. After all, Dotty was a friend of sorts, and I also thought using my designs in her home might be good for the company's business. We had just opened a showroom in Denver. Doing Dotty's house, I thought, would be a mutually advantageous job.

I soon found out that Dotty's ultimate dream was to belong to a local ladies' club where the members were the crème de la crème of Denver society. I had spoken at one of their recent meetings, and Dotty told me, "I do so want them to ask me to join. Maybe if I had a big wonderful house decorated by Carleton Varney they would let me in. Do you think they might?"

As we went through the house I noticed a lot of odds and ends that needed matching up. Dotty's bachelor apartment furniture during her stint as the gay divorcee, the draperies of the former owner, and the furnishings from their former house were all mixed together. But the work had to be done in a conspiratorial way, she warned. Her husband had to be treated gingerly if he was going to cooperate.

Bennie the cattle king was a smart guy, but he had no presence. Compared to Dotty he was a nonentity, and he had some qualities that made him, if not a social pariah, a definite embarrassment. He apparently had a gastrointestinal disorder that caused him to belch and emit a ghastly flatulence, which he did little to conceal. It also seemed he was tight with his money in spite of his initial spirit of cooperation. But Dotty assured me he could be handled. "Address everything to *him*," she instructed. "Don't talk to me when you discuss the decorating. Talk to *him*. Make him feel important. Then we'll get everything we want." There seemed to be no end to the devious methods his wife had perfected. If she wanted money for new draperies, she didn't ask him for draperies but for silver. He would then say, "All right, all right, buy the silver." If I mentioned some furniture that needed new upholstery, she would say, "Not now! Wait until he's had his massage." The mistress of perfect timing got her new upholstery.

In no time at all Dotty was coming to me with other problems in her life that needed solving. It seemed she hadn't slept with her husband Bennie in years, not even on their wedding night. They each had their own bedroom, but Dotty said she sometimes got lonely at night and let Derek and Rodney, the fourteen-year-old twins, sleep with her. "There's no harm in that, is there?" she said. Not only was there harm in that, I thought, but if the word got out, Dotty would never gain entrée into Denver's upper social strata. Social climbers, so goes the rule, must be on their best behavior at all times. Only those born into high society can indulge in kinky acts.

She had another all-consuming dream, which was to have the house written up in a glossy magazine. "Which do you think we should go for, *Vogue* or *Harper's Bazaar?*" She dreamed of having a garden party for Denver bluebloods and visiting celebrities. She dreamed of having her house included in a "famous homes" tour. She dreamed of ascending to the heights, and on her climb to social acceptance, my job was to hold the ladder. A photo I had signed *To Dotty and Bennie* was displayed in a prominent place in her living room along with autographed copies of all my books. I also found out she was going around town saying the most famous and expensive decorator in America was doing her house. My taste was infallible, my word was scripture, my advice was sought on everything from upholstery fabric to napkins to drawer pulls. Dotty was acting like a lost soul who had finally found her guru. And I was it.

Before the house was completed, Dotty and Bennie decided to have a photographer (chosen by me, of course) take pictures of the house, surrounded as it was by meadows of blooming narcissus and daffodils that Bennie had planted with the aid of a gardening service. They had high hopes of getting the pictures in *Vogue*. The photographer went to Denver without me because I was tied up in New York. When he returned, he told me Dotty had been heartbroken that I had not come. She had stood under a huge handwritten *Welcome Carleton* flag set up on her lawn and looked around at all the people she had invited to meet me and have me autograph their books and nearly burst into tears.

There were more serious disappointments to come. The house was finished. Dotty was off my mind. I was deep into several other projects when I got a call from Denver. Between sobs she choked out a story of how she had invited some of the ladies from that prestigious woman's club to see the house. "I left them alone and went upstairs. You know where that hole is in the floor up there? Well, I could hear everything they were saying." She sobbed pathetically. It seemed the women had given the house their seal of approval with one exception: Dotty's all-pink bedroom. I couldn't help wondering whether they might have caught wind of the bizarre sleeping arrangements. Was there an evanescence left in the room of the mother-and-son sleep-over, presumably dissolved? Was a young twin's Adidas poking out from underneath the ruffle of the dressing-room table? I couldn't understand what the queens of Denver society had found objectionable in that dainty bedroom, but whatever it was, it had to be changed at once. Dotty was not about to continue to sleep in a bedroom that had failed to be approved by Denver's duennas. Not only did she plead with me to take back everything and redo the bedroom, but she said I'd have to do it for free. Bennie's wallet was zipped, the books were closed, and he had told her not one cent more for the Taj Mahal of Denver, Colorado.

Dotty swung into a new undercover program to pry money out of her husband. She brought him to New York and told him she wanted a big emerald. I had a suspicion that emerald was to be laundered into another kind of green and used for a new bedroom, but Bennie wouldn't budge. He went to a jeweler's (recommended by me, of course) and sat with a face of stone, not even swayed by the opportunity to buy wholesale. Dotty got more and more desperate. She took limousines everywhere, had them billed to my office, then took me aside and whispered, "Work those limo bills into one of your decorating bills and send it to that bastard. I'll get money for the house out of him yet." It was obvious she was cooking up a new plan: divorce. She was going to squeeze him dry before leaving him and his intransigence was driving her nearly insane.

Then I did something that made her flip totally. I sent her a bill for the 25 percent service fee we had discussed at our first meeting about the house. "Why are you sending me a bill?" she said long-distance. "You're treating me just like every other client. That's all I am to you—a client!"

It was true that I'd done things for her out of friendship that I didn't normally do for my clients—like send her dieting aids she couldn't get in Denver or a couple of sets of eyelashes from the Joan Crawford auction—but a fee was another matter. It seemed I had also alienated her husband when I sent a photographer to shoot the house in full bloom before the daffodils opened up. In fact, he wanted to send *me* a bill—for those tardy daffodils that had failed to fulfill their one purpose in life, which was to provide a blaze of color hopefully for the pages of *Vogue*. Nor would he pay for the bedroom Dotty decided not to like. It seemed that he had been told by his clever wife that "the most expensive decorator in America" was providing them with free services. He told me this, then he belched.

I didn't sue. And Dotty failed to gain acceptance into the Beautiful People of Denver Society. I vowed never again to allow myself to be cast in the role of Pygmalion.

The next time the opportunity arose, with a fabulously rich couple and their new antebellum mansion, I was cautious. Once again I was off on a never-never-land trip into a world where money means nothing and offers little relief. No happiness— only toys that offer temporary pleasure. In my experiences decorating "Tara" I turned out to be not so much a Pygmalion as a security blanket, a therapist, and eventually *raison d'être*.

Her name for the purpose of the story was Melinda, and she was one of four sisters in a very wealthy South Carolina family whose fortune was made in lumber and mining. Melinda grew up on one of the small islands off the Carolina coast. When she was a child her father was driving her and a friend across a railroad intersection when a train struck the car broadside. Melinda's father was killed instantly; the two children survived. Perhaps this tragic memory affected the personality of this most unhappy of clients, for she tried to ease the pain of her existence with alcohol—and by building and furnishing one of the most lavish homes I ever worked on.

I met Melinda in 1963 when she was in her late thirties, although I would have guessed her age to be around fifty-five. She was married to a neurosurgeon and was fabulously rich. I think she had inherited the lion's share of her father's estate. She had a strong personality, but there was a sweetness about her too. She wore her blond hair in a pageboy style with bangs covering her forehead, a schoolmarm look that carried over to her clothing. Her dressmaker-made shirtwaist dresses were a little fuller than usual, and she always wore them with a belt. She bought her proper shortie white gloves by the dozen from Saks and her neat little spectator pumps from I. Miller. She wore no makeup, and her hair was already turning gray.

Several years later we met again. The neurosurgeon had tried to push his prim and proper wife out a window, and Melinda had divorced him. She introduced me to her intended, a man named Mitch, from upstate New York. Mitch was also divorced and was the father of three children. He was a handsome, well-educated man in his mid-fifties. He wore dark blue suits, was terribly quiet, and smoked a great deal. Between her divorce and her engagement Melinda had been in and out of several exclusive mental institutions. Once she believed she was "cured," she and Mitch were to marry. They did soon after, and moved into a small, unassuming house in Charleston, which Leon Hegwood decorated for them. Next the office did a small *pied-à-terre* for them in New York. It was on Fifth Avenue and had a French look to it with a lot of moldings and beautiful yellow silk draperies, a sofa upholstered in melon damask with soft yellow accents here and there. Melinda and Mitch came to New York only occasionally, and I didn't know them well. I knew one thing about them, though. They drank. A great deal.

The years went by. In 1970 Melinda asked Leon Hegwood to do a new house for her on James Island on the intercoastal waterway. At the time Hegwood had had enough of the wild world of decorating and had retreated to the serenity of his retirement home in California. I was in Honolulu doing the massive Sheraton Waikiki when Hegwood phoned to say he had heard from Melinda and would I like a residential job, something on the order of a modern-day Tara? I was intrigued and said yes. Thus I embarked on a three-year decorating job that was to end in tragedy.

Theirs was to be a huge fantasy house made of glass and steel. A Charleston architect had designed it, and I thought it was strangely conceptualized. The predictable front columns were crassly updated, and the back of the house featured balconies that looked out over the swimming pool. It looked like a motel. As Melinda and the architect were childhood chums, I kept my opinions to myself. It was a massive house that dwarfed its neighbors, for the lot was fairly small. When I asked her why she had bought such a small lot for such a large house, she said it had been the only lot available at the time. The lot was in the best location on the island.

The fantasy house had been constructed to fulfill not only the couple's dreams but also their future needs. Although the house was only two stories high, an elevator had been installed in anticipation of their old age when they expected to be too enfeebled to make it up the grand staircase. A phenomenally complex electrical system ran throughout. Everything, it seemed, was on remote control. The bathrooms were equipped with steam rooms, and all the fixtures had been bought at Sherlé Wagner in New York. The interior ended up costing approximately $2 million. Melinda and Mitch spent money as if they made it in the basement. They came to New York and went on shopping sprees. As long as they took their Antabuse tablets, things went fairly well; they did try to stay sober when they shopped. Often they would leave for Europe directly from New York, and I would be left with a shopping list that read like the index of a Neiman-Marcus catalog. Their house was to include everything their hearts desired, and their desires grew by the day.

On other occasions I would go down to South Carolina to stay with them in their little house while the new house was going up. Theirs was a rather sterile home, and I soon saw why. So were Melinda and Mitch. We would have meetings, but if business wasn't completed before cocktail time rolled around, it was put off until the following day. They would both get loaded and then the accusations would begin. It was like a scene from *Who's Afraid of Virginia Woolf?* Melinda insulted, accused, and threatened; Mitch sat there and passively took it all. He knew where the power was seated. "Show Carleton my balance sheet," she would bray at him. "I don't want to see it," I would reply. I knew how rich she was, but she had a habit of leaving evidence around to use in every argument. Her ugly side came out only when she was drunk, however. At other times she was prim and proper.

The day after one of these "eruptions," Melinda would be laid up in bed, wrapped in her Leron bedjacket recovering from the drinking binge. At one in the afternoon she would rise from her bed and stagger to the terrace overlooking the pool. She never had a house without a pool, although I never once saw her swim. As blessed night came around, another binge would begin.

She was rich all right. I once called her from London to tell her I'd seen a fabulous pair of silver andirons from Blenheim Palace on sale for $24,000. "Buy them" was the reply. I also got the go-ahead on a George I chair for $50,000 that was used as the model for all the other chairs in the house. The walls of the house were better dressed than all but the most fashionable women, in a Lampas fabric that cost $200 a yard. The chandeliers were

Waterford glass and the mirrors antique Chippendale; the rugs were from Beshar. The hi-fi system cost $150,000. Sculpture and paintings by the world's great artists adorned the $200-a-yard walls, but her favorite piece was something sentimental that touched me a great deal, an oak-leaf panel we had a local man do that was placed over the fireplace in one of the rooms. She was thrilled with it because it was made of wood that grew on what had once been her father's land. She took me to see her family's house, which a ladies' club now occupied, and showed me another memento of her father. It was a floor he had designed. It was composed of different kinds of wood that grew on his land, and it had his initials in the middle. I suggested we move that floor over to the new house, but for some reason the plan languished.

All the treasures we had bought for the house were put into storage to await installation day. A curious thing started to happen. I had a strong feeling that Melinda and Mitch were both falling in love with me. They were hugging me all the time. The building and decorating of the house, which had been their reason for getting out of bed in the morning and focusing their concentration on something tangible, was close to a fait accompli, and I sensed that I was now their sole reason for living. The couple seemed isolated from society, friends, and even family.

Melinda's big dream (after, of course, getting her house in Architectural Digest) was to give her beautiful new house to the local opera society after she died. Part of Melinda's fierce desire to spend was her determination to leave none of her millions behind after she was gone. Her sisters and cousins were jealous of her, she said. They had even asked her to sign her money over to them, but of course she had refused. She had a distant cousin and one aunt whom she liked. "All the rest of them are a pack of vultures waiting for me to croak," she said.

As installation day approached, my trips to Charleston became more frequent as did Melinda's check signing—which she did without batting an eye, no matter how many zeroes were involved. More frequent, too, were the kissing, hugging, and general flirtation. Mitch always drove me to the airport, and when we parted I couldn't help but feel sorry for him. I knew he was going back to that sterile house and Melinda upstairs in bed with her sherry.

It turned out that after three years of planning, building, and buying, the big new house was every bit as dreary as the small old house. They always kept the shades drawn. One of the more dismal sights in their house was the breakfast table. Melinda did not want any live-in help, and the maid would squeeze orange juice, toast a few slices of white bread, and lay everything out on the table. Neither Melinda nor Mitch ever came down to eat breakfast, and the food sat there all day while Sir and Madam recuperated upstairs in their separate beds.

With the house all but completed, there was nothing left to stimulate them from the outside world except me. In fact, I had a strong notion that all they did between my visits was drink. One night I arrived in Charleston with a large Picasso painting for the house. The plane had been delayed, and it was the middle of the night by the time I got a taxi to James Island. All the lights of "Tara" were ablaze, and in the vast living room, seated on two Georgian armchairs, were the master and mistress, stone sober. I had the wild thought that they had been sitting there for six hours awaiting my entrance. We hung the painting, and they could contain themselves no longer. Out came the bottle, and the toasts to Picasso began. As the two of them drank themselves to sleep I sat in their magnificent living room and contemplated the great piece of art we had hung on the wall, full of sadness for all of us, Picasso included.

It took three long years to finish "Tara," and when it was completed, did it make Melinda and Mitch happy? Within two months Mitch was dead, from too much booze and pills and the constant strain of his marriage. After his death Melinda felt she was to have one of her greatest desires fulfilled: "Tara" published in *Architectural Digest*. She asked me to come down for the photography session, but I couldn't make it. I sent down someone from our office to supervise the photography in my place. "It's just as well," she said rather coyly. "What would people say if I had a *man* in my house?" At first I thought she had taken a new lease on life and was about to embark on a career as the Merry Widow. I was wrong. Before the magazine could consider the pictures of her beloved house, Melinda was dead. I feel certain she took her own life.

Some of the estate was auctioned at Christie's in New York. Through a sealed bid, I managed to buy back a few of Melinda's pieces, although I would have bought even more had I gone to the auction. The family, it seemed, had hired a Washington antique dealer to evaluate the furnishings for estate purposes. The dealer vastly underevaluated all those treasures, then hired someone to buy them back at bargain prices. Eventually Melinda's furnishings found their way back to the antique dealer at incredibly high figures. I never learned what happened to Melinda's huge fortune, a rumored $200 million.

In decorating "Tara," I had fullfilled my obligations as a decorator, but I realized somewhere during the process I had been hired to treat patients, not clients. Melinda and Mitch, desperate souls who reached for help but never found it, had sought salvation through their decorator. I was to provide them with a little relief from their despair. Living in a newly furbished "Tara" had never been important to them, even though they went through the motions of building a cozy nest for their old age, complete with gilt elevator. No, living in splendour was never the object. They had hired me to provide them with some drama. Decorating the house had given them some focus. There were decisions to make, objects to buy, things to touch and see and discuss with great animation. I hadn't decorated a house for two people who wanted to live well. The purpose was all in the doing, and in the end "Tara" was nothing more than a fabulous mausoleum, the last act before shaking off their mortal coils.

Whether designing for a regiment of corporate executives or for a single woman, a decorator learns volumes about human nature. It is in the nature of human beings to create havens of comfort for themselves. Beyond that urge is a myriad of expectations. When they are met successfully, I'm a happy man. When they're not, I hope for a more successful chemistry next time.

Chapter 6

They Never Promised Her Gray Gardens

Home to Edith Beale was a prison where she was both inmate and warden . . . or was she? The sensation created by the documentary film *Gray Gardens,* which featured a close-up view of the bizarre life styles of Jacqueline Onassis's aunt and cousin, revealed to the world that even a Bouvier could live in a state of dishabille, but it asked more questions than it answered. Why *did* the two former madonnas of high society live as recluses in that sorry old house in East Hampton? The neighborhood is one of those places on the south shore of Long Island where the superrich spend languorous summers in an F. Scott Fitzgerald world of manicured lawns, tennis courts, rambling old frame houses, quaint shops of the "Ye Olde" variety, and garden parties around Olympic-size swimming pools. It is a community that spells M-O-N-E-Y, from the clean white beaches to the potato fields that border the mansions' big backyards.

In the midst of all this opulence, on a choice piece of ocean-front property, lived two eccentric women and fifteen cats in a state of not-so-genteel decay that was bringing down real estate values and making the neighbors very unhappy. After their impending eviction by local health officials had made worldwide news, Jackie and Lee, Ari and the Prince, the Beale sons and their families all joined the list of people who found the life style of the two Ediths an embarrassment.

Meanwhile, Cousin Edie's life, which had remained static for so many years, underwent some drastic changes. First there was the money, $30,000, rumored to have come from Aristotle Onassis, which was put into repairs on the house. Then came the film, which was released in 1974, followed by the death of her mother three years later. Shortly afterward, Edie embarked on an entertainment career, the fulfillment of a lifelong dream of being in show business. When I interviewed her for the *New York Post* in 1978, she was still on the roller-coaster ride of instant fame, and being Jackie-O's cousin, Edie's dizzy ride was longer and higher than it otherwise would have been. Of course, people were intensely curious about Edie herself, and I wanted to write a column about how her life had changed after the film, her mother's death, and her new career.

The night before the interview I caught her show at Reno Sweeney, a New York nightclub, and found her fascinating and a little touching. She came on stage in a red chiffon dress and with a big red rose in her hair, sat on a stool, and talked; that was her act. Frequently she would break into her ruminations and answer questions from the audience. "Were you ever in love?" someone asked, and Edie smiled wistfully, struck a pose, and sang "Falling in Love Again"—without accompaniment. The overall effect was spellbinding, as if some enterprising person had gone out to Gray Gardens, found Edie in the attic playing in her mother's finery, and transported her straight up to the stage. Sad, dusty, a vision from another era, yet fascinating—that was the impression of Edie I carried home with me that night.

The following day, a bitterly cold Saturday afternoon in January, I taxied to Greenwich Village with Vic DeLucca, a *New York Post* photographer, to interview Edie at the apartment of a kindly man who hoped to become her manager. It was a typical West Village apartment, small rooms attractively decorated but with a certain pretense—movie-set grandeur in a limited space. I've seen so many similar apartments over the years that before I enter one, I can almost predict the opulent overdraped windows, the harp in the corner, the potted plants hanging from the ceiling, the antique pillows heaped on the big velvet sofa that really belongs in a drawing room, the Byzantine bar with marble top and silver glasses all in a row complete with silk-tassled key that opens the bottom compartment, the coffee table with crystal obelisks, the big glossy books . . . the ambience on Waverly Place was all there.

Reclining on a damask chaise, dressed in a quilted kimono and pants, her hair tightly wrapped in a bandeau, was Edie Beale. She did not rise to greet me. In fact, she didn't move from her position the entire interview. Our host went into the kitchen to prepare some quiche, and I asked Edie about her relationship with the Bouvier family. She told me it was a family of great beauties. "My mother was a world-famous beauty," she said. "She was dark and looked Italian, like Jackie's father. My mother's sisters, the Bouvier twins, were also international beauties, but they have red hair and very light skin. They're terribly famous in American society, the Bouvier twins. People fainted when they saw them." But it was her mother for whom she had the greatest praise. When I had seen Edith Sr. in the film, I thought she came across as a rather daffy old woman, in contrast to her daughter's still quite striking manner. It was hard to relate the silly, pathetic old woman of *Gray Gardens* to the version of loveliness Edie described with such rapture. As she talked I was again intrigued by the resemblance to her most famous cousin. Edie had a very dramatic face, full lips, Egyptian eyes, heavy brows, and the straight high Grecian nose that Caroline Kennedy also inherited from the Bouviers.

But the Bouviers were more than a bouquet of international beauties. They were, Edie said, very closely knit. "We were a large family. I had a great many first cousins on that side. When we were young we had many family parties, birthday parties . . . we were all very close." Was the family still close? Edie sighed and made a gesture of helplessness. "I feel so badly about what happened," she said. "Just imagine, it was put on Telstar—the whole house! It went all over the world. Prince Radziwill and Mr. Onassis saw it in London. Jackie was in Greece. Lee was supposed to be looking over the whole place. Then Lee went and got a divorce. She had so much trouble we didn't see her more than two or three times, and the house was kind of destroyed."

I asked whether she was ever entertained by Jackie and Lee. "About a year ago Lee told me I must come see her in New York, but I didn't really want to. Too much water over the dam." As for her two brothers, she would have nothing to do with them. "I may never speak to them again," she said. "They sided with the authorities to get Mother out of her own house. They kept sending down powers of attorney that Mother wouldn't sign. Then the authorities tried to evict her. Can you imagine?" Edie said she feared her relatives and no longer trusted anyone. "They're dangerous, do you know what I'm saying? Mother was terrified. She wanted me to leave after she died. She gave me strict orders to go straight to Paris. 'You have to get rid of every cat and go live in Paris,' she told me. I said, 'Can't I take any cats at all with me, Mother?' and she said, 'No. You don't *need* any cats in Paris.'"

As to whether she thought her cousins also wanted her mother out of that house, the answer was an adamant no. "Not the Bouvier girls," she said. "They weren't in on it. They came forward because it went to Europe on Telstar."

Edie Beale's youth was one of great luxury and privilege. Her mother, a daughter of the prominent lawyer John Bouvier, Jr., Jackie's uncle, was a celebrated beauty, and her marriage to Phelan Beale, also a successful lawyer, was the social event of the year. Beautiful Edith bore two sons and a daughter she named after herself. Edie went to Miss Porter's and Spence, her mother's alma mater, and made her debut at the Hotel Pierre in 1936. "My father paid thousands of dollars for it," she said. "He didn't want to. He never spoke to me again afterward."

In those years all was not well with the Beale family. Edie's brothers left during World War II and went their own ways. Their mother left New York City to live in East Hampton year round, and saw her sons only when they visited her. "The war took them away and they never returned," Edie said sadly. "I was crazy about them. I brought them up." Then came a crushing blow. Edie's father went to Mexico and obtained a divorce from her mother, who then withdrew from the world for good. "I had taken charge of the house when I was seventeen," recalled Edie. "I had to run it. My mother was a singer and she didn't like to do anything domestic. She was a highly trained singer. Fifty thousand dollars was spent on her voice. She had no interest in American society. She was a very distinguished artist and I was happy and proud to work for her."

Instead of pursuing a career or marrying, Edie moved into Gray Gardens in 1952 and adopted her mother. For twenty years the two women lived there, summer and winter, the house slowly crumbling around them, and attracted little attention aside from the annoyance of the neighbors. Then in 1971 local and county officials, apparently responding to increased pressure from the residents of East Hampton, began eviction proceedings, the charge being "unsanitary conditions." This catastrophe came shortly after the two women's trust funds from the Bouvier estate had run out. Of course, Edie's version of what happened next was vastly different from the official account. "Do you want to know what was wrong with that house?" she said. "The raccoons had eaten the wooden shingles and the rain came through and the plaster ceilings began to fall—just a little bit in each room.

We couldn't get a plumber. We had no money. I had to bring up a pail of water in order to turn the handle on mother's toilet. So of course they took pictures of *that*," she said indignantly. And what was the real reason behind the raid, I asked? "A neighbor wanted to buy the house," she replied.

The first invasion was repulsed by Edie. Like Barbara Fritchie at the window, Edie held the health officials and police at bay. "'Go get a search warrant,' I told them. They came back two days later with a fake search warrant!" When I asked her what they were looking for, she said, "Two hundred things— everything and anything that could evict us. There were twelve people in on it and they were all paid government agents. It's no wonder that my mother is dead and I want to give up my citizenship." Edie had told reporters about the more sinister aspects of the raid, but she said they weren't interested in the truth. "I told them that truth was stranger than fiction. They told me they had to write certain things. I said, 'Why? Why?' and they said to me, 'Miss Beale, we want to keep our jobs,' and I said OK." Her mother had tried to hire a lawyer but could not afford his $3,000 retainer. The eviction was prevented with the help of Mr. and Mrs. Onassis, and the house was fixed up. Edie said she had found out from her brother's law office that the monthly food and utility allowance they were given came from Mr. Onassis.

Then came Albert and David Maysles, documentarists *par excellence*. According to Edie, Lee Radziwill brought them together because the Maysles wanted to make a film about East Hampton. "I didn't know what I was doing," Edie said. "If I had known what a documentary was, I would have left for Montauk and hidden in a beach house out there. I thought I'd look lovely, dancing to Spanish music in beautiful costumes and taking half a day to get ready. . . . I thought I was going to be the cat's pajamas. I didn't know it was going to be personal and I was going to be screaming at my mother. Those Maysles nearly killed me! A wave crashed down and almost broke my neck and they never used it in the picture. I got under it in time. . . . I saw them for three years straight and I nearly committed suicide. Directors are very dangerous."

But wasn't it true, I asked, that she and her mother had signed a very generous contract with the Maysles? She waved my question away with her hand. "Do you know what my mother said? 'My God,' she said, 'the Maysles are deadly.' Later on someone explained that to me. Do you know what Mother was talking about? A documentary means showing *stuff*, and oh my goodness, that's why poor Mother was in absolute agony. She kept saying, 'Don't you want some singing? Don't you want some music?' 'Oh no,' they'd say, 'We can't pay royalties on songs.' My mother damnéd them before she died. She wanted a used Rolls-Royce and she never ever got it."

Edie had seen *Gray Gardens* four times and eventually became so detached she wept over herself on the screen. "Why were the New York film critics so mean?" she wailed. "The people liked the film. They yelled and screamed and threw their hats in the air and everything. But the critics were very insulting." Perhaps, she thought, they were mean because they wanted to get back at her cousins. "They were mad because *Jacqueleen* [as Edie pronounced her name] married a Greek and they decided to show her up with poor relatives. They hated my cousin and took it out on me. They were very insulting. I cried. . . ."

The film came and went, the house was repaired, some of the cats were given away, and Edie and her mother lived on at Gray Gardens in relative peace. But Edie, who had had dreams of glory all her life, found her passion for show business had been inflamed by the film. While Mama was a singer, Edie was a dancer, and she and her mother had many heated arguments over where and how Edie should perform. Edie saw herself as a London music hall dancer and wanted to perform in nightclubs. Her mother was horrified at the idea. "You can't!" she said. "You'll be shot or kidnapped!"

"She told me all these terrible things," said Edie *sotto voce*. "She said the only thing for me was TV because I'd always be protected there. She was great on safety. I think I had nerve to disobey her, don't you?" Mama was protective, no doubt about that. In the movie Edie complained bitterly to the camera that her mother had driven away all Edie's lovers and forced her to live in seclusion as an aristocrat *manqué*, to which her mother countered by insisting her daughter stayed by choice. "You never fell for a man. France fell, but Edie didn't fall."

Edie never did marry. She spoke with great fondness of a niece who was extraordinarily beautiful and looked as if she could be her daughter, but Edie never found a man she could live with and have children and a life of her own. Instead, she lived with Edith Sr. from 1952 until her death in 1977. Mama was a witty, acerbic, and generally overwhelming person, and in tantalizing glimpses Edie revealed the two decades she had spent in her exclusive company. After a childhood spent in that rarefied circle of American aristocracy in which beauty and pedigree, especially for women, is more important than a huge fortune (that can always be attained through the proper marriage), Edie went from the best of everything to self-imposed exile with a bitter, disillusioned woman. What a shocking contrast between the two worlds for both mother and daughter.

What kinds of wounds caused them to make such a dreary choice? Several times as I looked at Edie reclining in a graceful but studied way on the chaise—the gray hair she hated covered in a turban, the bright red lip color rather touchingly asymmetrical—and listened to her reminiscences of times past, it struck me that she was like one of Chekhov's "Three Sisters" who had somehow wandered into a play by Tennessee Williams by mistake. The play was a tale of two formerly beautiful women living out their years on the far eastern tip of the American continent, a dismembered arm that stretches out for Europe, their gaze averted from tawdry, crime-filled, dangerous East Hampton to focus yearningly on London and Paris. Exiled Edith and Edie were two American ex-patriots-to-be who never quite made it back to Europe's cradle of culture. They couldn't have gotten much closer without leaving land.

"The only thing I wanted to do was travel." Edie sighed. "Go around the world all the time. . . . Isn't that funny? So I stayed in one place forever."

Edie adored her mother. Her admiration for her was close to worship. It was Mother who had given Edie her values: be cultured, be beautiful, be discreet, and be a lady. Edie achieved all but one, discretion. But then, her mother also failed, for when the Maysles came calling, both Beales said yes. Perhaps they agreed out of innocence, as Edie insisted, or perhaps they were desperate for a chance to make some money of their own to buy a little independence. Maybe it was unconscious revenge. For whatever reason, opening Gray Gardens to a film crew was not discreet, and on several occasions during the interview Edie was full of remorse, particularly about the effect of the publicity on Jackie's sensitivities.

Although Edie adored her mother, she also fought mightily against her. Like a perennial adolescent, Edie went from one extreme mood swing to the other. "Next to William Randolph Hearst my mother was the world's most famous collector. She collected everything," Edie declared.

"What things did she like to collect?" I asked. "Pictures, silver—"

"Everything," she said expansively, "down to tiny little things she'd buy at the five-and-ten-cent store."

In her next breath Edie spoke of Mother in a new tone of voice: "Mother never cleaned anything out, never threw anything away. The house is a storage warehouse." And three minutes later, on telling me she considered herself a bit of an amateur decorator: "I've been decorating my whole life. My mother was better than I was, but she never wanted me to touch her house. In later years things began to get kind of dilapidated and I had to try to get things to look a bit better, so I was always working."

And losing sleep too. After the Beales became famous, crackpots started calling them day and night, Edie said. "Last summer I moved to another side of the house." I was not able to get her to explain that security measure.

For two years, Edie and her mother argued about her dancing career while the workmen came and went, strangers in every room, more disruption of their privacy; it was even worse than the Maysles and their everywhere-peering eyes. When the carpenters, plumbers, roofers, painters, and repairmen finally left, Edith and Edie discovered they had been looted. "All the family heirlooms were gone," Edie exclaimed. "Beautiful chairs from China with curved teakwood fan backs—"

"Who took them?" I asked.

"The workmen," she said with impatience. "They weren't properly screened. East Hampton is one of the most terrible places! The crime! And the police never seem to be able to do anything about it," she said, her voice fairly dripping with sarcasm.

At last, having taken everything they coveted except the Big Prize, that twenty-plus-room beach house cum mansion, the world at large left the two women alone once more. Then Edie's mother died, and Edie was truly alone, with the responsibility for holding on to Gray Gardens all hers.

"Why don't you sell?" I asked at one point.

"I'm a European," she said. "We don't sell our houses. Americans do. They don't think anything of it. To me it's so personal it's like my left arm or my leg or my nose. That house is part of me."

Even so, she knew she could not possibly care for the house. She couldn't afford a gardener or housekeeper, and still heard the words of her departed mother inside her head: "When I'm gone they'll burn the house from under you. They're dangerous." Edie finally put the house up for sale. For half a million dollars. Needless to say, there were no takers. "Someone offered me $200,000 this summer but I didn't think it was enough," she said. "It's so beautiful, comfortable and unique. I'll never get another beach like it."

What did she do all day? I asked. She walked on the beach a lot, she said, to get the maximum benefit from the $2,500 a year in taxes on the property. She collected shells. "I'm a collector like my mother, but I'm trying to get over it. She gave me plenty of things. She gave me everything . . . there wasn't anything I haven't had."

"But what do you *do* all by yourself out there?" I asked. She told me she stayed up all night playing records, reading, looking things up. . . . "But I have to clean up. It's going to take another year. I pushed boxes around the whole summer but I could never get it right. It was always so junked up with Mother's things." She had turned their upstairs rooms into something hot and tropical, for Edie loved hot climates, she said, and she had made her mother's room a sort of shrine. "Mother loved Japanese. She sang *Madame Butterfly*. She bought Japanese kimonos. I tried to make the upstairs look like Tahiti or something, and in Mother's room I put Japanese prints up and I wrote something Japanese on the wall, 'The Death of the Samurai Warrior.' I wrote some poetry on the wall too: 'She's gone. She was human after all.'" The goddess had fallen, leaving her mortal child alone and unprotected.

Into the lonely chaos of Edie Beale's life came a man who told her he could get her booked into nightclubs. And he did. And here she was, performing in a New York in-spot and still in awe over everything that had happened.

"How were the reviews?" I asked the host, who had returned with trays of quiche and a green salad.

"Definitely mixed," he said. "The positive ones compared her to Gertrude Stein."

"Oh Jesus, Gertrude Stein!" came a mortified cry from the

sofa. "Oh my God, Carleton, what would you do if you were compared to Gertrude Stein? Do you think I should commit suicide this afternoon?"

Edie was eager to talk about her performance. She frankly admitted she was inexperienced and could be criticized by other entertainers for having made it to Reno Sweeney because she was related to Jackie and Lee. "I don't know what I'm like," she said. "It's simple and amateurish." She was very grateful to the night-club owner who had let her sing. "He called and asked me to sing and I just about died. I'd never sung a note in my life. Mother was the singer and I was the dancer." But she was excited about the offer and made a big decision: she would come out of her twenty years of solitude and spend the next twenty being an entertainer. Then, at age eighty, she would retire and presumably find something else to do. But show business was not all she had dreamed it would be. "I thought it would be different. I thought I was going to have lovely days just lying in bed. I think I'd be better at it if I could lie in bed all day. I always imagined doing this on television. I imagined getting up and doing this beautiful dance and then going back to bed."

I was intrigued by her idea. I visualized a TV screen and saw Edie lying on a many-pillowed bed, then rising and doing a dance full of chiffon, Tchaikovsky, and Isadora Duncan-style frolicking, then leaving the frenzy and drifting back to bed. I thought it a great visual idea, and told her so.

"They wouldn't let me do it. Television's too mechanized," she said, and asked about Robert Altman. She had heard a rumor that he had been in the audience the night before, and had become very agitated. "No directors! They drive me crazy!" Altman, she confided, had wanted to direct a sequel to *Gray Gardens*, and she had adamantly refused any and all offers to star in another film. The reason was Jacqueline. "You know, she felt terribly about the botch of that house. Lee was upset and she never took charge. I don't want to hurt poor Jackie's feelings. She's a terribly sensitive girl. She was terrified I was going to make another movie about the house after Mother died. I said, 'Jacqueleen, I wouldn't *think* of making another movie in that house.'"

But what Edie really wanted to talk about was her career. She was very skeptical of the audience's interest in her. Was it for herself, or for Jacqueline Bouvier Kennedy Onassis? Maybe Edie should change her name? "No!" said her prospective manager. She was also crushed that Rex Reed hadn't come to review her act, and had commented that he thought Edie was being exploited.

"I suppose Rex Reed thought I was unprofessional. You know, Mother might have said the same thing," she said.

"That's not it," I said. "Rex Reed didn't say that at all. He said the management should be embarrassed for exploiting you."

I was also fascinated by Edie's approach to pleasure. It attracted and repelled her at the same time. She had noticed that the audiences enjoyed hearing her talk about Jackie and how being First Lady had changed her. "Now and then I do say something funny," she remarked. "When they asked whether I was jealous of Jacqueline, the fame, the White House, and all that, I said, 'It began to dawn on me at one point perhaps Jackie was enjoying the whole thing.' I thought that was funny."

"I think you're enjoying the whole thing," I said.

"You're not unhappy in a nightclub. You're absolutely right," she replied laconically, as if being "not unhappy" was the ultimate joy. Later, when she spoke of her great desire to see London, she said timidly, "You think I'd better not satisfy these little desires, don't you? What do you think about going to Hollywood? They gave me the names of two studios—"

"I think you should continue what you're doing," I said.

"You want me to make money," she accused. "I want to be happy."

"Sometimes one helps the other," I said, and wondered to myself how she defined being happy.

At one point her prospective manager left the room for a moment, and she became very animated. Leaning over to me, she whispered, "They all want me to do what they want, but I want to do what *I* want, and I want to be a *rock dancer*. It's dangerous, but that's what I want to get into."

I was too stunned to answer.

"I don't want to go on being intellectual and singing. I'm a rock dancer! But I may be killed! Mother told me that. She didn't think I'd start taking pills, but I'd meet people who would be dangerous and I would need protection. If you get into the rock field it gets dangerous. You know the kind of people you meet—Mick Jagger and the Rolling Stones and all those funny people." She became very excited at this point and lowered her whisper to a hiss. "I've got to go to California to do this. I don't *like* what I'm doing now."

"But you were having a good time last night," I protested.

"I'm a good actress! But you've got to love what you're do-ing. I don't like singing and talking. I'm out of my *mind* when I dance, and I'm a rock dancer. I think I've got Negro blood. I'm half rebel. I'll tell them what I am."

"So then do it," I said, and I really meant it. After years of dreariness and self-denial and lack of excitement, Edie Beale was going for broke. She was going to do what *she* desired, not what someone else told her to do, and I was happy to hear her so de-termined to take charge of her own life.

"Do it," I said, "if it's really what you want."

"But I'll be killed," she wailed. "I'll be killed! You meet all these dangerous people."

"Crossing the street can be dangerous too," I said. "You'll be all right."

Then followed some rapid-fire questions about where she should tour. I suggested larger cities with more sophisticated audiences. Her prospective manager encouraged her to go to London. Edie wanted to go wherever it was very warm and people would let her be a rock dancer. "I have to get my own band," she said, "and that could take as long as six months. And I have to wait until my eye heals. The lens dried up, something everybody in the family has, and I had to have it removed. I have to get soft contact lenses because I can't dance with my glasses on. I'm going to do this maybe in three months—six months. I'm not going to rush it. I can't get any dancing jobs until I solve the eye problem."

Suddenly she seemed deflated. "I've got a long way to go. I hardly know what I'm doing yet. Don't you really think the big thing is who I'm related to?" I told her that to the contrary, I thought there was a strong audience identity and a great sym-patico. She looked skeptical, and I changed the subject. "When will you be going back to East Hampton?" I asked. She said in two days she had to go back to regulate the thermostat and feed the cats as she could not keep imposing on her friends to do it.

"How many cats do you have now?" I asked. "I heard you've given many of them away."

"Well, yes. Some," she said.

"Do you feel tied down because of the house?" I asked.

"Tied down is not the word. I feel as if it's my duty to take care of it, you know. They do those things in Ireland and En-gland, but they don't do them here." I asked her whether she had any special ties to the locale. "No, I loathe East Hampton, excuse my language. They killed my mother."

"Would you sell the house? Is it on the market now?"

"I took it off," she said. But she acknowledged that eventually she would have to sell it. "I don't have anybody to take care of it. There's a lot of crime there. I feel so bad about all that's happened. I'm not happy living in East Hampton. Why were they so awful to us?"

"But you turned it around and made it work for you," I said, trying to get her out of her sudden despair. "You've turned it into a very positive thing. Your life is exciting now, and you're back in the thick of things. Why don't you let me do an interview with you out at the house? We could show you and the improvements that have been made and you can talk about your new career."

I could tell she liked the idea, but she became very wary. "I think that would disturb Jacqueline greatly. I don't want to upset her."

"Why?"

"She pays my utilities and she gives me a food allowance. She did it for Mother and she never stopped."

"But the article wouldn't be done with a destructive intent," I protested. "It would show the good things that have happened to you. I'm not going to zero in on cats and garbage bags. I'll even help you arrange the furniture so everything looks right for pictures." She was very anxious to say yes but still evaded specifics. "Did you see the farewell piece I did on Joan Crawford?" I said, thinking it was a good example of how I could accentuate the positive. In the middle of an anti-Crawford tempest created by the media, I had written a sympathetic article about her in the *New York Post*. At once I realized I had made a big mistake, for Edie got on her high horse and denounced Crawford for being rude to Justice Douglas's young wife, stealing attention away from her, and for wearing the same light blue satin dress with a big bow on the bodice as Edie wore to a debutante ball.

"She grabbed the room, wearing *my* dress, stopped the dance and did a solo on her own. And I *always* was more or less in control of the room." And if that hadn't been enough insult, Joan Crawford had also been rude to Edie's mother in Saks by wearing her mother's hat! She attributed the coincidences to the fact that the Beale women and Crawford, née Lucille LeSueur, were all French "and I guess the French wear the same things."

Joan Crawford may have been a superb dancer and entertainer, Edie said, "but she wasn't a nice person."

"There's good and bad in everyone," I said.

"I bet you raved about her. I'm not going to read it. I bet you said she was utterly divine."

"Well, I'd like to do an interview with you and the house as an upbeat sequel, and I'd do it nicely."

She thought for a while and then said, "I'd certainly have to clean and fix the house if you're coming. It's very cute upstairs on the second floor now." She was fading away again. I asked her about the room she had at Gray Gardens when she was little. Could we see that too? She declined. It had never been cleaned or painted. "It's locked up. I can't let you in. It's dirty. It was a little room in the middle of the house—terribly cute, filled with pictures of ships. The one thing I wanted to do was get on a ship and travel."

"Could I come out on Wednesday?" I asked.

"I don't think the house will look nice until the weather gets warmer," she said. "I can't really fix it. It's very damp and you'll get very sick. You wouldn't want to go in Mother's room either. It's cold and damp there and we'll get pneumonia."

"I'd just like to write a story showing how the media overplayed the thing, making it into a circus and then moving on—"

"It's going to be cold and dirty and you're going to get sick," she said, her voice rising to a near shout. "We'll get sick marching around Mother's house in winter." In the next breath she was telling me where we could have lunch. Certainly not in East Hampton, which was "absolutely verboten" because they killed her mother.

"Shall we go to Southampton?" I said.

"I'll go anywhere you want," she said obediently, "if you're kind enough to take me out to lunch."

I said good-bye to her. We were to meet again the following Wednesday. On Tuesday I got a call. Edie Beale had changed her mind. She would not grant me an interview until spring, which of course meant never. I often wonder what happened to her. Listening to the tape of the interview that night with Suzanne, I was quite taken with the entire experience. Throughout the interview a radio somewhere in the house had been playing sentimental WPAT-type pop music, adding background effects that created an even more bizarre theatricality to the taped interview. With lush violins playing "Send in the Clowns" and a full orchestra delivering a peppy if muted Beatle song, "Eleanor Rigby," Edie Beale had told me of her life and her dreams.

I had met a sixty-year-old woman who wanted to be a rock star. Even though terrible danger awaited her if she followed her desires, she said she would see it through because dancing made her wildly happy. I really wished her all the happiness she could find.

I don't know where Edie Beale is now. In September 1979 she sold Gray Gardens to Ben Bradlee and Sally Quinn for something over $200,000. They are now doing extensive repairs. When I called the town clerk's office to check my facts, the gentleman at the other end of the line said, "It was a shame. When Edie was young, she was a beautiful girl."

Chapter 7

This Interior Rated X

Photographs of my interiors have not been limited to the readers of *Family Circle* and *House Beautiful*. I regret to say they have also appeared in a porno magazine—all because of a client I'll call Joe, the king of twine.

There is a certain kind of client who has bought everything and done everything and then finds out the only thing left to do is do it all over again. They are sufferers of the nothing-is-ever-enough-if-you-don't-know-what-you-want syndrome. A decorator by trade sees more of *la dolce vita* than people in most other professions, but of all the decadence that has flashed before my jaded eyes, the top award must go to Joe.

He was tall and skinny, an ordinary-looking guy with no sex appeal. He looked more like an unusually well-dressed shoe salesman than the self-made multimillionaire he was. Joe had cornered the twine market, then branched into a myriad of other businesses; and they had all made money. Lots and lots of money. By his early sixties he had ascended to that charmed economic region where you have to work hard to spend all your money before you die.

By the time I met him, Joe had done everything. He had seen everything. He had lived everywhere. He had residences in Chicago, New York, Paris, Palm Beach, and Switzerland, all identically furnished. He had or was to have six wives, also all identical. Joe was interested only in merchandise between the ages of eighteen and twenty-four. Between wives he had an endless supply of nubile women who rescued him from the throes of

---

Author's note: *Each of the characters depicted here is not only fictitious, but a composite of several people. Any similarity between an actual person and the character as depicted is purely coincidental.*

ennui. He had a Learjet and a large yacht and a stable of cars. He owned an island near Grand Cayman and another one off the coast of Greece. He had a ranch for his blooded horses and an avocado plantation in southern California. He even owned a rock group. The only thing he didn't possess was taste, but Joe knew there was virtually nothing in this world that was not for sale if you could afford it. Good taste was a commodity, Joe felt, and somewhere out there, someone would sell him some of it.

I met Joe when he was auditioning decorators for a job. The setting for the interview unawares was a party I had been invited to one snowy February evening at the home of Carlotta, whose parties always featured an interesting assortment of people. Carlotta was very successfully on the make, and her soirées were often pretty showcases for who was "in" in New York society. This particular party featured several of New York's leading decorators, including the late Michael Greer, whom Carlotta insisted on calling Michel Gruyère in an intensely French accent. Carlotta was Greek. The atmosphere in her apartment was a reflection of her homeland: heavy, coarsely woven Greek fabrics, banquettes, lots of incense and low brass lighting. Little did the decorators assembled at her soirée realize they were on display for a potential client.

That client was Joe Keene. Carlotta introduced him to me as an industrialist who lived in New Jersey. He had brought his wife, Leda, a delicate Scandinavian bloom in her early twenties. Joe, said Carlotta, was an old and dear friend. "We are like kissing cousins," the hostess murmured. I wondered about that. Carlotta had just shed her third husband and was shopping around for a fourth. I think she may have had Joe in mind, but that was not to be. What did work out was Joe Keene and me.

Joe had just bought a New York apartment in the Hampshire House on Central Park South, and he wanted it decorated. Cheaply. He wanted the very best, the top of the line, an apartment befitting an important industrialist—but he wanted it cheap. I quickly learned that arguing with him about the discrepancy between what he wanted (ultima chic) and what he wanted to spend was futile. I found a method that did work: buy what he wanted, have him declare it was exactly what he had asked for, then present him with the bill. It soon became as predictable as a comedy routine.

The office pulled out the stops. We marbled the floors in the living room, painted the walls a fabulous chocolate color, and upholstered everything in bright coral. I went to London and purchased lots of expensive accessories at Mallet. We gave him a contemporary library and a magnificent bedroom in a soft mauve, inspired by Mrs. Keene's youthful sweetness and purity.

Joe already had a huge triplex penthouse apartment on Park Avenue in the 80s where he had once lived with a former wife and their four children. After the divorce the daughters stayed with their mother, and the oldest son, Brad, chose to stay with his father. I once had occasion to be in Brad's room in that huge triplex apartment and saw a framed photo taken of him with his parents on an ocean liner. Across his mother's face Brad had scrawled "bitch-bitch-bitch-bitch." It was my first clue to the emotional state of the Keene family, and obviously all was not well. We had come to the triplex to remove a few pieces of furniture to the Hampshire House apartment, which was to be a *pied-à-terre* for Joe, Leda, and Brad whenever they were in New York. I looked around the vast, nearly empty rooms of that triplex penthouse, one of the most desirable apartments on Park Avenue, and wondered why Joe kept it. Even for people who find money no obstacle between themselves and what they want, it seemed an example of shameful waste.

I was also getting to know Mrs. Keene a little better. As work on the Hampshire House apartment progressed, Leda would come to the office to approve color schemes. She always wore high boots and very short Mary Jane dresses. With her deep red hair and big blue eyes and youthful innocence, she looked the picture-perfect wife. She fulfilled all Joe's requirements, or so I thought. Leda insisted that price was no object to her husband, no matter what kind of an act he put on, and we were to supply them with the finest of French furnishings, no matter what the cost. Although she wanted little in the apartment for herself, other than a mauve bedroom, her husband wanted a room for his son, who had just turned fifteen.

Up to the office came Junior. He was dressed in a shirt open to the navel, jeans, and boots. Unlike Joe, Brad was extraordinarily handsome. With him came the girl whom he was dating. The couple talked laconically about the look of Brad's room. I wondered whether provisions should also be made for the young lady, but it was obvious the son was doing everything to emulate the father. I wagered that the life expectancy of Brad's relationship with that girl would be shorter than that of a mayfly.

Brad was eager to be like his father in every way. He told me he was going to go into his father's business and carry on the family tradition. Success, it seemed, was the tradition begun by the father—success in business and success with women. I had already surmised from the mutilated photo in his room that Brad was not fond of his mother, but the relationship with his father was the opposite of his absence of affection for Mama. In return, Brad's father adored him and gave him everything he wanted.

When Brad went off to boarding school in California, Dad bought him a Mazda, which Brad liked to drive at top speed. On a beautiful fall weekend Brad crashed into a tree on the way to Santa Monica; he lived, but the young woman who was with him was killed. Brad's father was the first to hear about the tragedy. The parents of the dead girl heard the news not from Joe but from his secretary. Joe was late for a tennis game. That was the way Joe did things, with a lack of sensitivity that sometimes took one's breath away.

Long before installation day at Hampshire House, intrafamily problems hit the crisis stage. Leda had made it perfectly clear to me that she did not want Brad living with them. I thought this was a little strange. After all, Brad was her husband's unemancipated son. My perplexity was cleared up when the son casually informed me that he and Leda had had carnal knowledge. I assume that Brad's father not only knew about their lovemaking but approved of it. What was good for Papa was good for Junior, was Joe's philosophy, and when it came to giving his son everything he wanted, his generosity had no limits.

The situation was deteriorating rapidly. One day Joe telephoned me to say his wife had filed for divorce. By that time I had also begun to realize that Leda's wide-eyed look was more drug euphoria than innocence. In fact, she was hooked on pills, a whole pharmacy of them. Joe agreed to the divorce, and Leda made a quick trip to Mexico. Her ex-husband seemed rather smug about the affair, for Leda had not asked for alimony, as had his other former wives.

One day I came to the Hampshire House apartment to deliver a couple of lamp shades, and who should be lying on Leda's mauve and white bed drinking vintage red wine and speaking of dancing in TV commercials or on Broadway but Leda, an ex-wife turned mistress. I needed a day or two to adjust to the rapidly changing events. In the days that followed, Leda started going to theatrical agencies. She was taken on by a booking agent at one of the top agencies and instructed to collect a portfolio of her pictures, while dancing as well as playing. The agencies needed to see how she photographed and in order to get feedback from photographers they sent her for test shots. They wanted to see her in all kinds of pictures: Leda in modern dance dress, in evening gowns, in leotards, in nothing at all. There were to be close-up shots of Leda's sweet, limpid-eyed face, of Leda dancing through open fields of flowers in yards of flowing chiffon, of Leda rising like a wet nymph from the sea. When Leda heard about the need for some water ballet shots, she decided she must have them taken in Hawaii.

Joe gave her money to have her maid, clothes, drugs, hairdresser, and photographer flown off on Joe's Learjet to Honolulu and then on to Maui and the small island of Lanai. On Maui, she was thrown fully clothed into a swimming pool during a wild party. Someone called Joe to get Leda and her entourage out of there before they were arrested, and he came at once to the rescue, flew them out of Maui, and tucked his crazy little angel into her mauve and white bed. It seemed he had become her father as well as her sugar daddy, and he felt compelled to play all the roles she demanded of him. No matter what she did, it seemed, he forgave her. Whatever it was that she did to him, he couldn't get enough of it.

Like a concerned parent, Joe sent Leda to a New York psychiatrist to help her work out the drug problem she wouldn't admit having, but going into therapy only seemed to make Leda worse. Then she fell madly in love with a man from South America who introduced her to sadomasochism. The sight of Leda's bruised body drove poor Joe wild. He begged her to stay away from the kinky South American, but Leda had recently added Angel Dust to her pharmacopeia of booze and pills, and there was no talking to her. While things were still hot and brutal between Leda and her new lover, she decided what she really needed to straighten herself out was a loft in which she could practice dance. Joe agreed at once. A dancing studio was found in the factory district around So Ho. It was done up like something out of *New York* magazine called "The Ultimate Photographer's Fantasy Loft." In the window she hung a sign advertising her talents. The sign read ZARA'S DANCE STUDIO, the name Leda used as a professional dancer. Joe called me in to do all the work, of course, and we stripped the walls of many coats of paint, put in a tin ceiling, created a new kitchen, and raised the bedroom on a platform. One large room became Leda's studio, equipped with ballet bars, lights, backdrop paper, and camera equipment. Photographers came to *her* for test shots—some of the best. During the completion stage of the loft Leda's lover beat her badly, stole her money and the jewelry Joe had given her, and cleared out. I thought that was the end of that particularly shabby episode.

It was moving time again. No more funky loft for Leda; she needed the protection of the Upper East Side, and a respectable apartment was soon found, this time on East 57th Street. Again I was called in to do the interior design. Although Joe's apartments were always identical, Leda's were always different. This one was done in lilac: lilac lacquer walls, lilac floors, lilac sofa, and lilac balloon shades. We even lacquered her ebony piano lilac. I admit I was doing it a little tongue-in-cheek, but Leda loved it. She felt like Theda Bara. Leda was also looking a little lilac herself after an abortion, the inability to sleep, a lousy diet, and the heavy use of booze and pills. The further she fell into ignominy, the more Joe adored her. The more she degraded herself, the more trouble he had to bail her out of, the more he wanted her.

Then an odd thing happened. Just when her 57th Street apartment was about to be finished, Joe announced that he was not giving his pet any more money. When Leda heard this, she ran straight into the arms of the sadistic South American. The next thing I heard they were going to tie the knot.

Meanwhile, I was busy doing yet another apartment for the peripatetic Keenes, this time the fabulous Park Avenue triplex where Joe had once lived with a former wife, the one before Leda, and his children. After a few years in the Hampshire House, Joe had tired of the relative lack of space and lusted after that wide avenue and the three floors of penthouse splendour he had so foolishly abandoned. We spent about a million dollars on that job, and it was a showplace by anyone's standards. With Leda now gone, an advertising man, who booked models for conventions and industrial films, was hired to book young ladies for Joe's pleasure.

The arrangement worked as follows: Joe would tell the agent he wanted to do an industrial film for one of his many companies and interview the models himself. Joe was, after all, chairman of the board, and it was his good money that was paying everybody's salaries. The models would arrive every ten minutes on what is known in the business as a "cattle call." In the model's case, many are called but few are chosen. Into the foyer would step the young women with their leather portfolios, some of them mere girls who had left for the big city before graduating from high school. In those days of the Pepsi Generation youth was all, the younger the better, and modeling agencies snapped them up and sent them out, innocent babes in a jaded world of too much money and tired thrills. Some of them couldn't help but be impressed with Joe's white marble entranceway, the antique dining table, the comfortable cushioned sofas near the windows overlooking Park Avenue. Seated with a model on the coral velvet sofa, portfolio zipped open on his lap, Joe would offer the girl a drink and check her out. If she was pretty enough, he would ask her out to dinner where she would either succumb to the heady atmosphere of all that dough or she would not. Many of them did.

Those who did were led back to the apartment and Joe's bedroom where the walls were covered in gray suede, the floors with striped Edward Fields sculptured carpet, and the bed with Porthault sheets. Joe also had several thousand dollars worth of video equipment built into elaborate breakfronts in that penthouse bedroom. They had a remote control system he could operate by pushing buttons and gadgets on a panel hidden on the left side of the bed. Not only did Joe have a thing for electronic gadgets, he needed a handy on-off switch because he didn't film every conquest. "Sometimes I like to play it back to myself to see if I enjoyed it," he once told me. I'm sure the fare was better than most late-night TV.

Sometimes those innocents with their Kentucky drawls or healthy but fading California tans would return to the penthouse with their brothers and girl friends. Then Joe might decide to produce a full-length feature on a grander scale, after which he'd take the cast of thousands out to dinner, the doting papa surrounded by his adorable kids. He really loved them all. They made him feel good, but unless they were truly naughty, he didn't want to marry them. Ah, Leda, where is the young woman who can replace you in Joe's affections? Is there anyone anywhere as beautiful and decadent as you? Shakespeare had his Dark Lady and Joe had his Leda. He moved from house to house, from apartment to apartment, from ranch to island to penthouse, heart heavy for his darling Leda, the nymph he had cast out. Where was she?

For a while there was a stunning young woman from Larchmont. She was a little past Joe's cutoff age of twenty-five, but she was beautiful, intelligent, poised, cultured, and crazy about Joe Keene. He wouldn't have a thing to do with her. He wouldn't even take her to bed. She was too sane. He steeped himself further and further in kinkiness, upping the ante from *ménages* to more elaborate scenarios. Accouterments of every kind, battery powered and electrical, were bought and stored in his closets. (When a client requires you to design the interiors of his closets down to the last drawer, you can't help but know what's in them.) Joe was one of those clients who took particular pains about the design of everything, down to his shirt rods, which were laid out at a height that just cleared the flotilla of shoes below. There were black sock drawers, brown sock drawers, cuff link drawers, belt drawers, handkerchief drawers, each one laid out neat and tidy. And above the drawers was a locked cabinet for his *props d'amour* of various straps, costumes, whips, and molded plastic items. There are no secrets from one's decorator in these cases. Sooner or later everything comes out of the closet.

I did much more than color schemes and closet arrangements for Joe. I told him what linens to buy; selected his pots and pans; advised him on staff services; helped him put together parties; told him how to cook, what to eat, and what wines to buy. And there were other favors beyond the call of duty—like sending several yards of his living-room drapery fabric to a woman with whom he had just spent the night.

All the moving Joe did complicated matters. He exchanged residences with dizzying speed, and the only thing that made the moving easier on our office was his ordering all the residences to look alike. It was interior design by the dozen. The Lausanne home and Gstaad chalet were exact duplicates of the New York penthouse. The house on Grand Cayman had the same furnishings as the Paris apartment. Going from place to place for Joe was like going to stay at a series of high-class Sheraton hotels: whenever he turned the key in the lock of one of his many residences, he would instantly know where he was. Home. The only variance was that some of the homes were more elaborately furnished than others. For instance, not all his bedrooms were clandestine movie studios, only the ones in Paris, New York, and Palm Beach. The Paris bedroom was another exception: it was done in peacock blue velvet and satin. At the time he was in the company of a fashion model every bit as crazy as Leda but lacking that *je ne sais quoi* that compelled Joe to marry. He left her in Paris for a few weeks while he went to Iran on business, and while he was gone the apartment became the scene of a two-week party. When Joe came home to a pile of liquor bills and rooms strewn with the detritus of the marathon party, he found cigarette burns in the Edward Fields rug, drug paraphernalia in the bathroom, and a fireplace full of broken champagne glasses. He sent her packing. All his women were "on approval"; one indiscretion was all they were allowed. Except for Leda.

I was called to the Park Avenue triplex one summer morning to discuss another apartment Joe wanted done. This one was in Madrid. As was his custom, he greeted me in his striped Italian briefs, fresh as a rose from his scented bath. Joe was extremely particular about hygiene. He didn't even like to share a bathroom with any of his women, and each apartment had a powder room installed for them off the master bedroom. Joe was in a great mood that morning, and when I went into his gray and white bedroom I discovered the reason. There on the flounced bedspread was Leda, looking as lovely as ever. Hard living seemed to agree with her. I tried to ask her how she was, but she was barely coherent. Then Joe announced, "Leda and I are getting married again."

Of course, marriage would mean another new pad. Poor Joe never got his life together. Either his son was leaving and Joe wanted something a little smaller, or he was getting married and needed something larger. But that was not the reason for giving up the triplex. His business was not doing so well as it had been, and his expense account no longer covered all those residences. In fact, the house in Madrid would have to be paid for out of his own pocket, a fact he thoroughly resented.

I regret to say that by the time our office had installed everything in the newlyweds' new apartment, they had split again. In his grief Joe turned his full attention to that new dwelling place in Spain, and on one of my trips to Madrid I took my wife, Suzanne, with me for a little vacation. Joe booked us a suite of rooms at the Ritz, right down the hall from his. There we met Joe and his new woman. To simplify his life, he had begun to date prostitutes, nothing but the best that money could buy, of course. This one was from Madame Claude, the best Madame in Paris.

We went to lunch one afternoon at Las Cuevas de Luis Candelas in old Madrid with Joe and Mimi. The atmosphere was cozy, almost conspiratorial. After lunch, Suzanne and I went to the Grand Via for a little shopping, then returned to our room at the Ritz. As I was getting some papers together to take to the new apartment, Suzanne came in from the bedroom with a strange look on her face. "Have you been with somebody in this room?" she said. "Are you kidding?" I said. Not only didn't I want to be with anyone but Suzanne but we had spent the entire day rushing around, our only respite that cozy lunch with Joe and Mimi. "Well, I'd like you to step into the bedroom for a minute and see what I've found," Suzanne said in the understatement I've learned means she's really upset.

Suzanne opened the closet door in the bedroom. On the floor below my clothes was a pair of black lace panties. "Oh, oh," I said. "In Spain this is how couples let you know they'd like you to join them in a little *ménage a quatre*. And I think I know who did it."

I vowed to extricate myself from this particular client. Not only was he honing in on my private life, but he was also becoming harder to do business with. He hadn't liked the work a local Madrid firm had done on his apartment there and had refused to pay them. The firm had to sue to collect, and I was embarrassed that I had involved them in a hassle. Joe had also decided to sell all the furnishings in the triplex prior to giving it up, and had used the underhanded tactic of having the pieces undervalued to the point of ridiculousness, then sold at an out-of-the-way auction where half the people on the floor would be bidding for the bargains he was "selling." It's an old trick, and it often works. But I follow the auction notices, and when I saw there was going to be a sale of some familiar-sounding French pieces, I sent a friend of mine, an antiques collector himself, to that obscure gallery and had him bid against Joe's agents. They had been instructed to buy back the pieces for his personal use at a fraction of what his company had spent for them. I would have done better if my friend hadn't been outnumbered. Joe never knew who his toughest competitor was.

Joe was losing all his endearing qualities. The gilt had worn off, and underneath was a brassy, skinny man with Scrooge-like tendencies who showed no one any mercy. But he wasn't through marrying by any means. One of his brides was discovered in Bimini. They met on Tuesday and were married on Thursday. I don't know how long that marriage lasted, but the next time I heard from him he was going to marry a Swiss citizen who also happened to be his recently deceased brother's wife. His brother had gone to Paris to visit Joe one Christmas and had died in his apartment of a stroke. Joe had accompanied his brother's widow back to her home in Switzerland, and after a brief courtship had married her. This marriage, however, was not a matter of impulse as much as good business. Married to a Swiss citizen, Joe could own property in Switzerland!

Joe's life had begun a precipitous slide from *la dolce vita* into something a little more Old Testament, in fact, heading straight for Gomorrah. His next move was into a furnished apartment near the United Nations, although he held on to the apartment in Madrid but not the one in Paris. He was definitely paring his life style to fit the recession of the mid-70s, a life that continued to swirl around him in endless motion. His moves from residence to residence were a relentless game of musical houses, his moves from wife to wife a series of expensive misfortunes. Through all the exchanges one element remained constant: Leda. They're somewhere right now, I imagine, planning a new apartment.

The story ends in ignominy. Not long ago someone showed me a copy of a French porno magazine, the kind that puts the American versions to shame. One of the stories concerned the usual group of happy, enthusiastic gymnasts having their fun in a bedroom decked out in peacock blue velvet and satin. It all looked depressingly familiar. My guess is the photos were taken during that two-week party when Joe was out of town. From *Family Circle* and *House Beautiful* to a French porno mag. . . . I'm glad I'm not a decorator who leaves his signature all over his work.

Chapter 8

Allah's Radar

It's surprising to recall that less than six or seven years ago everybody wanted to go to the Middle East and make lots of money off the oil-rich sheiks who had in turn been making a killing off the precipitous rise in oil prices of the mid-1970s. These days, when the Middle East brings to mind streets full of angry demonstrators shaking their fists at the American government, it is difficult to imagine that not so long ago nearly every professional and technician I knew had been struck with "Middle East Fever." They envisioned the area as a place where the streets were paved wtih gold and faucets flowed with oil, and the craze to get a contract in Arabia or Iran spread through design firms all over the world.

Decorators in New York, Paris, and London all harbored hopes of doing a sheik's palace in Riyadh or a big international hotel in Teheran. Every day a new story was heard of a fabulous contract a designer had made with a wealthy oil magnate from the Middle East. The word was out that the oil cartel was having trouble finding ways to spend all that money. We *all* wanted contracts and went out to get them, including me.

I had seen some designs made by fellow decorators for a Middle East project. One had been done at the office of David Hicks-France. Madame Barbara Wirth and her partner, Christian Badin, had made an elaborate design presentation for a Saudi Arabian prince in which the sketches of rooms and salons were trimmed with gold beading. I took one look and knew how many long hours the office had spent preparing the design presentation—all on speculation. When I asked Madame Wirth sometime later whether the office had landed the job, she gave me a delicate Gallic shrug and said, "Perhaps next time."

What a disappointment, I thought. Those presentation boards had included samples of the finest brocades and damasks, and designs for chandeliers of the finest crystal had highlighted the main rooms of the palace. Forewarned is forearmed: the oil sheiks were not easily impressed. I wondered what the winning design presentation had looked like. Three-dimensional sample rooms with miniature furnishings? I never knew, but with my usual confidence I was undeterred.

At that time I had been doing the red, white, and blue Sheraton Boston. Bud James, president of the Sheraton Corporation, had told me several times, "Get ready for a trip to Lebanon. We're going to need someone to decorate lots of hotel rooms in the Middle East, and you're it." Sheraton, it seemed, had a lot of business propositions in the fire in Lebanon, Saudi Arabia, and Iran, and Mr. James believed in me. "Do you know the customs of the Saudi Arabians?" he would say. "You'd better start boning up on them." Mr. James had definitely gotten my Middle East juices flowing.

One day I received a telegram from the project manager for Sheraton in the Middle East, asking me for a fee price for designing the interiors of a new 240-room Sheraton motel-hotel structure in Riyadh, Saudi Arabia. I answered it at once, noting the fee price, 10 to 15 percent of the overall furnishing costs, plus travel and expenses. Four months went by. Then I received a second telegram:

MR. HARUN MULLAH, OWNER OF SOON TO BE BUILT SHERATON RIYADH, WANTS TO MEET YOU IN BEIRUT WEDNESDAY FOUR P.M.

"I'm going to Beirut," I shouted through the office, succumbing at last to a heady case of Middle East Fever. I chose Robert Allan, a young associate in his early thirties, to accompany me. He too was thrilled. I rushed back to my apartment in a high state of excitement and announced to my family, "I'm going to the Middle East!" For several days and several nights I dreamed of visiting holy places, of mosques and camels and palaces. I had heard much of the beautiful things to see in Beirut. A neighbor in my building happened to be Ambassador Gura, the Lebanese representative to the United Nations. He too was delighted that I was going to visit his country, and gave me names of people to see. "You are in for a fabulous experience," he said.

Another neighbor is Diane Lambert, a songwriter who is somewhat of a mystic. She came into our apartment one evening with a gift. "You must have this," she said. "I found it today in a junk shop on Third Avenue." I tore open the wrapping and saw a portrait of Lawrence of Arabia in a high kitsch tin frame. "What a coincidence," she said. "It's definitely in the stars for you to go to the Middle East."

I decided to go in high style, with a touch of romance. After all, I was heading into the land of the Arabian Nights. Suzanne had given me a big black cape. I would take it along. Those Arabian Nights on the desert could get chilly, and besides, I always needed something to huddle under on the plane, and airline blankets for a man my size don't make it.

The flight from Kennedy Airport to Beirut, Lebanon, via Rome was long and far from comfortable, even with my Dracula robe, as my sons called it, but I have always found long-distance air flight uncomfortable, no matter what. The truth is I dislike flying and would much rather go by land or sea. Notwithstanding the advantages of flying by night, first class, with a few drinks to ease me into sleep, I was awake all night. I spent the layover in Rome in the drafty Leonardo Da Vinci terminal feeling tired, cruddy, unshaven, and numb. Then back on the plane for another five hours of discomfort. Charles Lindbergh, look what you started. Man was not meant to fly. He was meant to travel in staterooms. I think Lindbergh knew what I know too, for he chose as his burial place a spot on the island of Maui. I have visited the burial ground of Lindbergh, which overlooks the sea, because it is close to the Hana Maui Ranch Hotel that I am now designing. Lindbergh found Hana on Maui—and selected that island as his resting place. I understand Anne Morrow Lindbergh has selected Maui as her final spot too, as has Sam Pryor of Pan American World Airways.

We arrived in Beirut at mid-afternoon, an hour before my scheduled appointment. From the air the city disappointed me; it was unattractive and a dryness seemed to occupy the land. I was parched before I landed. I had been to Israel a few years before and had enjoyed myself enormously. I don't know what my expectations were concerning Beirut, but even before the plane touched down I knew they didn't jibe with the reality of the place. Our hotel was the Phoenicia, a massive structure directly across from the Mediterranean Sea. The hotel was a kind of hodgepodge Arabic Modern in purple and tinny gold. The lobby duplicated all the clichés of the airline terminal with ticket counters and tour booths. The rooms were American of Martinsville in design with the usual matching headboards, luggage racks, and night tables. Still wearing the black Dracula cape, I threw myself on the magenta bedspread and said to Robert, "I'm done in. I've got to get some sleep. Do you think we can reschedule our meeting for the morning?"

Before he had time to answer, the telephone rang. It was Mr. Harun Mullah. He was in the lobby and wanted Robert and me to come down to the cocktail lounge for a drink.

"We've just flown in directly from New York," I explained to Mr. Mullah, "and we're exhausted. I don't think either of us would be much good right now for discussing the project. Could we meet first thing in the morning?"

"If you wish," was the curt reply, and hearing it, I was off to dreamland, unaware that I had made my first Middle East mistake. A whopper.

The next morning I went down to breakfast. The only thing recognizably Lebanese was the face of the waiter. Everything else was Yankee Doodle Dandy, right down to the cellophane wrapped prune Danish and the catsup bottle on every table. I was not feeling like myself at all—I suffer greatly from jet lag—and was just finishing my second cup of tea when who should arrive but my Sheraton project manager. The sight of him did little to perk up my spirits. He was in full charge of his senses, and in fact was much too cheerful. I ordered a third cup of tea and hoped for better things to come. We were to meet Mr. Mullah at ten A.M.

Lebanon was not at all what I had expected. I had been prepared to enter another world, one where women wore veils, where people shook your left hand (or is it your right hand?), and did not drink hard liquor. All around me were people in Western dress, dousing their eggs with catsup, shaking with their right hand (or left hand—I don't remember), and making chirping sounds with their lips whenever an attractive woman walked by. It was a sound that reminded me of my student days in Madrid where men made that suggestive noise and touched their penises with their left hand. I disliked it then. Finding it again in Lebanon, where I thought women were treated with the greatest deference, did nothing to enhance my jet-lagged mood.

Nevertheless, I had not traveled all this distance to do less than my best. I was not about to offend a client. At ten o'clock we joined Mr. Harun Mullah in a second-floor lounge. He was of medium height, dressed in a khaki suit somewhat Brooks Brothers in cut. With him was an American-born architect from Rome, a pleasant fellow who was designing the exterior of the Riyadh Sheraton.

"What hotels has your company done?" Mr. Mullah asked me. I rattled them off: the Sheraton Waikiki, the Sheraton Boston, the Greenbrier, Dromoland Castle, the Berkshire, the Plaza, the Mark Hopkins . . . a roster of wonderful inns, each unique, each a source of pride to me, to anyone who called himself an interior designer. No expression crossed the face of Mr. Harun Mullah. I didn't know whether he knew of the hotels or whether he had even been to America. Suddenly I regretted not having brought any pictures or presentation materials. I simply hadn't thought it was necessary because Sheraton, for whom we had done so many successful hotels, had recommended our firm for the job. Having been flown in all the way from New York, I had also assumed that this was not an audition. In my overly confident mind I was as good as hired. I soon discovered my error.

"Would you be able to fly this afternoon to Saudi Arabia to see the hotel site?" Mr. Mullah asked. The thought of another three hours in the air did not thrill me, but both Robert Allan and I agreed to make the trip. After all, we were in the Middle East, and Beirut had been a disappointment. We might as well grab the chance to see more of the Middle East.

If we were doomed to another three hours of sitting, we were determined to get a little exercise while we waited for Mr. Mullah to call us back with the details of our flight to Saudi Arabia. We left the Phoenicia and walked over to the George Hotel. Unlike the depressing Phoenicia, the George was a fabulous Old English hotel decorated with big leather Chesterfield sofas with the familiar Draper Number 9 brass nailheads. The lobby walls were outfitted with antique bracket light fixtures. The place had charm, character, and a wonderful old patina. Little did we know its days were numbered. The George was to be demolished in the impending civil war, along with much of that unhappy city.

We walked in the fierce late morning sunshine of Lebanon and sat on a bench overlooking the Mediterranean. It was March, neither hot nor cold, and for the first time since I had left New York I began to unwind. The area is one of those spots on the globe that is so steeped with history it seems to hang in the air, one of the reasons I found the ticky-tacky glitter of the

American-style hotel decor so oppressive. I thought of the Phoenicia's lobby with all that purple, gold, and acid green and was convinced it was some imported designer's concept of how Western-style furnishings could be given an Arabian look. The look is unsuccessful anywhere, but particularly depressing in Arabia.

It was time to return to our hotel room. On the way back I stopped in a little shop to buy some trinkets for the many people on my list I wanted to present with some authentic Lebanese treasures. I was in for another surprise. The prices, from the smallest trinkets to the big brass urns, were much higher than identical items I could buy back in New York on lower Broadway and Eleventh Street. In fact, I could buy them there for half the money!

The swimming pool at the Phoenicia was deserted except for a French woman clad in a skimpy bikini. Two local men were nearby, chirping and fondling their genitals. We passed through the lobby, looking neither left nor right, and returned to our room. The visit was beginning to leave an acid taste in my mouth. A mid-day Bloody Mary did little to remove it, to say nothing of relax me. We sat and waited for the phone to ring. When it did, Robert Allan answered. I could see by his display of facial fireworks that something was very wrong. The conversation was short. Robert hung up the phone and said, "That was Stanley, our Sheraton man. Harun Mullah has decided not to give us the project."

"Why?" I cried.

"Stanley said something about Arab temperament," said Robert. "A quick yea or nay and that's it."

Stanley's answer didn't satisfy. Then we got another call, this time from the American architect in Rome. Very sympathetically and apologetically he explained to us that by not having seen Harun Mullah immediately upon my arrival, I had deeply offended him. Trying to cheer me up, he suggested my staying on in Beirut for a while as there were lots of projects starting up. Waiting for jobs to pop up in and around Beirut did not appeal to me. I was crushed. In fact, I was overwhelmingly disappointed. I was at the time not a man who could take rejection easily.

I had been turned down by Harun Mullah! I had flown all the way to Lebanon to be rejected on a whim! I had to get out of there fast. The only way I can cope with rejection is to plunge myself into work. Instead of departing for Saudi Arabia, I was off with Robert Allan on Middle East Airways for London and a good night's rest. I hadn't even unpacked. We were airborne less than twenty-four hours after our arrival in Beirut, and all the way to London I drowned my sorrows in Bloody Marys. It didn't help matters that the three passengers in the next row were the French sunbather and the two chirping businessmen from the poolside Phoenicia.

Upon arriving in London we headed straight for the Westbury Hotel and a little homey familiarity. I was greeted by General Manager Allen Fairbrass and my housekeeper friend, Elsie Lumsden, the one who went with me to Omar Sharif's interview in the hotel's Hartnell suite. I was jet-lagged to the earlobes. The kindly Elsie and Mr. Fairbrass took one look at my ashen face and called a doctor, who came up and gave me a tranquilizing injection. I was out in minutes, and in two days was back to my cheerful self and heading for New York.

Back at the office, I continued to have tantalizing offers of work in the Middle East dangled before my crossed eyes. Several letters arrived from the Sheraton Corporation, one discussing a project in Abu Dhabi, which I answered positively. Nothing more was heard. Apparently word had reached Sheraton President Bud James that Carleton Varney was a guy who kept sheiks waiting. Although my *faux pas* could not be forgiven, Mr. Mullah did pay my $14,000 bill for travel, time, and hotel expenses within a matter of days. I admired that. He never gave me the time to admire anything else. And five months after my abortive trip to Beirut, Lebanon was in flames.

Back home, I took out the picture of Lawrence of Arabia, the one given to me by neighbor Diane Lambert as a talisman for my trip to the Middle East. The good-luck charm had become some sort of omen, a warning maybe. . . . I took it to work and hung it on my office wall.

Several months later, I was enjoying a little peace and quiet listening to my neighbor's cows moo at my farm in upstate New York when I received a long-distance call from Susan Senis, the wife of a Spanish portrait painter friend of mine, Enrique Senis Olivar. He had painted King Juan Carlos of Spain, the Onassis sisters, and my beautiful wife, Suzanne.

"Carleton," Susan said in her sweet, birdlike voice, "you must fly to Paris *tout de suite*. Enrique is painting the portrait of a Saudi Arabian prince tomorrow morning. His relative is King Saud."

"*The* King Saud? The one with the dark glasses?"

"The very one," she said breathlessly. "You must be here to talk with the prince. He is building a palace for himself in Jedda and I've told him all about you!"

I could envision her enthralling description of me to the Saudi Arabian prince. He couldn't possibly have resisted. Nevertheless, I had my doubts. I stared ahead at a picture on the wall and thought. I thought about Harun Mullah and the dismal aftermath; I thought about princely titles. There were lots and lots of princes and princesses in Saudi Arabia, I had learned, and being a prince doesn't always mean being near the head of the line of succession.

The prince got on the wire.

"I'm planning a trip to Paris in October," I told him, "and I'll be happy to met with you then."

"I will be in Paris only until October 11."

I could sense he was annoyed that I wasn't going to fly right over to meet him the next day. Here we go again, I thought, offending sheiks and princes by keeping them waiting. Voices buzzed in the background.

Susan Senis came to the phone. "Please, Carleton, you have offended him. You must offer to see him soon, if not tomorrow, then the next day."

"The soonest I could possibly fly to Paris is next week," I said, feeling like I was getting pulled into something feet first. "Tell him I'll meet him, but I'll be bringing an associate and he's to pay our expenses," I said. Susan repeated it, and I heard him go "Hah!" in the background. *Faux pas* after *faux pas*.

"He says tell him I'm not investing anything if he's not investing anything," Susan relayed to me through the telephone. In other words, the prince wanted me to speculate and foot my own bill. More complicated negotiations took place over the wire. In the end we compromised: he would agree to a delayed meeting, and I would see him on my October trip to Paris.

I continued staring at the picture on the wall. It came into focus. It was the Lawrence of Arabia in the cheap tin frame. Was it a magic picture? Was it luring me into another Middle East adventure?

The prince had been kind enough to have us picked up at the Charles De Gaulle airport. His driver looked as if he had come straight from Regine's nightclub: about twenty-one, French, and the spitting image of Mick Jagger. As he careened his master's car to Neuilly, he asked me whether I had met the prince before. I said I had not had the pleasure. "Have you met the princess?" he asked. "No," I said. "Would you like to?" he said meaningfully. "I'm on my way to meeting them both," I said somewhat primly. The driver was supremely impressed with his employers. He was even a little pompous about it. Some of their importance seemed to have rubbed off on him. I could not figure out what kind of scene I was getting myself into. I vaguely wondered, what would Dorothy Draper have done? I got no answer.

The prince's apartment was a duplex connected by a spiral staircase of the kind that can be bought ready made in America. Long brown shag carpet was wrapped around each step, giving the appearance of a spiral of covered toilet seats. The overall style was Early Chrome. A table in the corner of the living room was chrome and mirror over which hung a wild wall mounting and a Bronx Renaissance lamp. The light fixtures were all chrome with naked bulbs hanging out all over the place. On the wall was something beautiful: the two portraits by Enrique Senis Olivar of the prince and princess and their children.

The elderly houseman who had opened the door motioned me to sit down on a modern sofa covered in brown crushed velvet, an uncomfortable seat for the sofa's back was the same height as its arms. I was offered a drink of coffee or Coca-Cola. I accepted the coffee, which was served in the proper Arabian manner in very small glasses on a brass tray. Honey drops were served as sweetener.

The prince could not have been more than twenty-four years old. He was thin with big dark eyes, and was dressed in a caramel-colored gabardine suit, the kind worn by Wall Street brokers and college professors from Ohio: American all the way. He had also been educated in America, but retained a lot of his Arabness. In fact, moments after I walked into his apartment, he said, "Why do you Americans give money to Israel? Don't you see you take away money that should be going to the needs of your people? Your cities are dying and you keep sending the money to Israel."

His complaint was directed completely at me. I myself had passed the legislation and signed the bill, put the money on the plane, and flown it to Israel. I was fuming. What an obnoxious twerp is this kid! I sat on the uncomfortable sofa clenching my teeth and acting as charming as I knew how.

The princess arrived, a vision with dark, wide eyes and olive skin. She held out a tiny hand to greet me but did not look at me directly. Nor did she speak any English, but she smiled and nodded a lot. She became animated only once during our brief meeting, when she showed me the portrait Enrique Senis Olivar had painted of her. There is something of the macabre in the paintings of Senis Olivar, and the look of the princess contained it in full measure. Her fingers showed veins and her face showed a strong jawbone line. The Senis Olivar touch was also present in her costume, and surely he must have selected it for her. She was clad in a scarlet robe with a monk's rope around her waist. Her black hair and expressive eyes were most prominent and seemed almost ignited by the scarlet robe.

Then the prince showed me the plans for his enormous palace, and again I was amazed and annoyed. These plans are the most cockamamie things I've ever seen! I said to myself. Nothing makes any sense! The dining room is next to the bedroom, the kitchen is right off the fancy front entrance. How do you do, Sir and Madam. Will you hold this spoon while I help you off with your coats? This was one obnoxious, arrogant prince, I thought. What a know-it-all. And why does he get me so riled up?

"How do you work?" he said to me as I pored over the strange plans. I explained that the palace could be done at full retail price, and that the profit for my firm would be the difference between wholesale and retail. He then reminded me that he wanted the whole thing done within a year. "How much is your fee if it's not the difference between wholesale and retail?" he asked me. "A set fee, I believe is the term."

"Seven hundred and fifty thousand dollars," I replied with a straight face.

"Is that for the furniture?" the prince said with admirable calm.

"No," I said. "That's for the fee." The meeting had turned into a showdown. The way I figured it, the fee wasn't high enough. I knew I was dealing with the kind of person who really got my dander up, and the year I spent working on his palace would mean a year of increased blood pressure and quite possibly the shortening of my life. All things considered, $750,000 would barely do.

"And the furniture?" said the prince, sneering a bit. He was doing well for a mere stripling. Heaven knew what he'd be like in another ten years. "What do you think the furniture will cost?"

"Well," I said expansively, "you can furnish anything inexpensively, or you can buy the earth. Knowing your style," I said, casting what I hoped was an inscrutable glance around his living room, "and the quality of the pieces you have, I think you'd end up spending about five million dollars." After all, the young man had called me in to decorate a palace. He said nothing, but his stare said, "Let's go another round—hotshot decorator." He was not one to let an American make him feel as if he could not afford anything he wanted.

"Would you and the princess like to see an apartment I'm doing right now?" I asked him after several minutes of conversation. "I'm doing one with Barbara Wirth at the David Hicks office. We can stop by and pick her up. She has the key."

He agreed at once. We proceeded to collect Madame Wirth, then went to the Avenue Victor Hugo. The prince walked around an apartment so elegant that people naturally lowered their voices as they walked in it. The place was impeccable, a little too perfect for my taste. Finally the prince said, "Nice, but not my style." It was obvious the princess loved it. She spoke rapturously to her husband in Arabic, and he gave her curt replies.

After the tour, the prince dropped Barbara Wirth and me off at the David Hicks Boutique, which is frequented by anyone who is anyone in Paris. Again the prince pronounced judgment, picking up items and saying, "This is tasteful. This is not tasteful." He dropped me off at my hotel door and drove off with his beautiful princess. I never heard from him again.

When I got back to my office, I took the picture of Lawrence of Arabia and hung it in the bathroom. The office bathroom is a cheerful place. The walls are decorated with photographs, clippings, little sketches, and other items, most of them humorous. It is the ideal wall on which to deflate pretension. Or, I hoped, to remove an evil curse. Once more Lawrence had beckoned me to the sands of Arabia. This time I had managed to stop short at Paris, but I had a feeling the spell still lingered.

When I received a letter about decorating a private residence in Abu Dhabi for yet another prince, a letter accompanied with two pages of impossible and outrageous requirements, I laughed uproariously and threw it in the waste basket.

But decorating in the Iran of the Shah was another matter, and altogether not unpleasant. The name of the complex was Zomorod, which means emerald, and it was to be built at Farahzad, a satellite city on the outskirts of Teheran, named of course for Empress Farah. Zomorod was to be a high-rise luxury housing development consisting of several buildings, a joint project of Bank Omran—supervising authority of the area—Starrett Housing Corporation (of Starrett City fame) and an Iranian firm, Azgara, owned by three Iranian brothers. My firm had won the bid to design the lobbies, card rooms, interiors of the elevator cabs, lounges, planting areas, club house, model apartments, and hallways of all the Zomorod buildings. Several American, English and Parisian firms had been interviewed, but Dorothy Draper and Company got the job.

At last I had done it: a for-real job in the Middle East. Not some chimera in the sand, no heavy speculating, and no *faux pas!* Lawrence of Arabia came out of the bathroom and went back on the conference-room wall. The spell had been broken by the dependable *salle de bain.* I spent days running around Manhattan getting things for my first visit to Iran. To *Persia!* To the land of my childhood books. To flying carpets and forbidding mountains and desert societies. Glistening beluga, glazed Islamic tile and peaked arches, the fabulous Peacock Throne, the bazaar where women still wore the chador, pistachios, and Omar Khayyam. Tents, pearls, emerald navels, camels, and some of my favorite art and architecture. I was also looking forward to the social activity, for I had run into Arlene Dahl on one of my shopping trips. She was going to Iran too, to launch her new perfume, Dahlia, in Teheran. She and I had worked together on radio programs and knew each other socially as we had many friends in common, and so she suggested I contact her at the Teheran Hilton. She would get me invited to all the parties being given for her fragrance. "You're sure to meet the Shah and the Empress at one of them," she said gaily.

How frivolous all that seems now. I was headed for Iran at a time that would later always be referred to as Iran right before the revolution. Arriving at the airport I was a little alarmed at all the checkpoints the passengers had to go through, waiting on line at each one for endless procedures to be followed. Getting into Iran was like being admitted into an armed fortress, only the fortress was the size of a country. Teheran airport had many portraits of the Shah and his empress on the walls, smiling serenely high over the passengers. In every building I visited, from a terminal to a barbershop, I found their portraits prominently displayed. I asked my American employer why pictures of the Shah and his empress were all about. He told me that the royal family owned or controlled just about everything in the country. Including the hotels.

In effect, then, I was, indirectly, in the employ of the Shah of Iran, for it was he who controlled the Bank Omran, supervising authority of the Farahzad lands.

My two staff members and I proceeded, not to the Teheran Hilton, but to a huge, bizarre apartment rented by Starrett, which had been decorated by a California woman who had married an Iranian. The lady decorator told me she was stuck in Persia. I'll call her Claire. She and another friend ran a business in Teheran, just a small decorating firm to keep them busy and bring in a little money. That apartment seemed like miles from everywhere, though it was in a Teheran suburb. Teheran had grown so fast the city was more farflung than Los Angeles. The only other person I came in contact with was the maid, and she spoke only Parsi. I was stuck there, miles from downtown Teheran with no car, a situation I find healthy to avoid, particularly in a foreign country. My bedroom window faced a highway, and all night long trucks filled with concrete and machinery, or something heavy and loud, went up and down the road. I had been told Iran was having a building boom. Everywhere you looked new high-rises were going up. The city seemed to quiver with anticipatory fever.

I had lists of fabric houses to see, none of which had anything I wanted. From the first look of the apartment where I had been staying, I got the feeling good furnishings were difficult to find in Iran. If you wanted quality, you had to import it. There was one woman artist whose work I liked. Her name was Monir Farmanfarmihan, but aside from her, buying anything local for my Zomorod project in a Western style would be next to impossible. When I searched out-of-the-way shops hoping to find some bargain pieces, I found the prices laughable. A used American sofa was priced at $2,000. So much for Iranian second-hand stores. It didn't take long before I concluded I'd have to have everything brought in.

Everywhere I went, I felt under surveillance. Before I had boarded the plane, I had memorized once again the unspoken rules of conduct for Americans in Iran. I wasn't going to slip up this time. But these rules were nothing like "Shake with your left hand" or "Refuse no food." These orders smacked a bit of fascism: Do not criticize the Shah or his family. Do not create a disturbance or draw unnecessary attention to yourself in public. Do not be in the company of people who do any of the above. I found the Americans who worked on the Starrett project at Farahzad very guarded in their attitude. It is every American's birthright to complain about the boss, the government, the working conditions, the hassles of living in a foreign country. These people didn't complain about anything, and I found their guarded attitude very unnerving.

Another strange moment was when I went out to the site where Zomorod was to be built. The site, while some distance from downtown Teheran, was actually within the city but in the middle of what I felt was a desert. Will anything really be built out here? I thought. The wind whipped the sand dunes in all directions, and the sun beat down on our heads without mercy. The car was surrounded by shimmering heat waves. I began to think the project was years away from discussing fabrics and color schemes, as I had also been clued into the slow rate of construction in Iran. Experts had to be called in for everything. The only really plentiful resource was labor, though it was unskilled; there seemed to be an endless supply of that for the Shah's luxury housing complex.

Another incident occurred during that trip that exemplified for me a touch of the sinister among the lighthearted Iranian elite. Although I did not get to see Arlene Dahl or the royal family on that trip, I did pay a visit to a couple who traveled in the highest Iranian social circles. He was Iranian and an art dealer, she was French, and both were utterly charming. They invited me for cocktails to their all-white villa. It was an elegant place with lush greenery and fine pieces of furniture, paintings and sculpture, an oasis of charm and expensive taste. But behind the high front gate three mastiffs prowled on long chains, just out of reach of a visitor's heels. At a word from their master they whined and cowered, still showing their gleaming teeth. Dogs don't frighten me, but the sight of those Baskerville hounds in the yard of that beautiful villa in the dense quiet of the most exclusive suburb in Teheran was a disturbing note in an otherwise peaceful atmosphere. However, the presence of those dogs didn't bother me as much as my host's startled response when I jokingly asked why there were no portraits of the Shah and his empress among his Brueghels and Kandinskys. The man was truly frightened, and I instantly regretted my joking remark.

After that first visit, my associates and I got to work on the interior plans for the Zororod buildings. The job was to entail three years and many trips to Iran. We designed and purchased all American-made furniture and furnishings for the public lobby spaces and sculptured tapestries to hang on the lobby walls. Chandeliers purchased in France were to hang from the lobby ceilings. I even took a two-day trip to Milan to select tiles for the model apartment kitchens and bathrooms. I was also doing work on an apartment for a gentleman I'll call Hassan, work for which I will now surely never be paid.

Hassan loved all things American, and he could afford to make shopping trips to the United States and buy away. His penthouse in the luxury Zomorod complex was designed to be the ultimate in chic Western styling. It had mirrored ceilings, motorized beds, the finest mohair fabrics, and indirect lighting everywhere. The family room, dining room, and library were each on different levels, all in Norman style. Hassan's three brothers were a little unhappy over his ostentatious style. "I don't think he should be making such an elaborate statement," said the oldest brother, Mahmond, but Hassan did what he pleased, ordering everything custom-made from America.

On subsequent trips to Iran I made sure I stayed at the Teheran Hilton, for I did not want any more out-of-the-way apartments. The Teheran I saw was the enclave inhabited by the wealthy, and to be wealthy in Iran before 1978 invariably meant you were loyal to the Shah. Loyalty to the Shah meant hanging the royal family on the wall and never speaking negatively of him. Most people never spoke of him at all. Consequently, the Iran I knew was a country of bustling construction projects, seemingly endless supplies of money, and restaurants like Leon's Russian Grill, an understated place with white tiles on the floor and white tablecloths, a place that served the best blinis and beluga with a vodka appropriately called Caviar. For dessert there were incomparable Persian melons sprinkled with lime juice. Sometimes Hassan and/or the Starrett people entertained me at Darband, a restaurant that looked like a castle and was located in the most chic section of Teheran. It was a favorite watering spot for the international set. The disco music was deafening; everyone gyrated and drank and had a good time. Iran before the revolution. Before the face of the white-bearded man who looks like an El Greco cardinal became a dart board, before the hostages, and before tens of thousands of angry Iranians began shaking their fists for the world's television cameras. The Teheran I knew in 1977 was as different from Teheran 1980 as the Winter Palace before and after 1917.

Art and culture congregate around vast wealth. On one of my many trips to Teheran I was invited to the opening of the Teheran Art Museum where none other than Vice-President Nelson Rockefeller and Empress Farah Dibah greeted the guests. I think now of the resentment that must have smoldered among all those soon-to-be-revolutionaries by the presence of these two people in their city. One was married to the dictator they were planning to overthrow, and the other was a prime symbol of American imperialism, which they despised with equal fervor. Empress Farah was also a thorn in the side of the more conservative Moslems because of her outspoken espousal of women's rights. That night she was dressed with impeccable good taste, and her jewelry was stunning without being ostentatious.

The same lack of ostentation could not be applied to the homes of the typical wealthy Iranian. Calling them palaces or châteaus would be more accurate. One was a scaled-down replica of Versailles, an extravagant home in a neighborhood of extravagance. The owners were, I was told, out of favor with the Shah. Like most of Iran's elite, they loved French furniture, the more ormolu the better, and like all Iranians who had the means, their house was built and furnished in the style of the American robber baron, ostentatious to the point of humor. The miniature Versailles even had an outdoor swimming pool complete with subterranean game room from which one could watch the swimmers in the pool through a glass wall.

On my last visit to that house, the owner arranged to meet me in private, or perhaps the emptiness of the house was part of a larger and more urgent plan. That afternoon he told me that his wife, sister-in-law, children, and most of the staff were out of the country. A maid dressed in a black and white English maid's outfit brought me iced tea, and I sat and listened to the silence of that enormous house until the owner finished a telephone call. Then we toured the empty rooms. He was agitated that afternoon, an unusual state of mind for such a serene man. Taking me into his library and closing the door, he asked in a low but casual voice, "On your way home, will you be stopping in Paris as usual?"

I said I would.

"Would you do me a favor? Would you deliver some papers to a gentleman there?"

I said yes because I was unable to say no. I had found him and his family gracious and very kind, and I sensed he was in trouble. In spite of my great reservations and all the warnings I had received, I agreed to carry an envelope out of Iran for him. His relief was obvious. He assured me there would be no danger. After all, I was an American, in the employ of the Starrett people as well as the Azgara Company, and I knew all the right people. I was most assuredly above reproach, he said, and he would never forget the great favor I was to do for him.

No matter what assurances he gave me, I was scared stiff. I had been warned many times not to get involved in internal Iranian affairs, and here I was, doing a favor for a man whose entire family was reportedly out of favor with the Shah. I had been seen on several occasions going in and out of his home. Was I going to be followed on my return to the Teheran Hilton? Had his library been secretly bugged? Was this whole arrangement a setup? On the taxi ride back to the hotel I craned my neck right and left to see whether anyone was following me. My knees were shaking. I imagined the taxi driver himself was a member of the Savak, the Shah's secret police. The incriminating papers were not even in my hands, and already I was falling apart! Some espionage agent I was going to be.

Two days later I returned to my hotel room and found a large manila envelope on the bed. It was addressed to a man in Paris. His name was Iranian, and his address was on the Avenue Foch. At least there would be no clandestine rendezvous in Paris dives. My courier service was definitely going to be first class, a thought that did nothing to assuage my nervousness. Two hours after finding the envelope on my bed, still worrying about who had secret access to my room, my agitation turned to numb fear. I was having lunch with one of my Starrett associates, and he told me the brother of the man at the miniature Versailles had been placed under house arrest. "I'm sorry to hear that," I said with unbelievable calm as my heart did flip-flops in my chest. Why was he telling me this? Was my associate aware of what I was about to do? Was he giving me an elaborately casual warning, or was the information merely part of a random and rather boring chat about who was in and who was out, Teheran style? I had absolutely no way of knowing. All I knew was I was leaving Iran early the following morning, and in the next twenty hours I would have to be supervigilant.

My thoughts kept returning to that empty house. It was obvious to me now that the women and children were not merely on a vacation jaunt. I wondered where my friend was now. Had he also fled? All I knew was that I had been seen on numerous occasions visiting that house, the occupants of which had apparently fled the country. But why? What had they done to curry disfavor, and what were they about to do? Worst of all, what was my role in their plans?

For twenty hours I was followed by everyone I saw. Waiters, taxi drivers, strollers, the nice couple down the hall—they were all after me. I packed my suitcases four times before I was satisfied with how it looked when I opened it. I didn't want that large manila envelope too exposed, but I didn't want it to look as if I were hiding it either. Finally I slipped it into a file folder marked *Model Kitchens: Zomorod* and laid two layers of clothing over it.

I always left Iran in the early morning, taking off just as the sun rose. On every visit, rarely staying beyond two or three days, I was always so eager to leave Teheran that I did not sleep the night before for fear of missing my early morning flight. That particular night, not only did I not sleep, but I couldn't even sit in a chair and wait for the hours to pass. I paced that night away, and left the Hilton by taxi with my incriminating luggage while it was still pitch dark. All the way to the airport I lectured myself: Be cool, don't act suspicious, you've done this dozens of times before, the checkpoint guards paw through luggage all day and you're just one more American interior designer with a suitcase full of sketches. Look nervous and you're done for.

I went through each checkpoint with remarkable aplomb. Not too casual, just sleepy and a bit impatient. By the time I boarded the plane I was wondering to myself whether I might have a career waiting for me in the CIA. I was a little amazed at my cloak-and-dagger talents. Maybe I'd bring along my big black cape next time. As I basked in my mood of self-congratulation the plane started taxiing down the runway just as the sun came bursting over the desert. As soon as I heard the thud of the wheels as they were tucked under the plane's belly my exultation turned into a severe case of delayed fright, and the jitters began again. However, before I could get too concerned about my shaking knees and the Bloody Mary I could barely hold, I was already nodding off.

I was safe. I hoped my friend and his family were safe too. Through the fog I was aware of a winsome Irish hostess in an

Iran Air uniform covering me with a blanket. An angel of mercy. The next thing I knew she was standing over me and saying in her lilting voice, "We'll be landing at Orly in a few minutes, sir." Never have I been so glad to touch down anywhere. I experienced another twinge of fear when I had trouble locating my baggage at the Orly terminal. Other than that minor delay, the rest of my mission was a piece of cake.

I hand-delivered the envelope as per instructions to the Avenue Foch address, put it in the hands of an elderly Iranian servant, and watched him disappear through an elegantly furnished foyer. I never saw the man himself. I never again saw my friend who lived in the miniature Versailles in the most exclusive suburb in Teheran. I do not know what the manila envelope contained. I only hope my cooperation helped them evade the Shah's secret police. Perhaps someday I will know whether it did.

There was to be one last visit to Teheran. In June of 1978 I went out to the Zomorod site and supervised the finishing touches of the paint and wallcovering job on the first building to be completed in that massive project. Tenants were about to move into those $180,000 cooperative apartments, and everything needed to complete the job was coming in by ship from New York and other points west. The drapery fabric, sofas, tables, and chairs were all on the high seas. The lobby chandeliers and mirrored walls had arrived and were being installed. The final touches had been selecting art for the public lobbies, and I had included some paintings by Monir Farmanfarmihan, Iran's best-known woman artist, along with the obligatory oversized portraits of the Shah and his empress, of course.

As I arrived at the bustling construction site in the desert the carpets were being installed in Building Number One. Zomorod had become a reality, and I thought it was somewhat of a miracle. I remembered standing on the site three years before as the wind whipped sand in my face and I despaired over anything ever being built out there in the desert waste. Now six buildings had gone up, in different stages of construction, and Iran's upper class was clamoring to move in. Already there was a waiting list for apartments. That June I worked with the owners and architects on plans for the swimming pool and restaurant complex, all under construction. All that remained to design was the club house, plans for which I would make in New York.

I returned to my hotel at the Teheran Hilton on a blazing hot afternoon, drenched with perspiration from my walks around the

Zomorod construction sites and an unusually slow taxi ride in the gasping heat. Traffic had been heavy that day. I didn't know why. Once I had showered and relaxed in my air-conditioned room, I put a call through to my office. My secretary was both alarmed and relieved to hear from me.

"What's going on over there?" she said. "Are you all right?"

"Everything's fine. Why?" I said.

"There's rioting in Teheran. It's all over the front page of to-day's *Times*. Haven't you heard?"

I had heard and seen nothing. From my isolation in the Teheran Hilton, and the circles I traveled in, none of them includ-ing a route through the bazaar, I was unaware of anything un-toward happening in Iran. I was in the middle of a revolution and didn't even know it. As it turned out, I wasn't the only one. Of the people whose opulent houses I had visited, many were to leave the country, but many others, unable to grasp the serious-ness of the situation and unwilling to trade their comfortable existence for the uncertainties of exile, remained behind. Six months after my last visit to Iran, the Shah fled and revolution swept the country. Of the hundreds executed in the aftermath, I was sure I had been in the homes of some. I studied the blurred photographs in the newspapers of the blindfolded men standing before the Ayatollah's firing squads and wondered whether I had ever had coffee in their villas or met them at one of the glittering social functions before the revolution.

I often wonder about the art dealer and his French wife, and the family who lived in the miniature palace of Versailles, and Hassan and his brother Mahmond. I wonder if anyone is living in the ultra-chic Western-style penthouse in Building Number One now that big-spending Hassan has fled the country. I won-der whether the shiploads of furnishings that were still on the high seas when I last left Teheran ever arrived. Are the sculptured tapestries hanging on the lobby walls? Have the hostages been moved to Farahzad and kept under guard in the still unfinished buildings? The isolated location would be an ideal place to hide a group of people and fend off another rescue attempt.

When the plans to rescue the hostages were thwarted be-cause of equipment failure in a sandstorm, I couldn't help but remember how the professionals and technicians I worked with in Iran were contemptuous of the lack of technical know-how among the local people. When there were buildings to be built and finery needed to adorn them, it was good old American know-how that was called on to do the job. The elite who prospered under the Shah lusted over all things Western. They couldn't get enough of the look, and they had plenty of money to buy it, even if it all had to be imported from across the Atlantic. How ironic that the good old American know-how they admired so much failed in the face of the Iranian sand and wind—or as one revolutionary called it, Allah's radar. Now all the professionals and technicians from America have fled, with the exceptions of the fifty-three who have been hidden away. Gone also are the Shah, his family, and the beneficiaries of his rule. Left behind are the millions of angry people who rarely benefited from American know-how.

The saddest part is that it looks as if the people of Iran have yearned and fought and died for freedom only to have exchanged one tyrant for another as the whole world holds its breath and wonders whether we're heading into a new Dark Age. My experience in Iran taught me about the ephemeral quality of the "good life," but more than that, it demonstrated to me how in the struggle for power it it always the ordinary citizen who suffers most. There is little that remains of a tangible nature from all my experiences in the Middle East. The most obvious reminder is that picture of Lawrence of Arabia that still hangs on the office wall in its cheap tin frame. I don't know what message it is trying to convey anymore. I wish I did. I wish someone did.

Chapter 9

My Client, God

Do you recall God's warning in the New Testament against building castles in the sand? This story is about a sand castle and the man who wanted to live in it. He also called himself God, but that claim turned out to be a horrifying case of mistaken identity.

For many years the McCune home in Scottsdale, Arizona, has been referred to by local residents as "San Simeon of the Desert." Without question it is one of the largest and most elaborate homes in America. Built for wealthy Pittsburgh scion Walter McCune, the 23,000 square feet of marble, glass, and semiprecious stones is situated on a hill rising above Paradise Valley with vistas of the spectacular Arizona desert and mountains on either side. The estate far exceeds even the opulent imaginings of a Coronado, who marched through the Southwest in the sixteenth century looking for just such mansions of gold.

If you had $5.8 million to put into a dream house, what would you ask for? Mr. and Mrs. McCune desired the best of everything plus the fulfillment of all their fantasies. One fantasy, as they dreamed of El Dorado on long Pittsburgh winter nights, was to ice skate in the 120-degree Arizona summer. And so it came to pass that the manse included an indoor ice rink, 25 × 45 feet, with his-and-her dressing rooms and marble showers, all overlooking an outdoor Olympic-size swimming pool, for those skaters who might have a sudden penchant for some water sport in liquid form.

As the wind whistled through the smokestacks of their Pennsylvania coal town, the owners envisioned a lush tropical paradise blooming in the sand dunes and sagebrush of Arizona. It was given unto them: A landscape architect from Hawaii was called in, and he created a ready-made jungle of towering palms and verdant bougainvillea. He sent divers to the bottom of the Pacific Ocean to bring up a 4- × 6-foot chunk of black coral and transport it to one of the many fountains that watered the tropical vegetation on the 33-acre estate.

What else would a person want when the shimmering blue Arizona sky is the limit? The McCunes desired the ultimate kitchen: 76 feet of counter surface; 100 cabinets with 40 drawers; 6 sinks, 2 each of dishwashers, freezers, refrigerators, and ovens; and a towel rack with a built-in dryer. The McCunes planned to entertain a lot in their desert castle. It was a kitchen fit for a king, or at least a four-star restaurant.

They also desired separate accommodations for the children. *Voila!* Ten rooms off a long corridor, complete with separate children's laundry, kitchen, and dining room, plus quarters for nurses and governesses. Fireplaces were another important item. No one seems to have counted the total number of fireplaces in those thirty-odd rooms, but some are of marble; others are of native stone or the finest mahogany; and one is implanted with chunks of native amethyst, copper, and gold ore, which once inspired miners to come to this forbidding territory where it is said that even a grasshopper can die of thirst.

Mrs. McCune wanted a nice, roomy bedroom about 65 feet long with a fresco on the ceiling portraying the children as cherubim. She got it. Her bed was designed around and built on an electric turntable from which she could follow the sun setting over Camelback Mountain. Her "lazy susan" closet had rotating clothing rods on a turntable, the kind used in dry-cleaning establishments. Her shower had 6 gold shower heads, and her Roman bath was of pink marble, 4 feet by 6 feet, the walls and floor of which could be heated whenever a chill was felt in the desert air.

The garage was designed to accommodate a fleet of 10 medium-size cars; the pool house was equipped with soda and beer on tap; and other requests were 26 bathrooms, a dogs' "ready room," a commercial laundry, massive Monel metal doors leading to the foyer, floor-to-ceiling glass for optimum view of the surroundings, 20,000 square feet of patio, a built-in vacuum system throughout the main house, over 3 miles of copper heating coils, and a temperature control system powerful enough to cool the place to 65 degrees even when the thermometer outside the mansion read 120. The 150-ton cooling apparatus was big enough to regulate a variety of temperatures in a 200-bed hospital, and if the desert air got too dry, a humidifying system corrected things. The humidifier was so powerful that when it was set at 55 percent during testing operations, rain began to fall throughout the house.

Construction took many years, its cost per square foot soaring to the top of the charts. But before the dream house was finished, Mr. McCune died. For years the house languished on the market, an unfinished monument nobody could afford. Even at a bargain $3.75 million (a big reduction from the $5.8 million it cost to build) Previews, Inc., the Tiffany of realtors, could not find a buyer.

Every decorator in America knows the McCune estate of Scottsdale, Arizona, and every one of us would commit any crime short of a felony to do that house. . . .

One morning in 1973 my receptionist buzzed me on the intercom to say that a Mr. David was calling. Assuming the caller was Mort David, godfather of my eldest son, Nicholas, and a member of our board of directors, I picked up the phone and said cheerfully, "How are you, Mort?" There was a pause at the other end, then I heard a sonorous voice say, "I am not Mort. I am Emmanuel David, and I am calling you from Washington, D.C." Small warnings in my life invariably go unheeded; from the outset my relationship with Emmanuel David was to be one of mistaken identity. But it is always hard for me to think sinister thoughts, especially so on a beautiful morning in my sunny office with its poppy-and-rose wallpaper and with a wife at home about to bear our second child.

"What can I do for you?" I asked Mr. David.

"I'm about to purchase a home in Arizona," he said, "and I'd like to talk to you about your decorating services."

"What would the job require?" I asked. Doing a house as far away as Arizona has to be worth the travel.

"I'm buying the McCune house," said Mr. David. "The one on the hill opposite Senator Goldwater's house. Do you know it?"

Did I know it!

"I would like you to come to Washington to talk to me about doing the house," he said.

For a moment I hesitated. Because of my syndicated column, my name is familiar not only to those with legitimate requests but also to anyone who can shell out a quarter for a newspaper, including the numerous nut cases in our fair land, an inordinate number of whom seem to have come through my door over the years. My wariness has caused me to require references and a retainer before going out of town, plus having a member of my office accompany me to a first meeting.

Mr. David told me I had been recommended to him by Donald Gartenhaus, one of Washington's leading furriers, who has a beautiful store in downtown Georgetown. I remembered him well, and my suspicions were allayed at once. I even agreed to go to Washington to discuss the house without a retainer. After all, the McCune house is not just a house, and I thought a simple trip to Washington well worth a little speculation.

On a gray election day in 1975, Brian Norris, an English-born assisting architect on my staff at the time, and I boarded an Eastern Airlines shuttle for the capital. Our rather unlikely destination was the Holiday Inn in Georgetown, where Mr. David occupied an entire upper floor. Or so he said. From what he had told me, this was where he and his family had been living for the past year, paying the motel bill each day in cash. I thought his payment system a little eccentric, but over the years I have found that very rich people have a lot of strange customs concerning money, and if doling it out in cash was the way Mr. David wished to conduct business, so what?

We arrived at the Holiday Inn and waited. And waited. Just as I was about to succumb to .the severe depression prolonged exposure to Holiday Inn decor invariably causes, unrelieved in this instance by as much as a Bloody Mary because the bar was closed, Mr. David appeared. He was dressed all in white and weighed about 300 pounds. His long hair was braided into a pigtail down his back. Behind him came seven silent, immaculately groomed children ranging in age from sixteen to four, all holding hands. On a cue from their father, they said hello, almost in unison. Mr. David then brought forth his wife, Rachel, a rather plain woman with downcast eyes. I was introduced one by one to the children, whose names were Rebyca, David, Joseph, Debbra, Joshaha, Elezbath, and Rachal. The unusual spellings of their names was a later discovery. At the time I thought them charming and well-behaved, a pleasure to behold compared with many wealthy clients' offspring, who are as likely to bite one's hand as shake it. My temporary paranoia vanished. Norris just looked at mother, father, and seven children all in a row and said nothing.

"Come to the meeting room," Mr. David said, "where we can talk undisturbed." We left his little flock and retired to an

upstairs room, which turned out to be done in the ubiquitous
Holiday Inn decor that makes me break out in a rash in minutes:
gold stacking chairs with gold anodized frames, fold-down tables
shaped like boats, and cheap vinyl wall covering. I could not
imagine a more unlikely setting for discussing the interior design
of San Simeon of the Desert.

Emmanuel David eased his huge frame into one of the gold
chairs and began talking. The first thing I noticed were his eyes.
They were compelling, and seemed to bore their way into my
very soul. I found the man unnerving in the extreme, a mood
dispelled only by the presence of a waiter bearing the dreary
chicken salad sandwiches for which Holiday Inns are notorious. I
decided it was time to cut the mystery and get down to business.
When Mr. David took his next big bite of sandwich, I broke in
and said, "One of the things I always have to know about potential clients is who they are and what they are. Could you tell me
that?"

Mr. David paused for a long time and then intoned, "That is
one thing you must never know. You will never be told what I do
for a living. You must never ask me again."

"But I must know something about your credit—" I protested.

"If you want to do this house, you will find you will be paid
in cash for everything you do, ahead of time if you so desire, but
what I do and who I am and where my money comes from, you
will not be told." I found myself getting very uncomfortable,
whether the cause was the vintage chicken or the ersatz gold or
Mr. David's melodious voice and x-ray eyes I do not know.
Nevertheless, my rational self kept thinking of the marble palace
high above Paradise Valley. What a feather in my cap—a verita-
ble plume!

Sensing my discomfort, Mr. David said, "All right, I will
show you one thing." He drew out an old, worn leather wallet
and produced a Utah driver's license. On it I read his name.
There was nothing else in the wallet but a sheaf of bills as thick
as a deck of cards. Not much proof of anything. However, those
kids *were* charming, he had the plans of the house from Previews, that most prestigious of real estate agencies, and he had
agreed to pay me in advance if I so desired.

As I was debating whether to take on the job, Mr. David
began asking me questions that made it obvious he was also still
debating the relationship. How did I get started in the design

business? Did I have lots of rich clients? How large was my company? Did I own the firm? Was I married and did I have children? Instead of balking at some of the more inappropriate questions, I found myself answering them all. The barrage had become at times an interrogation and at others a confessional, and again I was unnerved. I had the distinct impression that he was trying to get into my head and find out what kind of person I was. Could it be he was trying to discover quirks and foibles that he would later use against me for his own ends? And what were those ends?

When the meeting was over, I was chagrined to discover that he had found out much more about me than I had about him. The only personal question he had deigned to answer was where his children were schooled, a logical question between parents. "I educate my own children," he said quietly, "as I brought them unto this earth: by myself, without interference from the corrupt outside world." Brian and I exchanged looks. I wondered how his wife had felt about her husband's midwifery seven times over.

As we were about to leave, he gave me the impression that I had been hired, now that he had found out all he needed to know about me. "Nothing in the house is to be used," he said. "Everything must be new. I don't want anything in it that has once belonged to another soul. Furthermore, nothing is to be purchased from a catalog. Everything must be custom-made."

"Everything must be custom-made" is the stuff of designers' dreams. I had apparently stumbled on the ideal client, the ideal house, and the use of his private plane to transport all those custom-made furnishings directly to Arizona! Nevertheless, I was not so dazzled that I forgot to ask for a retainer. I told him $25,000 would be needed to get started, and Mr. David nodded in agreement. "It will be forthcoming," he said in his archaic, rather ministerial way. We departed with a hearty handshake. Mr. David's hand was soft and fleshy, and the gesture had gone on a trifle too long. Why did the man unnerve me so?

By the time I arrived in New York I was a complete maniac. I had had a couple of shots of vodka on the plane in an attempt to settle down. Here I was, about to decorate one of the most fabled palaces in America for a man who would not reveal his identity, a man who attracted, repelled, and thoroughly mystified me all at once. There was another reason for my disturbed state of mind. One piece of information had been left out in my response to Mr. David's interrogation about my private life: Suzanne had just given birth to our second son, Seamus, and he had Down's Syndrome. We had both been devastated by the event, which had come without warning. I have never been a particularly religious man, but the tragedy had caused me to stray into new and frightening areas of thought familiar to anyone who has been struck with the news that he and his wife have brought a mongoloid child into the world. I found myself stumbling down streets thinking, "Why us? How could we bring such imperfection into the world?" At such times people begin to question their worth and often seek professional help, having found themselves such imperfect creatures. That was my state of mind during those nightmare weeks, and it was absolutely the wrong time to meet an enigmatic and disturbing man like Emmanuel David.

I couldn't wait to get home to talk to Suzanne. Every night I tried to bring home diverting office stories to get our minds off our tiny infant in the very nice upstate private home instead of in the newly decorated nursery. That night I was bringing her some real diversion, and I knew that between her insight and my detective mind we could puzzle out the mystery of the David family. By the time the sun rose, we had concluded he was yet another nut case. I don't remember my dreams that night, but they could not have been any stranger than the reality of the day.

Emmanuel David wasted no time. The calls began: "How are you, Carleton? This is Emmanuel. Let us discuss the house. I wish to soundproof the children's wing and build a wall, say, fourteen feet high around the property. And a guest house for you and your family when you come to visit." He also provided me with an unsolicited critique of the "Room of the Month" series I was doing for *American Home* magazine. His taste was impossible to determine because it was a long string of contradictions. One day he wanted big, sweeping rooms; the next day he wanted something small and intimate.

Mr. David said he was an art connoisseur and wished to hang a Frankenthaler here and a Gottlieb there; he would purchase them by taking his private plane to fancy auctions. At the end of every telephone conversation, he would sign off with, "Don't be checking up on me now, do you hear?" I wasn't.

For six months we exchanged calls, and calls came more and more frequently. Then he started calling my home. If I wasn't there, he would speak to my wife. He began calling in the evening and on Sundays. He asked me constantly how Nicholas and Seamus were, inquiring particularly after our institutionalized child. And still Mr. David had not closed the deal on the house, which, of course, was the reason why he had yet to send me my $25,000 retainer. That at least made sense to me, but why he had to call so often did not. Yet I seemed helpless to prevent him from intruding into my private life.

As the months passed, my suspicions began to multiply. Finally I called the furrier Mr. David had named as a reference. I told him everything. "Donald, I'm going crazy. This man is calling me every day. What's the story?" Donald Gartenhaus told me that Emmanuel David had come into his salon with his wife and had ordered several mink coats. In the course of the business David had mentioned that he was buying the McCune house in Arizona and that he was looking for an interior designer. Don had recommended me. Did I ask my friend whether Emmanuel had paid for the mink coats? I did not. Maybe I really didn't want to find out. The calls kept coming.

By then I had other people in the office listening in on my conversations with the persistent Mr. David, if for no other reason than to convince myself that it wasn't all an eerie dream. Although David was becoming increasingly strange, I still wanted to do that house, the El Dorado of the Southwest. I too was suffering from some Coronado symptoms.

Seeking further information about my mysterious client, I called the Scottsdale, Arizona, office of Previews and spoke with a woman who confirmed that Mr. Emmanuel David also existed for her. He was indeed interested in the house, and a closing on the house was due, if not in the near future, soon after. The deal, she said, was to be in cash. "I've even flown to Utah to have lunch with him," she added.

"But he won't tell me anything about himself," I protested. "Not only that, he lets me know in a kind of threatening way that I'd better not try to find out anything about him." I was relieved to hear her say that she had received the same warning and had felt the same chill. When I hung up, I felt slightly better about the situation but still knew no more about Emmanuel David than I did at our first meeting in the Holiday Inn.

Then one day he called with a request. "Reserve the Presidential Suite at the Waldorf-Astoria. We're coming to town to look for furniture." Aha! I would get to see Mr. David on my own territory! Now he'd become real enough. I called Frank Wangerman's office at the Waldorf, and he advised me that he had a five-bedroom suite at the expected stratospheric rate. "We will, of course, require a deposit," he said. There was no way I was going to advance that kind of money to anyone as elusive as Emmanuel David. I called Emmanuel back and gently explained that the Waldorf required a deposit. "I will send that," he said.

I set about making plans for their visit. When I told him about the suite of rooms, he advised me of the sleeping arrangements. Two of the children, he said, were to sleep in the master bedroom with their parents. I don't approve of that kind of sleeping arrangement. In fact, when I design hotel rooms, I opt for less sleeping space and more rooms in order to offer parents privacy, if for no other reason than that parents need a break from their children when they're going through the rigors of traveling with them (and I guess that works the other way around as well). The arrangements were made, pending the arrival of Mr. David's deposit to the Waldorf. I was getting close to finding out, once and for all, about Emmanuel David, and I was sure the glib and sassy atmosphere of Manhattan furniture showrooms would dispel all cobwebs.

Nearly eight months to the day after our first meeting at the Holiday Inn, Emmanuel David and his clan canceled out. Their trip to the Big Apple for furniture was not to be. I don't remember why. I just remember saying to myself, "When will it all end?" Suzanne and I had both observed that Emmanuel was becoming increasingly spiritual. Certain phrases were creeping into his conversations, such as, "I feel a good spirit about you today, Carleton," or, "How is your heart? Have you listened to it today?" It was beginning to get a bit cultish for me.

My mental condition was still not the greatest. I continued to fight the guilt feelings I had about bringing a handicapped child into the world, to say nothing of the wrenching guilt that comes with having your infant in a foster home rather than home cuddled in your arms. Emmanuel David seemed to capitalize on my weakness and continually asked me in a solicitous way that I found offending, "And how is the little one? Will he ever get any better?" Yet I did not hang up on him. He commanded my attention. In spite of my better judgment, my irritation over his constant telephone calls and his invasions of my private hurts, I was compelled to listen. I couldn't figure him out. Who was Emmanuel David? Where was he born and who were his parents? Where did his money come from, and why weren't his children in school? All perfectly natural questions, and in an increasingly stubborn way I wanted answers.

Suddenly Mr. David stopped calling. An assistant named Matthias David called for him instead. After the second call, I began to feel utterly bewildered. The man was making my head swim. I told Suzanne about it, and on hearing the assistant's name, she instantly solved the riddle. "Carleton, don't you get it? First David, then Matthias . . . and his wife's name is Rachel, and the kid's names are—" We ticked them off, all seven, their names spelled so peculiarly, as if they'd just been copied from a Dead Sea Scroll: Rebyca, David, Joseph, Debbra, Joshaha, Elezbath, Rachal. All biblical names . . . a religious man with a Utah driver's license . . . the real estate dealer's lunch in Salt Lake City . . . the urgency for secrecy and the home births and the self-educated children. Mr. Emmanuel David must be the new head of the Mormon church!

I did the next bit of sleuthing and called the Mormon church center in Salt Lake City. Fortunately, I had remembered reading that the previous Mormon leader had recently died and a successor was about to be named. A secretary came to the telephone with my answer: Mr. Emmanuel David was not the new head of the Mormons. In fact, no one at the center had ever heard of him.

Then who was he? The question was beginning to consume me.

Next I was convinced that Mr. David was involved in a cult, a thought that frightened me. One morning Matthias called again, this time to tell me that Mr. David wanted me to fly to Utah to see another house he planned to buy in Salt Lake City while the McCune house was being decorated. I didn't say no. On the other hand, I didn't say yes. I was confused about what to do. If I said forget it, I'd never find out who Emmanuel David was, and I'd never get to do that desert mansion. On the other hand, if I flew to Salt Lake City, I might be killed in some unspeakable ritual cult sacrifice. The newspapers had been full of them. All over the West satanic cults were running over the mountains and through the canyons. What was happening to religion? I did manage to get the message across to Matthias (who, by the way, was the disciple who replaced Judas Iscariot) that I must see my $25,000 retainer before I went all the way out there. In some crazy way I thought my insistence on a fee would prevent the trip from happening.

Matthias called one day and said, "You'll get your retainer when you meet Mr. David in Salt Lake City. Now, here are the arrangements." When I continued to balk, I heard from Emmanuel himself. "Trust me, Carleton," he said, "You've got to trust me." I said nothing. Then I heard a long-distance whisper: "Very soon now, Carleton my friend, I am going to tell you who I am." My heart started pounding in my head. "I'll call you at one this afternoon, your time," he said, every word heavy with meaning.

So we were to have a one o'clock showdown, an hour past high noon. At 12:55 I alerted everyone in the office to stand by on an extension. The telephone rang at 1:05, and every ear in the place was pressed to a receiver.

"How are you, Carleton?" he said, amused, a man about to spill a secret. "How's your health?"

"Just fine, I'm fine," I stammered.

"Good. Have you given any thought to who I'm going to tell you I am?"

"Are you the head of the Mormon church?" I asked.

"No, no," he chuckled with indulgent condescension. "Let me give you a clue." Then a loud voice came through the wires: "'And they worshipped the dragon which gave power unto the beast: and they worshipped the beast, saying, Who is like unto the beast? Who is able to make war with him?' Do you understand me now, my friend? *I* am that power. Head of the Mormon church indeed." He laughed softly. "Let it be known, first to you and soon to the world, for I am about to go on television. All will know soon enough who I am, but first I reveal myself to you." There was a pause as my entire staff inhaled. "Surely you must know by now," he said gently, "that I am God."

I started shaking all over. I was limp. "You're insane," I told him, and he said, "Trust me, Carleton, trust me. Trust me and I will heal Seamus."

"Stop calling me!" I shouted, and hung up. He called back, but I was already on my way home. My paranoia was out of control. Here I was with a crazy man on my hands who thought he was God. Who knew my wife, my children, my address, and God knows what else about me—an absolute whacko who might do anything!

Once I reached the safety of my own four walls I pulled myself together and called the FBI. They were less than helpful. What could they do? I gave up and prepared to tough it out on my own, but Emmanuel David never called again. Nor did his disciple, Matthias. My grief began to heal; the bizarre affair with the David family and the desert estate were relegated to a part of my memory where I store things I don't want to think about. And I rarely did.

Two and a half years passed. One morning, while I was up at my country house in upstate New York, I got a call from Ed Evers, an assistant who had been with me during the nightmare. "Did you hear the news?" Ed asked breathlessly.

"What news?" I said.

"Well, I want you to go out and buy a *Daily News* right away. It's all over the front page."

I got the paper. The headline story was about a woman who had thrown seven of her children off a balcony of the International Dunes Hotel in Salt Lake City and then jumped after them. None of the children had screamed; all had fallen obediently to their deaths. One little girl was in critical condition, the others were dead. The father's body had been found two days before in a pickup truck, its gas pipe attached to a garden hose that ran inside the cab through the window. The suicide's name was Bruce David Longo, also known as Emmanuel David.

Newspaper accounts of the tragedy included familiar scraps of information: the father paid his hotel bill of $90 a day at the International Dunes in $100 bills. Although the family had been living there for over a year, no one had more than the briefest contact with them. One would expect a family with seven children, the oldest only sixteen, to make a little noise now and then, but not the Davids. The hotel manager reported the children were completely submissive to their father and did not even say hello unless he told them to. They even had to ask his permission to reply to his questions.

Ninety dollars a day times 365 days is $32,850. Where did Bruce Longo, aka Emmanuel David, aka God, get his money? My paranoia about cults proved to be well founded. Emmanuel David was heavy into being a messiah figure. When I suspected him of being head of the Mormon church, again I was on the right track. After the president of the Latter-Day Saints died in 1970, Mr. David had reportedly been very agitated when he was not named his successor. At the time he had a small group of disciples. But then, Bruce Longo may have thought, so did Jesus. He often tested his loyal followers by sending them into the arid Utah wilderness to ask God whether Emmanuel David was indeed not the harbinger of the Second Coming. On other occasions he told them he was more than that: he *was* the Second Coming.

At the time he was preaching to his tiny group of followers near the town of Manti, Utah, and when residents heard rumors of a 300-pound messiah in their midst, they began to get curious. All they could discover was that the group, rumored to number thirteen, was led by an apostate Mormon who was sometimes seen waving a long sword and threatening to lop off many thousands of infidel heads. Curiously, his main source of income seemed to be from a knife factory owned by one of the members of the cult.

I was also impressed to read that the FBI had been investigating a David Longo for alleged telephone and mail fraud. I wondered whether his file included a memo about my frantic telephone call in 1974. People around the International Dunes Hotel were also fascinated by the mysterious Emmanuel David. The manager found him brilliant and well-versed in current affairs. Maids had been told not to enter the David rooms until after eleven in the morning because the occupant and his wife were writing a book late at night. Waitresses at a nearby French restaurant were not so impressed. They said he was a big eater, a fussy eater, and a braggart. But he always tipped well, and they were intrigued by the two bodyguards who accompanied him at all times. During one meal, Emmanuel David had informed his waitress that he was of the House of David.

People who had known Emmanuel David when he was David Longo spoke of his commanding personality and his emotional instability. After he had claimed to hear voices and have visions, his doctor father had him admitted to a psychiatric hospital. Discharged and deemed fit for college, he attended Brigham Young University, met his Swedish wife, and changed both their names. Henceforth, Bruce was to be called Emmanuel and Birgetta, Rachel. When his first son was born, he blessed him and called him a prophet sent by God. The children kept coming; Emmanuel left the church, became a religious leader, met me, and then vanished. His death by his own hand was reported on the front pages only because of the tragic murder and suicide it inspired two days later.

When police entered the Davids' hotel rooms after the tragedy, they found everything neat and tidy. Clothing was folded in trunks along the walls, the remnants of a take-out order of chicken from the night before was in the refrigerator, and the children's bedrooms were decorated with their own crayoned pictures. The mystery of Emmanuel David remains unsolved. At least, clarification of the mystery has never reached me. The last I heard, the one surviving daughter has been mute since the tragedy. The chief of police at the time of the accident seemed to know no more about David than I did five years before. "We haven't been able to find out much about him," he reported. "He just claimed to be God, period."

In the spring of 1980 the still unfinished McCune estate was sold at last, after nearly fifteen years of standing empty. The new owner is North American Properties of Phoenix. The selling price was $2,455,000, "a steal," according to a local realtor. What the property will be used for is as yet unknown, but for me the McCune home of Scottsdale, Arizona, is forever connected in my mind with children and grief and death. "In my father's house are many mansions," says the Bible. I hope the new owners will bring happiness and life to that long-empty palace in the sun.

With President Carter at the State dinner for Jack Lynch, Prime Minister
of the Irish Republic.

"The Dorotheum" in the Metropolitan Museum. For years
museum goers have been coming here to relieve their sensory
overload under Dorothy's fabulous birdcage chandeliers, and
reporting "dreadful food, wonderful ambience."

Mrs. Carter and her grandchild stop for a moment in the State Dining Room to see the lilac and red decor I planned for Prime Minister Thatcher's state dinner.

Chapter 10

Sweet Charity

When I started to work for Dorothy Draper and Company, the office was not involved in theatrics like decorating luncheons, state dinners, and charity balls. Whether Mrs. D. had ever been tempted to pursue such projects I don't know, but I certainly was once I became president of the company. I was still entertaining my dream of becoming an ambassador, or the scenic designer of a Hollywood or Broadway extravaganza. My ambassador dream was never realized, except for the heavy diplomacy involved in being an interior designer if one is to survive in the business. But my dream of designing sets over and around and on top of which Ginger Rogers, Betty Grable, Gene Kelly, and their more modern counterparts would sing and dance their hearts out came close to being realized. At least, close enough to temporarily satisfy my yen for set designing.

My first charity ball was held in 1961. I had been involved wtih charitable organizations since my arrival in New York in the late 1950s and had met the charity heavies like Mrs. Robert Sarnoff and Mrs. Owen Cheatham. In time I even found myself one of their number, and my name was included among those on benefit committees for charities like the Boy Scouts and Project Hope. But my debut was the gala Polonaise Ball for the Polish Mutual Assistance League.

Involved in the plans were luminaries like Mrs. Artur Rubinstein and Lee Radziwill, for the annual ball was always attended by every Polish count, countess, baron, and baroness in New York. Geraldine Shephard handled public relations for the Polish Mutual Assistance League, and she suggested me for the decorating job. I was off and running for the first of what would turn out to be many charity balls, and I decided to do it up in the last word in Old World elegance and formality.

The Polish colors of red and white were employed throughout. The ball was held in the Starlight Room of the Waldorf-Astoria, and it was a smashing success except for one minor detail. I had been so busy planning all the formalities, I had forgotten to pay attention to what I was going to wear. I was not Polish nobility and thus had no red and white honor stripes dripping with ribbons and medals to wear across my chest. For some inexplicable reason, I arrived wearing a navy suit. No one had told me the evening was to be black tie, but I should have been able to figure that out for myself. For days I had been practicing the polonaise with an authentic Polish countess during several warmup sessions before the party, but when I approached her in my navy suit, she refused to dance with me. I have never forgotten the ignominy of that moment and have never attended a charity ball since in anything but a tuxedo.

The second Polonaise Ball was held in a small ballroom in the New York Hilton, and that one I did all in black with gold lamé. Each table was decorated with golden torches hung with golden apples, and the black napkins were tied with gold ribbons and laid on gold lamé tablecloths. I was quickly succumbing to charity ball fever. With every succeeding ball and every mention of my name in the society columns, charity committees got on the phone and wanted me to design their next affair. I soon discovered that word of my fee—zero—and my ability to scare up free suppliers of fabrics, flowers, and table favors were two of the motivating factors. As for myself, I was getting the urge to do set designs out of my system.

One of the most lavish occasions was the premiere of the film *Lord Jim*, which starred Peter O'Toole and Dahlia Lavi. It was held at the now demolished Astor Hotel, and in keeping with the film's exotic subject, I turned that room in the Astor into a jungle. The tables were decorated with baskets of bananas on which sat brightly colored toy myna birds. The room was filled with lighted fountains and jungle greenery, and it seemed as if every celebrity in town walked into my little jungle in honor of *Lord Jim*. The guests included Tennessee Williams, Judy Garland, and, of course, the stars of the film. That night Suzanne wore a white gown with a white maribou jacket, and as we walked through the cordoned entrance to the movie house across from the Astor

Hotel, we got a heady dose of Star Fever as flashbulbs popped in our eyes. They popped as much for Suzanne as they did for Dahlia Lavi.

More theater parties were to come. For *A Man for All Seasons,* which starred Paul Scofield, I divided the Tower Suite, a sky-high Manhattan restaurant, into four sections. *Autumn* had an orange tent over the bar and a cluster of small pumpkins on the brown tablecloths. (Fortunately the party was held in the fall. Pumpkins are hard to come by at any other time, even for endlessly resourceful me.) *Winter* was all ice blue tablecloths, white napkins, and centerpieces of white styrofoam snowballs and icicles placed in mirrored containers. Hothouse yellow and pink tulips bloomed on the pink tablecloths in the *Spring* section, and *Summer* was a centerpiece of fruits topped with a pineapple on melon table linen. All night long, people danced and tablehopped from season to season.

The movie connections began to snowball in a series of galas, all decorated gratis by me. I have always had a soft spot in my heart for things Irish, especially after designing the interiors for Dromoland Castle, and when the Irish Georgian Society asked me to do the party for the premiere of *Finian's Rainbow,* I couldn't say no. I created a hunting breakfast for them at the Rainbow Room atop the RCA building. And then there was my all-white party in the Hilton grand ballroom for the premiere of that seven-hour-long Russian-made *War and Peace.* The ballroom was swagged in miles of white silk edged in black. Tables were also draped in white silk, and the centerpieces were gold candelabra tied with black velvet ribbons and bowls of red roses. A red rose was laid at every woman's place setting. My objective had been to turn the New York Hilton into the czar's summer palace in Saint Petersburg, a near impossibility, but no one seemed to notice as they downed their caviar, vodka, and borscht.

Why did I do it? Prestige. Fun. A chance to pull out all the stops. And of course, a chance to play set designer. For *Oliver,* I turned Tavern on the Green into a slum. Caldrons filled with dry ice boiled and bubbled around the dance floor, the walls and windows were covered with burlap, and at the entrance to the restaurant I placed pushcarts laden with cabbages. *Voila!* An English street scene viewed through mists and cobwebs. Each guest took home a record album of the film's music score plus a toy pocket watch similar to the kind Oliver and his fellow urchins hawked in the film. Everything—watches, cabbages, burlap, cobwebs, and all—were contributions from suppliers. When I do a charity affair, everybody gives. Including me.

Goodbye Mr. Chips was close to my heart. As I mentioned earlier, I had done a stint at teaching right after college. The film starred two of my favorites, Petula Clark and Peter O'Toole. This party was also held at Tavern on the Green, and again I transformed the place from the floor up. I borrowed antique school desks from the New York City Board of Education and displayed them in the lobby for the dinner dance. Tables were covered in an English flowered chintz with coordinating napkins, and guests took home small blackboards, pencil boxes, crayons, and a record of the film. Tavern on the Green became Broomfield for the night. This is part of the fun of decorating charity balls: instant transformation into something fantastic, no holds barred.

Ethel Merman has always been one of my favorite clients, and so it was a real thrill for me to decorate a Project Hope party for her. I chose "Everything's Coming Up Roses" as the theme, and filled the Plaza Hotel's Grand Ballroom with hundreds of balls of pink roses and hung them from the ceiling. I used 10,000 roses in all, and the effect was sensational. I brought in a florist from Cleveland, Don Vander Brook, to decorate the party because no florist in New York could put his hand on so many roses all at once. Don did such a memorable job that I was determined to use his services again—and I did. He decorated the November 1979 dinner President and Mrs. Carter gave for Britain's Margaret Thatcher at the White House. I have given that party the Carleton Varney Academy Award for best-decorated set.

The last Project Hope party for which I provided the decorations was in honor of Amory Houghton of Corning Glass. The dinner dance was held at the Plaza Hotel, and I did a subdued look befitting the gentleman who was once our ambassador to France. Tables were draped in a Carleton V ice blue on white snowflake pattern, and each table was accented with a centerpiece of delicate flowers in a grouping of small test tubes.

Not all balls work out as planned. A Palm Beach socialite once asked me to decorate the lavish April in Paris ball at the Waldorf. She was married to a man whose mother had once owned the Hope diamond. I was looking forward to doing the extravaganza and was disappointed when the socialite did not keep our appointment. Later I think I pieced together why. I had once been called in on a minor decorating job at her Fifth Avenue maisonette. She wanted to remove the kitchen and install a sofa bed, but when I presented her with our estimates, which were reasonable I thought for such a small job, she declined. The price was too high. In spite of my reputation for delivering charity ball decor for next to nothing, she had neither forgiven nor forgotten: a minor irritation in a series of enjoyable assignments.

One of my recent successes was a benefit for Lincoln Center. I worked in conjunction with two dynamic Marys: Mary Lasker, once a client of Dorothy Draper and the woman who donates all those flower beds in the center mall on Park Avenue; and Mary Wells Lawrence, the advertising magnate and wife of the president of Braniff Airlines, Harding Lawrence. Flowers are one of Mary Lasker's passions, and we discussed the floral arrangements for Lincoln Center in great detail. The tablecloths were to be in a pink and white peony sheet fabric donated by my friend, Fieldcrest president David Tracey. I suggested quince blossoms in tall glass cylinders for table centerpieces, but Mrs. Lasker disagreed. She wanted pink and red carnations because of their vivid color. The atrium of the New York State Theater and reception area is architecturally beautiful but decoratively as cold as its concrete walls. I thought carnations were too old-hat for the affair, and the Lincoln Center people went along with me. I was wrong and Mrs. Lasker was right. The big bold carnations would have been prettier.

The most dazzling party of all was held at the Waldorf, a benefit for Retarded Children of America, and based on the theme of Blackglama's ads, "What Becomes a Legend Most." One of the legends was to be Ethel Merman. I designed a table fabric of the six women selected as the most legendary of the legends: Judy Garland, Barbra Streisand, Marlene Dietrich, Ruby Keeler, Joan Crawford, and of course, Ethel Merman. The champagne glasses were to be of the popular silver plastic variety, and each was to be imprinted with the six women's names. Somehow the manufacturer decided that six names were one too many from a cost point of view. Without consulting me, he eliminated Ethel's name. She was not delighted over the omission.

The entertainment for the evening was a parade of legends, and I found Blackglama's newest, Raquel Welch, the most impressive, although Hedy Lamarr, who had not been included in the original Blackgama campaign, came in a close second. It has never failed to amaze me how the more durable beauties can pull themselves together and come out smashing. The last time I had seen Hedy was at a party I went to in Chelsea, near the Chelsea

Hotel. My editor at Bobbs-Merrill was then Bob Amussen, who was also best man at my wedding, and he had invited Bobbs-Merrill associate, Roxanne Loder, who it turned out was married to Tony Loder, Hedy Lamarr's son. And so it came to pass that I was sitting on the sofa next to the legend herself. It was in the days of Mondrian dresses and high white patent leather boots, and Hedy was dressed à la mode in a white dress with red graphics. She was in a depressed state. She had disliked the book *Ecstasy and Me,* and she wanted to find a publisher who would buy "her" autobiography. "I want to tell it my way," she said, "but it seems I've already been done!" I didn't think she looked well that evening, and I felt sorry for her publishing troubles. Nevertheless, when I saw her at the ball that night, she looked as exquisite as ever. Some women seem to be blessed with a continual ability to postpone the deleterious effects of aging, and Hedy Lamarr is one of them.

Word of my charity ball design successes may or may not have reached Washington. One day, about three years ago, I got a call from the White House. It was Gretchen Poston, social secretary to Rosalynn Carter, and she made an appointment for me to visit with her at the White House. I had wanted to do a story on the new First Lady and her decorating and party ideas for my syndicated column. Instead, I got my story *and* the job of designing some of those parties. I was thrilled. I look on White House affairs as the ultimate American gala, and I can't go to 1600 Pennsylvania Avenue without feeling a little overwhelmed.

One of the first things I learned about decorating for White House affairs was that protocol extends to everything, down to the color of the napkins. Protocol at the White House is a bit like throwing birthday parties in a family of many children: what you do for one you have to do for the rest. Consequently, each party I do has to be the same and yet different: equally charming, yet befitting the country and the occasion. Even the music is carefully screened by Mrs. Poston. You don't want the band to strike up "The Lady Is a Tramp" at an affair for the Queen of Wherever. The press loves to pick up such *faux pas.* After all, they've got a story to write, and the pickings are sometimes considered slim.

The first decorating help I gave the White House was for a 1978 state dinner for President Portillo of Mexico. The entire affair was to be held south of the border. As the color of the State Department's china is indigo blue with gold trim, I chose a slate blue silk moire fabric for long round table skirts. The look was to be understated elegance. White House-owned Vermeil candelabra, from the attic or cellar or wherever in the White House, were sent to Mexico for the centerpieces. Floral arrangements were fullblown white roses, and the candles were also white. I like white candles at truly formal affairs only. The flowers were arranged in silver bowls that once belonged to Mrs. Andrew Jackson, and the silver was Pat Nixon's King Charles flatware. The blue, white, and gold State Department china dated from the Roosevelt administration. That's what I love about decorating White House dinners: everything has a meaning and a history. And why not? When America presents its best at a party, it should reflect its glorious past and, sometimes, its glorious present.

After the Mexico dinner, I received another call from Gretchen Poston. She told me with a certain urgency that she wanted to talk to me about a special party and would be coming to New York by plane that afternoon. Later she canceled. The following day the calls started again, on a rather peculiar note: had I ever designed a party I wasn't sure was going to happen? "No," I told her. "But why not?" The party in question hung in the balance of the success of some negotiations in progress. It concerned nothing less than the signing of the Egypt-Israel peace treaty. The deal was simple enough—no treaty, no party—although everyone was optimistic about a successful conclusion.

I started thinking. I didn't want to go with a look that was either Israeli or Egyptian; rather, the decor would reflect the time of the year. All over Washington the forsythias were a blaze of sunshine yellow. It was a color that connotated peace and hope, as well as the constant sunshine of the countries the party would hope to honor. As I formulated ideas, Israel and Egypt signed their peace treaty, and the celebration was on. We didn't have much time, five days to be exact. One hundred forty tables were covered in long tablecloths that featured a forsythia pattern. Lettuce green napkins were tied with yellow and white striped ribbon with an olive branch tucked into each. The gala took place under a huge yellow, white, and orange tent, and forsythia and white tulips were everywhere.

After that dinner, designed and executed in a whirlwind five days, Gretchen Poston and the White House staff knew I was a man of my word. When I said I would do something, it happened on schedule. During the treaty dinner I had been in Aspen with my wife and sons on a ski trip—my promises to them are equally binding—and to compensate for my inability to attend, Suzanne and I were invited to the White House for a state dinner in honor of Prime Minister Ohira of Japan, to be given on an upper terrace of the White House, outside the State Dining Room, overlooking Washington, D.C. This was a dinner I did not decorate, and consequently I could relax and enjoy myself completely. Prime Minister Ohira liked all things American, especially cowboys. When asked what kind of menu he would like, he answered, "Buffalo steak." He got it, barbecued, plus barbecued beef and chicken with two kinds of sauces: a sweet and pungent Georgia variety, of course, plus Mrs. Robert Strauss's special Texas sauce. She had spent a weekend making it in her Watergate apartment. The buffalo did not turn me on, but the rest of the meal was superb, including Mrs. Strauss's sauce.

Suzanne looked ravishing that night. She sat at another table with President Carter's national security adviser, Zbigniew Brzezinski, and the President himself must have taken a momentary fancy to her because as he greeted her in the receiving line, he touched her hair and complimented her on the way she had used flowers in her hairstyle. It was a magical evening, a little cool for spring, but delightful nevertheless. It was even marked by a kindly exchange between two designers, moments I always fondly remember. Gloria Vanderbilt was there with her escort, Bobby Short, who was the entertainer that evening. Gloria told me how she loved the Playtime collection of fabrics I had designed for children. She said she wished she had designed the fabrics herself. That's the sort of comment that rarely passes between designers, competitive as we are, but Gloria impressed me with her kindness, and I liked her for it.

My next White House project was Mrs. Carter's First Lady's luncheon for the senators' wives, planned for the Rose Garden. In keeping with the locale, I designed a rose-patterned fabric for the tablecloths of pink roses and green latticed ribbons on a yellow background and named the design "First Lady." I also hand-painted roses on all the pink and yellow napkins. Each table was set with an antique basket filled with red and pink roses, which happened to be the colors available in the Rose Garden at the time. Lillian Hermel, a collector of antique baskets, had loaned me her prize possessions for the luncheon. Mrs. Carter and I were most appreciative.

The guest list was a glittering one and included Mrs. Lyndon Johnson and Mrs. John Warner (Elizabeth Taylor). All proceeded without a hitch until it was time to set the tables. I then realized that the napkins, each painted laboriously by hand in New York and sent Air Express in a box marked *Urgent,* had not arrived. I dashed into the office of Rex Scouten, head usher of the White House, and started making telephone calls in an attempt to locate the wayward napkins.

As I waited and waited, having been put "on hold" by a clerk in the baggage office at National Airport, Elizabeth Taylor Warner walked in, also in need of a telephone. She was going to New York after the luncheon and needed some help getting calls put through to her home in Virginia in order to have some clothes reach her in New York. Her manner was pleasant, and the dynamism was still in the face, but she did not look "well put together." I was used to the likes of Joan Crawford, who dressed to the nines to go out and buy so much as an egg. Taylor had come to the White House First Lady's luncheon in a serape-like wrap that covered her body to a great degree.

She took care of her business and then joined the guests, who were already drinking their preluncheon champagne. Still no napkins. My calls to New York had traced the box to the plane, and somewhere en route or at the airport were those napkins. Like many people who are in a line of work where success depends on an accumulation of just the right details, my anxiety over a box of napkins can grow to alarm and then to ruination. Besides, they'd taken hours to hand-paint.

At last, one of my assistants, David Laurance, found the box marked *Urgent* sitting at the Eastern Airlines baggage office. The Eastern delivery folk rushed the napkins to the front door of the White House just as the guests were about to file in to the East Room. Bad weather had prevented our using the Rose Garden. Two minutes before they sat down, we got the napkins on the table. The luncheon was a success.

Another frustrating moment came during yet another state dinner, this one for Jack Lynch, the prime minister of Ireland, and his wife. It was held in November 1979 in the State Dining Room of the White House. I left New York with photographer Richard Champion on the shuttle, and we arrived slightly late due to air traffic. When the taxi dropped us off at the East Gate, the one I always use when entering the White House, I discovered I did not have a clearance. The telephone calls began. Half an hour passed as clerks tried to figure out what kind of computer error had caused my temporary banishment. Finally we were allowed in, and when I arrived in the State Dining Room I found the tables had already been covered with cloths in my ginkgo-leaf pattern of Celadon green leaves with melon berries on a white background. Another snag: Gretchen Poston informed me the cloths were too long. I had made them to skirt 72-inch tables, and it turned out that the tables being used were 60-inch. Varney, with the help of Mrs. Poston's staff, to the rescue: out came the scissors and the error was corrected. Part of a decorator's training is making instant adjustments, and after a while nothing short of a major explosion fazes me in the least.

There is a special room in the White House basement where the masses of flowers used daily throughout the rooms are arranged. I visited my florists, Madderlake of New York, who were down there busily putting together the floral baskets that were to be used as Irish country garden centerpieces. Along with long grasses and woodland moss my floral designers used white snowberries, seeded eucalyptus, peach melon Rieger begonias, white freesia, blackberries, and heather. They were beautiful. Chief Usher Rex Scouten sent members of his staff over the White House lawn to gather some ginkgo leaves, which I scattered about the tables, particularly under the leaf-wrapped votive candles.

Five days before the dinner, the Americans had been taken hostage in the American embassy in Teheran. The First Lady was in Thailand on a fact-finding mission for her husband, visiting refugee camps there. In her stead, President Carter's mother, Miss Lillian, was to be hostess for the dinner. I met the First Mother in the State Dining Room as I was arranging the tables. Gretchen Poston introduced us, and Miss Lillian asked me what I was doing with all those ginkgo leaves. "It's a special kind of tree," I said. "It's one of the few that can be either male or female." The idea of sexuality among ginkgo trees seemed to appeal to Miss Lillian a lot, and as she shook my hand she peered into my eyes and said, "Are you married?" "Yes," I replied, to which she said, "Damn." She was dressed in light blue, and I found her bubbly and talkative and radiating charm. There's a lot of life there, and her disarming nature dispels stuffiness at every turn.

Although I was disappointed that Rosalynn Carter was not there to see the tables, Miss Lillian put her hands in mine in the receiving line that evening and told me, "This is the prettiest dinner I've seen at the White House." Mrs. Lynch, wife of the

Irish prime minister, agreed with her and also embraced me. I guess older women are attracted to my round teddy-bear face. Earlier that day I had told Mrs. Lynch that I had used the ginkgo leaf in the decor because it reminded me of the Irish shamrock, and she in turn had complimented me on my work at Dromoland Castle. She and her party were obviously pleased that the President had selected me to design the dinner. Heady stuff. I do love those White House functions!

President Carter was somewhat preoccupied that night, as was to be expected. He is a gentleman of great charm in the southern tradition, and when Suzanne and I went through the line he greeted her with a big "Hello, Beautiful" and me with a simple "Hello, Carleton." Oh well, Miss Lillian had liked me better.

Each affair at the White House is planned around a theme: a person, a season, an event, a locale. For the May 1980 First Lady's luncheon I planned my decor around the guest speaker, Erma Bombeck, and I wanted an atmosphere as humorous and endearing as she is. I designed the color scheme around the tulip colors that would be available: lilac, rose pink, cantaloupe, pink, daffodil, and red. Hermie Powell and Jerry Crute, two friends from Richmond, Virginia, painted the drop cloths for the tables. The women paint them in an unique way by sometimes standing on a ladder and splashing the cloths with color, then hand-painting tic-tac-toe squares, scribbles, zany wildflowers, and whatever the imagination dreams up at the moment. The napkins matched the underskirts in the five tulip colors. The centerpieces were matching shades of tulips in glass fishbowls. Gifts were small baskets filled with tea napkins and cans of lemon, orange, spice, cherry, cinnamon, and peppermint tea. There was a flavored tea for each table color. A tradition of last-minute snags seems to have been instituted with that first luncheon in the Rose Garden for this annual affair. This year the napkins were not the trouble, but the guest speaker, around whose whimsy the entire affair had been designed, was sitting in the lobby of her hotel, the Hay Adams, waiting to be escorted to the White House while the staff made frantic calls to the front desk only to be told she had already checked out. All was well once Erma Bombeck arrived, and the luncheon was again a huge success. Until Mrs. Bombeck arrived, Gretchen Poston would not let me leave the White House for National Airport. There was a possibility I would end up as a substitute speaker for Mrs. Bombeck.

I have found that the Carter family has been willing to dispense with the usual diplomatic stuffiness that has typically surrounded White House functions. Can you imagine their giving approval to a lilac and red color scheme for a state dinner? Mrs. Carter did so without batting an eye. I can't say my color scheme did not generate some alarm among the staff, but Rex Scouten, the head usher with whom I had worked successfully on other affairs, had assuaged the more horrified members of his staff with a simple "Trust him." However, I was advised to use the word *lilac* rather than *lavender*. "Lavender is too fey," I was told by Enid Nemy of the *New York Times*.

The dinner was for Margaret Thatcher, prime minister of Great Britain, and the color scheme had evolved from a comment Mrs. Carter had made about a nosegay someone had sent her. As the affair was to be held over the Christmas holidays, I was racking my thoughts to find a way to avoid the usual holly and red candle decor. When I heard Mrs. Carter's delight over a nosegay, or a "tuzzy-muzzy," as it is called in England, I decided to plan the decor around it. Red and lavender: anemones, of course, and under the anemones, a lilac cloth. I decided to have them channel-quilted for a rich effect. The matching lilac napkins were scalloped-edged in red, and on every woman's place setting was a tuzzy-muzzy of dried flowers and lace. The tables were further enhanced with white freesia among the anemones, to give the bouquets a little more substance, and a circle of votive candles around them, each one in a red glass orb on a small brass stand. Whenever possible I go for low lighting at a table; it is more flattering and more conducive to conversation. The Christmas theme was present in the form of ceramic pears that held mints and nuts. I left out the partridge. And there was more Christmas, far more lovely and meaningful than a forest full of Christmas trees, in the beautiful holiday music we heard after dinner when Sarah Caldwell conducted the U.S. Marine Corps Band and orchestra and singers from the Boston Opera.

The success of my White House design assignments has come about because the President and his wife agree with me on many aspects of design and give me free rein, with their ultimate approval of course. They too dislike sitting down to white linen tablecloths, white napkins, white candles and flowers. Many residents of 1600 Pennsylvania Avenue would have thrown up their hands in horror had I asked permission to decorate with antique quilts and basketry and porcelain ceramics. The Carters liked the ideas from the beginning. They also like to have their tables reflect American culture, particularly American crafts. I wholeheartedly agree. Those ceramic pears at the Margaret Thatcher dinner were made by New York's Barbara Eigan, and Lillian Hermel provided the antique baskets at the 1979 First Lady's luncheon. It's good to spread the prestige around among artists, for being able to say you've "done the White House" is always impressive.

Pleasing everybody everytime, as Lincoln said, is impossible, and trying to do so is folly. Sometimes people are easy to please, like the prime minister of Japan and his request for buffalo meat. Nearly everybody was pleased with the JFK dinners, as long as they got invited, because Jacqueline was a woman of exquisite taste. On the other extreme was Eleanor Roosevelt, who also had exquisite taste but didn't give a hoot, and would serve heads of state frankfurters at Hyde Park. Shock tremors reverberated in society's parlors around the world. Lyndon Johnson's taste was big, broad, and loud, like Texas, and a function under his administration might mean being whisked off to his ranch and a hundred-mile-an-hour tour in an open car around his acres prior to a chile supper that cauterized your insides. It was not everybody's idea of an evening out. At the other extreme was the Nixon White House and its penchant for the traditional Thanksgiving approach of white on white with white. There's nothing wrong with starched and white, but it should just be one more decorating scheme, used no more frequently than lilac and red. For the decor of a party I planned for Ronald Reagan during his campaign for the Republican presidential nomination, I colored a ballroom at New Jersey's private Fiddler's Elbow Country Club of Bedminster, New Jersey, in white, aqua, blue and red to work with the permanent overall decorations I had planned. Mr. Reagan and his wife, Nancy, stayed at the Club as guests of my clients Ronald Schiavone and Ray Donovan. Unfortunately, the Reagans stayed in a room where the decorations needed a bit of upgrading. As of this writing, the room is planned for a redo come 1981; and maybe, if Mr. Reagan succeeds in his quest for the White House, we might redo it in the presidential manner. Who knows?

Anyway, according to all reports, the Reagan party at Fiddler's Elbow was a success, and the candidate raised some $175,000 for the National Campaign Treasury. I don't think I can credit the decorations for the money raised.

No matter what the success from a design point of view, the success of a dinner from the guest's point of view may have nothing to do with color schemes. Recently I ran into artist Louise Nevelson at La Samanna in the Caribbean, and the subject of White House dinners came up. She had attended the Pierre Trudeau dinner and had been unhappy about the affair because she had not been seated at a table of "interesting people." "When the Fords were in the White House, Shirley Temple Black came over and was so excited to see me that she rearranged the place cards so she could sit by me," she said. Apparently the Carters didn't permit that sort of thing. Louise was so bored she left before the entertainment.

I have thoroughly enjoyed my White House decorating jobs. I found President and Mrs. Carter to be sincere, delightful people with a sense of style that is truly American. I would be happy and honored to decorate for any President or First Lady, for I believe the White House must always stand proud and beautiful. As for Charity and me, I love to do her affairs because I can let my imagination take off on high flights of fancy. I'd never want to live in an all-black-and-gold-lamé room or have ten thousand roses suspended from my ceiling, but for one evening, pulling out all the stops is fun. And it works. Instant magic looks easy but takes a certain kind of unconventional thinking and an ability to surmount the unexpected. May I have the next dance?

The Grand Hotel. The place holds a special spell over me. It is on the water, has 100 years of charm and super owners Amelia and Dan Musser.

Blenheim? No, just Dorothy Draper's "Little Shack in the Hills of West Virginia." The Greenbrier is often called the most magnificent hotel in America, and I agree.

Club Photos—The Greenbrier

Dromoland Castle became my home in Ireland. The castle was one of the most important design jobs of my career.

Bernard McDonough, owner of Dromoland Castle, is seen standing, left; in the jaunting cart is Patricia Barry, castle manager, with driver; George Walsh, castle advertising manager, stands at right.

Chapter 11

Inns and Innkeepers

George Bernard Shaw once said that the great advantage of a hotel was that it was a refuge from home life. I couldn't disagree more. Perhaps such escapism appealed to Shaw, but not to me. The modern-day traveler who seeks a room at the inn is too often reduced to relating to his hotel room as a place to sleep and perform ablutions. Alas, many hotels, especially the giant chains, from the high-rise on the beach to the highway motor inns, are not happy places to stay—and nothing at all like home.

Dorothy Draper and Company is renowned for its hotels. I doubt if there is a man or woman alive who has decorated more hotel rooms than I have, and among the inns I love most are three of which I am especially proud. One is a castle in Ireland, the second an enormous summer home on an island, and the third a Georgian mansion in the hills of West Virginia: Dromoland Castle, The Grand Hotel, and the fabulous Greenbrier.

These three hotels are special because they are unique. They blend with their environment and at the same time are enhanced by it; they could no sooner be transported elsewhere than could a hill or a mountain stream. By contrast, my most frustrating moments in decorating hotels have been designing rooms that could have been interchanged, and were. Doing design for that system is a bit of an anachronism anyway. A decorator is trained to think in terms of personal statement, the more custom tailored the better, and the big hotel chains tend to think in terms of uniformity in vast numbers.

I call the look that often results in a marriage between designer and large-scale innkeeper *Esperanto,* a style everybody is supposed to understand and nobody does. A Hilton room in Teheran might look like a Hilton room in Buffalo. That's Esperanto, the universal decor, and a style that leans toward ersatz French ormolu. Worse, everything must match, like Joan Crawford dressed up. Chests, night tables, chairs, luggage racks, and headboards are all cut from the same piece, and are stored in warehouses chock full of repros for hotels all over the face of the earth. The vision of Esperanto, the language everybody was going to understand, just doesn't make it. Nobody understands it. Nobody *wants* to understand it, and certainly nobody wants to spend the night with it. By contrast, here are the three hotels and their keepers that exemplify for me the ultimate Home Away From Home.

The Grand Hotel

When I take on a hotel project of the kind that dreams are made of, it tends to be one where I can reflect the local environment, use local artists and craftspeople, and translate and pull together the tastes and personality of the owners. The Grand Hotel on Mackinac Island off the coast of northern Michigan is one of my most successful translations. I like it for personal reasons as well, because I have a particular fondness for summer hotels. I met my wife, Suzanne, at one in New Hampshire, the Balsams at Dixville Notch where I played busboy to her waitress. My boyhood was also spent in a summer colony atmosphere. My home town of Nahant on the North Shore of Massachusetts was filled with white frame houses with long porches and vistas of the sea. That is also the look of the fabulous Grand Hotel, the only inn I've ever done that appears in Ripley's *Believe It Or Not.*

When I first took on the project of decorating and restoring the Grand Hotel in 1977, I didn't even know how to pronounce Mackinac. I soon learned it is a local shibboleth to separate the ins from the outs: pronounce it Mackin*aw* or you're labeled an outsider. The word is Indian for "turtle," which is roughly the shape of the 2.5 × 3.5-mile island. Not a car will ever be seen disturbing the sylvan atmosphere of Mackinac Island, where the pace of life is more serene than on the nearby mainland. Nevertheless, when I heard all motorized vehicles were banned from the island, I wondered how I would furnish the hotel. There must be a solution. After all, people had furnished inns for thousands of years without cars and trucks, and if they could do it, I could do it.

I was in my office one day in the fall of 1977 when Irene

Frank, our receptionist, buzzed me to say a man named Dan Musser was on the line. It turned out he was the nephew of the grand old gentleman who owned the Grand Hotel, Stewart Woodfill, a bachelor well on in years. His nephew Dan was his right hand, the man who really took care of the day-to-day operations of the property, which is open from mid-April to mid-October for guests from around the world.

What Dan Musser had in mind for me to do was nothing short of completely restoring and redecorating the interiors. I was more than interested; I was excited. I wanted very much to do one of the unique hotels of America. The Grand Hotel, according to Ripley's *Believe It or Not,* has the longest porch in the world, 800 feet of it. From the brochures I saw the hotel was a white clapboard building with handsome white columns all along that 800-foot porch. I could count 34 of them. From the air the Grand Hotel looked a bit like an enormous floating riverboat. I took one look and decided that this was the hotel to turn into America's ultimate summer inn by providing it with all the antique charm it so richly deserved.

I first visited the place in 1977 as the season was winding down for winter. There I met Dan and liked him immediately. He was in his forties, a handsome man, with merry brown eyes and an air of charming sincerity, and I considered him a good omen. I was right. As I looked around the place my own childhood memories came flooding in: sunshine, wicker, geraniums, ladies in straw hats, collecting shells in my bare feet with my jeans rolled up. That was the way I saw the hotel, through the nostalgic mists of my own—and everybody's—childhood summers, whether real or wished for.

I had yet to meet the real owner, W. Stewart Woodfill, or Uncle Stewart as he was affectionately known to all but Dan, who called him Boss. Uncle Stewart's house was separate from the hotel and had a long porch too. It was a big white frame affair that had old bamboo chaises with umbrella shades on the porch, right out of the 1920s. So was Uncle Stewart. In fact, he was quite the dandy in his English burgundy dressing gown, white sneakers dyed black, and blue and white polka dot ascot. Uncle Stewart wore sneakers because he was afraid of losing his footing. His hair was snow white and his complexion the delicately pale patina of the well-preserved elderly person. A walking stick stood by his chair, and he sat in it, looking as if the house had been constructed as a background to his life. He was a grand old man all right, as befitted the lord and master of the Grand Hotel.

Uncle Stewart gave me a shrewd looking over and then launched into the story of how he himself had been decorating the Grand Hotel over the years. *He* thought the place looked just fine, and I found him so endearing I didn't want to let him know his decorating prowess left much to be desired. I didn't want to tell him that the lobby of his hotel looked like the Roxy Theater with its feather-and-scroll carpeting in red and gray. I didn't want to tell him that over the years the interior of his hotel had completely lost the magic of its exterior.

Uncle Stewart had bought the hotel many years ago, at a time when it was on the verge of bankruptcy, and revived it to the point where it now draws around a half million visitors a year. That was an incredible accomplishment, and I couldn't help but wonder why the special touch of class about the white-haired gentleman wasn't reflected in his furnishings. Nowhere in sight were the big wing chairs, wicker furnishings, and original fly fans that would have given his hotel the look of a summer colony. The Grand Hotel really needed me, and I knew it, and I love to be needed.

"Bring that black chair closer to me," Stewart Woodfill commanded. The chair was covered rather garishly in black vinyl. I pulled it, but it wouldn't budge. Then I realized it was bolted to the floor.

"And that, my good man, is how I want the furniture in my lobby to be!" Uncle Stewart said triumphantly. With chairs bolted to the floor? I wondered. It reminded me of my school days, that rather rigid era before Summerhill and Open Classroom when desks were bolted down in rows to prevent talking and cheating. Was that the kind of uptight atmosphere Mr. Woodfill really wanted?

It's true that there's nothing more disconcerting than seeing a lobby you have spent much time arranging to look "just so" completely ruined by garrulous convention goers who in their unbridled affability drag chairs near to heighten the atmosphere of good will. On the other hand, I feel that the test of a good furniture arrangement is to inspect a room after there's been a party. If everything is in a different place, the arrangement hasn't been right for conversation in the first place. When I told Uncle Stewart this, he seemed delightfully agreeable. He smiled his first smile. He liked me. I hoped.

We talked some more, and I discovered many of Uncle Stewart's decorating ideas were from another era, perhaps the one he remembered most fondly. He had a penchant for gold and red velvet and flocked walls, the dreaded Fontainebleu of Miami Beach look.

He then invited me to see what he called his real house. It was a little cottage behind the Grand Hotel where he lived during the Mackinac season. It consisted of one big room and a small bedroom. On a table in the tiny bedroom was Uncle Stewart's dinner, a bowl of stewed prunes. The cottage was so sparsely furnished it seemed like a parsonage with its clean, bare white walls. I later learned it was controlled for proper temperature and humidity—and germs too! Uncle Stewart was a bit of a hypochondriac. The most astonishing aspect was the collection of walking sticks that completely filled the large room. There must have been four hundred of them, canes of tortoise, canes with silver heads, canes he told me had been given to him by Harry Truman and Winston Churchill and other greats who had been his guests at the Grand Hotel over the years. He called his canes "walking sticks" and he was oh so particular about this. He was very proud of his collection in an almost childlike way, totally without egotism. In general, the old man reminded me of Ronald Colman, and I had a feeling he blanketed all his eccentricities with graciousness and cordiality.

After the meeting, Dan Musser and I got down to business. On the first round, Dan wanted me to do the lobby, card room, main dining room, and several suites. All the work had to be done on the off season, as the hotel would be open for guests the following April. The fact that the island had no cars did not turn out to be a problem after all. We would container everything and ship the containers over on the ferries that go from St. Ignace and Mackinac City on the mainland. The island also had a small airport, but while I use it when I come and go, the furnishings wait until the ice is off the Mackinac Straits.

The Grand Hotel is loaded with authentic charm. It is constructed entirely of wood, and many of the corridor floors are uneven and slant downwards. Never mind, the construction is so solid it was built to last forever, and over the years all the necessary fire precautionary devices have been installed. The hotel's flower is the geranium. Outside the dining room windows are boxes full of yellow and orange marigolds. At my first visit I determined that the geranium and the marigold would be the floral themes of my decor.

There are also many birds on the island, which is something of a bird sanctuary, and I used birds as another theme in my design. Third, and most important, was the light. Quality of light is very individual; what might work in Honolulu light would be a disaster in London light, and what might look good in New York or California would not work in Mackinac for the same reason. The air of Mackinac Island had an aura all its own. Whether it was a reflection of the water and all those square yards of gleaming white enamel, or a combination of all the elements that made the light unique, I don't know, but that indefinable quality would be my number-one cue when it came time to design the plans.

For the lobby I created white Georgian dadoes and painted the columns white semigloss enamel. I designed a new carpet, for the old feather-and-scroll had to go. It was replaced by salmon red and pink geraniums intertwined with a trellis of green leaves, all on a black background. For furniture I purchased English Georgian antiques, including a $21,000 breakfront I had found in Texas. I filled the breakfront with china in a tobacco-leaf pattern, and it looked sensational. Texans have a way of buying great English furniture in London and flying it out to their ranches and sprawling suburban homes. The dealer from whom I purchased the breakfront had in turn bought it from Mann and Fleming of Mount Street, London. Everything about the breakfront was traditional except for a small sign, a small, peculiar sign that Uncle Stewart affixed to it himself. It read: *This breakfront was built in London in 1710 and purchased in 1978 for $21,000.* Apparently the elderly gentleman felt that if you had just spent that kind of money for a piece of furniture, people should know about it. Dan and his lovely wife, Amelia, were opposed to having this bit of historical information affixed to the breakfront, but Uncle Stewart had the last word.

For those lobby chairs, all of which were not to be bolted down, I selected an upholstery of sky blue and placed the chairs around black coffee tables trimmed with gold, à la Draper. Lobby sofas were covered in a rich green velvet with skirts trimmed in heavy black twisted fringe. Georgian wing chairs were placed in pairs by the white columns where they fairly glowed in their salmon red cotton upholstery.

English library tables were used as lamp tables behind the sofas. I also purchased a pair of black end tables from the Joan Crawford auction to use in the lobby. Getting into the spirit begun by Uncle Stewart for annotated furnishings, I affixed a plaque to each one that stated it had been purchased from the estate of Joan Crawford, who had won acclaim in the film *Grand Hotel*. Other features of that wonderful lobby were white balloon shades at all the windows hung at a height that would always permit a vista of the Mackinac Straits, several fine Chinese coromandel pieces, Chinese export lamps, eighteenth-century mirrors, a George I tea table, and some Irish wood-framed eighteenth-century benches.

The birds of Mackinac Island inspired my Audubon bar and lounge. Through Sotheby I purchased many original Audubon lithographs, each mounted and described in detail. These were hung on dark green felt-covered walls above Chippendale furnishings also covered in dark green. Wing chairs and Hepplewhite cocktail chairs were upholstered in one of my own plaids of red, yellow, green, and deep blue. The lamps were leather riding boots mounted on black bases, for I thought the lamps with their red string shades were particularly appropriate on an island of horses and carriages.

One piece of furniture I had not included in my plans but quickly accommodated was Uncle Stewart's chartreuse wing chair. It was located to the right of the front door as you entered the lower-level check-in lobby, and served as a combination throne and reviewing stand for the old man. He wanted to know firsthand how business was going, to see his guests come and go and conduct his own census. In fact, he was forever asking the hotel staff questions about occupancies in other hotels across the country. He would even check up on his own by calling hotels long distance and asking whether they had any vacancies and what their house count was.

By the summer of 1978 Uncle Stewart's chair was in readiness by the front door, but he used it only infrequently. He didn't eat in the hotel, preferring his own menu served in his own room by trusted staff, and although he continued to have a keen interest in every detail of managing the hotel, he was becoming less energetic, more ready to take long naps than sit by the door and survey the comings and goings.

Dan Musser planned and built a new kitchen one of those first winters, and I found out Mackinac Island is magnificent in the winter as well. The summer houses are deserted, and the snow falls on them like powdered sugar on gingerbread cottages. The silence of the place is even more awesome because of the dense snow, and the sleigh bells of the horsedrawn sleighs that provide the occasional visitor with transportation are the loudest noise on the island in winter. The off season of 1978 was also a busy time of filling all those orders before the big April installation. Rugs, draperies, lamps, sofas, beds—everything awaited the first ferry through the broken-up ice to Mackinac Island. The hotel opened its 1978 summer season to much acclaim, and that fall played host to the Annual Resort Committee Convention. Representatives from the top resort hotels around the world gathered at the newly refurbished Grand Hotel to talk about their industry.

I, of course, was eager to hear what all these "experts" thought about the new decor at the Grand. Amelia Musser, who headed up the program for the wives of the resort hoteliers, asked me several months before the meeting if I would agree to be a guest speaker. I was flattered. It was a great way to meet all the resort owners, and I thought some were likely candidates for clienthood. Besides, I love talking to anyone interested in design, especially a captive audience.

Uncle Stewart put in one of his rare public appearances at a cocktail party during that convention. For all his idiosyncrasies, he still had a charisma that swept people off their feet. With a warm smile he came up to me and congratulated me on a job well done, although I knew he had withheld his praise from Dan and Amelia, as he apparently held them culpable for the change in the first place. In spite of his graciousness, I don't think Uncle Stewart will ever forgive the removal of the gray and red Roxy Theater carpet from the lobby of his beloved old hotel, as well as a lot of other sad and tawdry stuff that was whisked away with the carpet. Although he liked the new Grand, he resented change. He especially didn't like growing old and being out of command. Nobody does, but I think Uncle Stewart looked on the hotel as a woman he had saved from the ignominy of bankruptcy or, horrors, demolition, and it was hard for him to see someone else sprucing her up.

It was during that cocktail party that Uncle Stewart, dressed in his Ronald Colman outfit and sitting by a big chair near the fireplace, announced that 1978 had been his last season at the Grand Hotel. He would soon leave for the more agreeable climate of Phoenix, Arizona, and had sold the hotel to his nephew Dan Musser.

The summer of 1979 saw the Grand Hotel transformed again, this time into a sound stage for *Somewhere in Time*, a movie from Universal pictures starring Christopher Reeve, Jane Seymour, and Teresa Wright. It is a story about a young man who falls in love with the photograph of a beautiful woman for whom he travels back in time to 1912 to meet. In many ways, that was what I felt I too had done, traveled back into my memory to re-create a symbol of a bygone day and restore that slightly shabby rambling rose to its previous bloom. For the modern-day scenes my decor was fine for the movie set, but when it came time to go back to 1912 the white dado was stained brown and all my furnishings were taken away. When the filming was over, the movie crew put everything back to normal again, and I'm anxious to see the film, the closest I have come so far to realize my yearning to do set design.

The winter of 1979–80 brought still more changes to the Grand Hotel and its grand restoration program, and there were more to come. Just before my speech to the women hoteliers at the 1978 Annual Resort Committee Convention, Amelia Musser had told the audience that she and her husband and Uncle Stewart had tried to decide for some time what to give the Grand Hotel for its ninetieth birthday. After much debate, they decided that I would be the birthday present. I was deeply touched. I had never been anyone's birthday present before, and I also hope to be around for the hotel's 100th birthday in 1987 when all my work will be finished.

Dromoland Castle

I once was visited by a quaint gentleman carrying a Wall Street attaché case who asked me whether I would be interested in decorating the *Queen Elizabeth II*. Then he left, leaving behind a lot of question marks hanging in the air and his attaché case on the table. After it had been there for several days with no word from its owner, I opened it. It contained dirty underwear. Consequently, in 1962, when I was visited by a similar gentleman, wearing a beige and brown tweed suit and a battered brown felt hat and carrying an attaché case, I was on my guard at once.

"My name is Bernard McDonough. Do you decorate hotels?" he said.

I told him yes, Dorothy Draper and Company had done many a hotel, and then the questions began to rain. Did we only decorate *specific* kinds of hotels or did we only do hotel chains, and did we do hotels that weren't really hotels, and did we, for instance, do old Irish castles? By this time I was both intrigued and confused by this fast-talking man who seemed to be in a big hurry. "Would you like to see Mr. Hegwood?" I said. "He's president of the company." He said yes at once, and we proceeded to the conference/reception room and Mr. Hegwood. The room was then as Mrs. Draper had designed it, with black walls, an emerald green carpet, a big white conference table (which I still own), and chairs covered in her favorite black patent leather.

Mr. McDonough introduced himself and immediately got down to business. "I have bought a little place over in Ireland," he said. "Would you come over and decorate it?" I could see Mr. Hegwood was not at all intrigued, but he said nothing. "I have very little time," continued Mr. McDonough. "My plane is out at Newark Airport. Can either of you go out to my home in Parkersburg, West Virginia, to discuss the project?"

Hegwood was not at all thrilled by the prospect of dropping everything and flying to Parkersburg, West Virginia. In a state of momentary recklessness, I said I would go, and Leon was clearly taken aback by my eagerness. Perhaps Mr. McDonough saw the skeptical look on his face, for he said, "If you want to know anything about me, call the bank of Marietta, Ohio, or the bank of Parkersburg, West Virginia. When I come back you will be ready to go," he commanded. And when would that be? "In an hour," he said, already out the door.

Fortunately, I was living on East 64th Street at the time, and had just enough time to run home, pack an overnight bag, and be ready for—anything. Before I went anywhere, however, I rang up the bank of Parkersburg, West Virginia. "Mr. McDonough's credit is unlimited," said the bank officer at the other end of the line. "Anything he wants, give it to him." I relayed that to Leon Hegwood, hopefully without a glimmer of the I-told-you-so feelings I was having about my hunch that this particular tweedy man with the attaché case had more to offer us than a pile of laundry.

The pilot awaited at Newark Airport, and in no time we were in the West Virigina hills and at his home, where his wife, Mary, greeted us. The house was a newly built white Georgian structure overlooking the hills and dales of the countryside. We spent the evening in the sunroom talking about castles. For such was the "little place in Ireland" so whimsically described by my client. Its name was Dromoland Castle, located in County Clare at Newmarket-on-Fergus, a few miles from Shannon International Airport. Mr. McDonough wanted to turn the castle into a resort hotel, and living so near the Greenbrier, which is also in West Virginia, he had concluded that the firm of Dorothy Draper was for him.

I learned that evening that my client had made his fortune in shovels, shoes, cement, and shipping. When I told him what the bank officer had said, he smiled with satisfaction. Just before I retired to a guest bedroom decorated in soft Williamsburg colors, he asked me abruptly, "Well, how much do you want to decorate the castle?" The remark came so swiftly I was momentarily taken aback, but managed to say, "First we need a retainer of five thousand dollars." He promptly whipped out his checkbook and handed over a check for that amount. I too had been swift to do business. Before I left, I had one of the secretaries in our office type up a simple contract, which I produced on the spot. He signed, and we retired to our rooms soon after. I went to sleep in that guest cottage dreaming of castles, leprechauns, mists on the moors, and soda bread.

The following week Leon Hegwood and I were on our way to Ireland and Dromoland Castle. Long ago it had been the seat of the O'Brien kings, direct descendants of the legendary High King Brian Boru. I read in the local papers that Mr. McDonough had bought the estate for £175,000, although he never confirmed that amount to me. He had bought it from a very British lord and lady. Much to the dismay of the local residents, the tweedy and knickerbockered lord and his sweater-set-and-pleated-skirted lady had turned Dromoland into a kind of exalted guest house in which, at a price for bed and breakfast, one felt greatly honored to be allowed to spend the night.

The former owners and their maiden daughter had not been successful running their high-class inn, what with rising costs in Ireland and their reputation for stinginess. The lord and lady were well known for their watchfulness, and a story was told me of the butler in his stiff white jacket who carefully watched what each guest ate and drank, noting down every extra glass of wine or stout in a little notebook. Those extra glasses, or "jars" as the Irish call them, were bound to appear on the bill. The lord's bookkeeper. the jolly Mr. Foley of whom I later became very fond, told me the owners' parsimony was the result of a very difficult time making ends meet. Their ideas were too grand for the times, and at last they sold Dromoland and much of its lands, retaining a small part of the estate on which they built a Georgian house that overlooked the castle and tennis courts. How envious they must have been in the years to come as from a virtual front-row seat they watched the refurbishing of Dromoland.

In 1962 the castle was primitive all right. My room at the Old Ground, a nearby hotel, did not have a private bathroom, and I soon found the lack of such essentials common in Irish country hotels. The first thing Mr. McDonough wanted to do was talk about the addition of some basic creative comforts, all the while worrying about the quality of workmanship among the local people. "I want seventy luxurious rooms with seventy baths," he said. I looked at the magnificent exterior of that castle with its 1,500 acres of wooded land and vowed I would turn Dromoland Castle into a model for guest accommodation in Ireland.

Already I was thinking in terms of "I" because Leon Hegwood was not happy in that cold and rainy climate. While Mr. McDonough and I searched for furnishings and craftsmen, carpet houses and plumbers, Mr. Hegwood longed for New York and all the comforts of advanced civilization. He departed shortly thereafter on Aer Lingus, leaving me to hunt up possible design sources in Ireland for the work to be done. Although much of the refurbishing of Dromoland came from materials made in America such as fabric and wallpaper, the furnishings themselves were made in Ireland from models we air-shipped to Shannon and Dublin.

While Leon Hegwood didn't dig the old sod, I did. I wanted to find out all about the country. I wanted to meet Sybil Connolly and Irene Gilbert, Ireland's best fashion designers in the 1960s. I wanted to meet Seamus Keely who wrote under the pen name Quidnunc in the *Irish Times*. I wanted to meet Brendan Behan and John Huston and see the Cliffs of Moher and visit the Aran Islands.

I did meet Behan and Seamus Kelly at a bar named Davey Byrnes in Dublin. Behan lived up to his well-known reputation for being drunk. I also succeeded in meeting John Huston when he came to Dromoland Castle. I loved his craggy warm face and white hair. He was dressed in a dark green velvet tuxedo and seemed to go with the decor. I also lunched and dined with Sybil Connolly on a couple of occasions. We are still casual friends, and whenever I have a friend visiting Dublin, I always suggest he drop by Sybil's beautiful home in Dublin's Marion Square to give my regards.

After a few trips to Ireland, I came to love the place. There is a warm, protected feeling driving along those narrow roads through the gentle rain. The Irish seemed to embrace me even though I'm half English and half Lithuanian, and thanks to Tom McInerney of Limerick, my friend and colleague who served as my Ireland liaison while I was decorating Dromoland, I was made an honorary member of the Shannon Rowing Club at Limerick. Many was the evening I spent singing Irish songs, drinking a jar of stout, and having a general good time in Ireland, and I loved stopping at the Royal Hibernian or Jury's Restaurant for prawns, soup, and Irish soda bread when I'd go on furniture and accessory shopping trips to Dublin. After all, I was still leading the freewheeling life of a bachelor in those days, and I did love decorating that castle. In fact, I think of it now and feel compelled to buy a house in Ireland, an urge I usually quell because I'm the kind who wants to buy a house wherever he goes.

Mr. McDonough, I discovered, was quite the industrialist. He owned about eight companies and a number of other properties in Ireland, among them the Clare Inn and the Shannon International Hotel, both decorated by yours truly. He was also a philanthropist, and bestowed the Bernard McDonough School of Law to Georgetown University. Therefore, I was not surprised to find him a great believer in the power of money and a wielder of authority, which came as naturally to him as did making heaps of money. One time when I was dining at the Clare Inn, Mr. McDonough, who had been drinking a very good bottle of red wine, demanded I cut my hair "like a normal young lad." This was the 1960s, and long hair was definitely the style. The Beatles did not impress Mr. McDonough in the least, and when I informed my client that I liked my hair exactly as it was, he put down his glass and said in a very loud voice, "Young man, get that hair cut to a normal length, and I'll give you $25,000 right now." I knew he meant what he said, for I'd seen him give away thousands of dollars on a whim. He once gave an Irish Airlines stewardess $5,000 for being nice to him on an economy-class flight to Dublin. (Mr. McDonough traveled exclusively with "the people," even though he probably could have written out a check and bought the airline.)

Needless to say, I turned down his offer and kept my locks. I wager that had I cut my hair and taken the $25,000, I would have lost his respect for good. He had other eccentricities. The man detested the American institution of the secretary screening the busy executive's calls. If I called him, his secretary put me through to him without interrogation, and he expected the same treatment from me. "If I ever call your office and someone asks me who I am, I'll hang up and take my business elsewhere," he once told me. All the receptionists at Dorothy Draper were instructed to put him right through. Fortunately, he had a distinctive voice. Although he was generous with his money, the man demanded much attention. He scrutinized every stick of furniture that was bought for Dromoland Castle, even though he knew little about interior design. If there was any hesitation on our part, he would bark loudly, "I want to see what I bought." Every decorator knows this rule: the less a client knows about decorating, the less he should see until it's finished, and sometimes I would hold out on him. If I refused to show him something, he would not hesitate to threaten to put me on the next plane back to New York.

He also had the irritating habit of calling in everybody he knew for opinions as the castle was being refurbished. I was given advice by Irish bankers, brokers, his business associates, and casual acquaintances. He seemed to thrive on all that attention, and we gave it to him.

There was something of the leprechaun about him in his Irish tweeds that bagged and sagged in odd places, and he had a twitch in his right eye that started up whenever he was nervous, giving him a charming youthful look. Yet, despite his energetic appearance, he worried a great deal about his health, particularly his blood pressure. Occasionally I was called upon to give him medical assistance. Sometimes he would order me up to his hotel room at the Royal George in Limerick, where we stayed while the castle restoration was taking place. He had a spygmomanometer in his room for testing blood pressure, and I would proceed to wrap the tape around his arm and pump the little rubber ball. I made sure, however, not to let this extra little service get to be a habit, for I knew he was a man who liked attention, and my medical training is very limited.

Eccentricities and all, I found Bernie McDonough endearing. In fact, he became a sort of father figure for me. He was an older man and took to calling me "son," and our relationship lasted beyond Dromoland to his inn, his hotel, and then his house, an old friary at Newmarket-on-Fergus that he turned into his own residence. One evening Mr. McDonough invited me to Glebe House, as it was called, for dinner. We sat at a beautiful Chippendale dining room table I had purchased for him, and Bernie served us a boiled steak he had fixed himself. It was horrendous. Although he made no claims about being a gourmet cook, his attitude was, if it's good enough for me, it's good enough for them. At least he had fabulous taste in wine.

Over the years, I would have to say that Dromoland Castle has worn better than both Bernie and me. His eyes have weakened to the point where he needs brighter lights around him. Several years ago, he became short-tempered with some of the staff and ordered them to change all the light bulbs to a higher wattage. His tolerance level also decreased as the years went by. He had a habit of stalking in and out of rooms in the castle or the Clare Inn and shouting imperiously, "I'll give anyone a hundred dollars who can see what's wrong with this room! Can't you Irish see what's wrong?" The staff would shudder, look around, and say nothing. I happened to be on one of these inspection tours and said, "Here's something wrong. There's one curtain hook off the rod." "You're absolutely right," he said, and handed me the hundred dollars. I took it.

His unpredictable nature sometimes astounded me. The Limerick Inn, another of his Irish hotels, this one constructed by him and decorated by me, was given away because he refused to comply with some fire regulations he thought were unfair. He would not install the required equipment unless all the other local hoteliers were made to comply as well. Instead of opening the inn, he gave the property away to an Irish family. I never found out why or how, and knew of the gift only from a number of Irish acquaintances.

One of the reasons Mr. McDonough was so enamoured of Irish real estate, of course, was his own Irishness. He was proud of his roots in Galway, and I always believed that restoring Dromoland Castle was his way of celebrating that heritage for all the world to see and enjoy. In fact, one of the reasons we worked so fast, finishing the castle in six months' time at his insistence, was to ready it for the visit of America's first Irish Catholic President, John F. Kennedy. I was installing the furnishings when a flock of Secret Service men arrived along with other members of the Kennedy administration.

The Secret Service decided the castle grounds were too expansive to offer the President proper security, a disappointment to me and, I assume, to Mr. McDonough, but he offered the group a tour, which I led. Letitia Baldridge, Jacqueline Kennedy's White House social secretary, came behind me with her group, and everyone oohed and aahed. Tish Baldridge especially loved the green walled entryways and the soft lawn green color of the V'Soske carpeting in the drawing room. Later, Dromoland Castle was dubbed an "in" place by Suzy Knickerbocker. She was the first to write about the castle in the American press, and arrived one summer with a suitcase full of wigs to spend an evening or two with me discussing who's who and what's what in Ireland.

I have high praise for the local men who made it all happen. During the Dromoland project John Spencer, Joe Loge, and Joe Perrica and I would sit in those dingy, drafty rooms all through the winter months, the little Bunsen burners and a peat fire going but doing little to warm us, and supervise the Irish workers, who had never worked on a project like the restoration of a castle. The company air-shipped wallpaper and curtain and bedspread fabrics from New York, and the bathroom fixtures were flown over from Canada. However, I am a great believer in keeping the old and mixing it with the new whenever possible. After all, old things are part of the castle's history. At the public auction conducted for the former owners, I bought back ginger jar lamps, desk chairs, and many paintings. The family portraits also remained, for they seemed so much a part of Dromoland it didn't make sense that they be anywhere else but on those dark green walls.

Over the past eighteen years I have done a number of other projects for Bernie McDonough. He doesn't interfere with me anymore, and trusts my taste. In turn, I honor his attachment to his personal effects and never try to change them. I do the job without ever seeing him during the course of it, and receive a letter from him afterward telling me how pleased he is. However, he still brings everyone in, from his banker to his butcher, and says, "Well, what do you think?" I'm not sure that's such a bad trait.

The Greenbrier

Once upon a time there was a winding river whose banks were covered with briers. The river had curative powers known only to the Shawnee Indians, who visited it regularly, zealously guarding its healthful magic from intruders. The first white man who dared to claim the springs as his own (a strange and bewildering custom to the Indians, who could not conceive of land ownership) was one Nathan Carpenter. Word about the curative powers of the waters that flowed among the abundant briers spread rapidly among the settlers, who soon began to visit the springs whose sulphurous contents brought them such relief. The Shawnee Indians were outraged by the invasions of whites to their magical waters, and murdered Nathan Carpenter in revenge. His wife, Kate, and their children managed to hide in the mountains and escape.

Eventually the white settlers wrested the land from the Indians, named the waters and the town that grew up around them White Sulphur Springs, and became part of West Virginia. Early in the last century, the area became a spa, and a lavish hotel was built to accommodate the likes of the Jeffersons and the Clays, the Jacksons and the Van Burens. It was designed to be the New World's finest copy of the French château, and replicated the Amboise of the Loire Valley built for Charles VIII. Presidents Tyler and Fillmore made it their summer White House. In 1858 a new hotel, the Greenbrier, was built on the grounds of what was then called the White Sulphur Springs Hotel, which served as the backdrop for the Grand Belles, glamorous debutantes of their day. Those days of melon and champagne under the magnolia trees came to a bitter end with the Civil War when troops from both sides occupied the hotel, depending on the results of the last battle. After the war, the Greenbrier was restored to its old glamour, and General Robert E. Lee made his summer home in one of the cottages.

Once again the lovely old Greenbrier was racked by war. In World War II the government requisitioned it, first for a center for diplomats of enemy nations and later as an army hospital. By war's end the hotel was a shambles. Into the fray stepped Dorothy Draper, who began the largest hotel rehabilitation program in hotel history. When the Greenbrier reopened in 1948, the guests who came to the celebration included Massachusetts Congressman John F. Kennedy, his mother, and two of his sisters, and one of the first guests in the newly decorated restored hotel was Dwight D. Eisenhower.

Today the hotel is an attraction not so much for its rich history or the curative powers of its springs but because it is seen by many as *the* most sensational hotel in America. People tour its rooms and exclaim over its many treasures of cloisonné pieces, old porcelains, a portrait painted by a daughter of Gilbert Stuart, and the masses of eighteenth-century furniture I myself have brought over for the Greenbrier during the years. Nowhere else in this country is a hotel more beautifully maintained.

Recall your last hotel stay. Was it in a room decked out in orange and brown? Remember, if you can bear to, the overwhelming smell of carpet cleaner that invaded your nostrils on opening the door, the strip of paper across the toilet seat meaning heaven knows what, the orange polyester bedspread, the plastic laminate furnishings, the paper-thin walls through which you heard an unwanted late-late movie, the bas relief toreador and bull on the wall, the gray-speckled draperies and the brown-speckled carpet, the plastic daisies in the bathroom, and the mustard-colored lamp by your bed of futuristic molded plastic knobs, like warts on a pickle, its shade by F. W. Woolworth, basement housewares. Remember how you took one look and decided you needed an aspirin, went to the bathroom, removed the plastic-wrapped plastic glass above the toothbrush holder, drew yourself a drink of lukewarm water, and felt no better.

Such is hotel living at its dreary worst. How different from bedding down at the Greenbrier where the big Testa beds have warming comforters folded neatly at one end, one side covered in an English flowered chintz in contrast to the snow white candlewick spreads. Works of art hang on the wall, and at every bedside is a crystal decanter of cool spring water. At night each elevator landing bears a moon-shaped sign with a face drawn on it saying, "Sh-h-h-h, it's sleepy time down South." A certain care is taken at the Greenbrier, a loving attention given, that is rare in this day of impersonal uniformity.

I first saw the Greenbrier with the person who rescued it from the ravages of wartime use, Dorothy Draper. We had taken the mid-afternoon train from New York that went through the pleasant Allegheny Mountains, making stops at every little village on the way. After a Pullman sleep, we awoke to find ourselves at White Sulphur Springs where hot southern rolls, biscuits dripping in butter, fat, spicy sausages, Virginia ham and coffee awaited the famished and wrinkled decorators from New York.

My first look at the Greenbrier staggered me. I had never seen a building quite that enormous, quite that grand. It was everyone's fantasy Georgian antebellum mansion, the one everyone dreams of occupying, from which women emerge as Scarlett O'Hara and men stride through the library as Rhett Butler. This was the realization of that dream of the Old South, and Mrs. Draper had, with her usual sweeping statement, added a few more layers of glamour. Her characteristic large-scale moldings were around all the doors and employed as ceiling cornices, as she was then in the midst of her "Bolection Moulding" era. The place had room after room of the most beautiful spaces I have ever seen. I still feel, twenty years after I began working at White Sulphur Springs, that the Greenbrier is the most beautiful hotel in America. I believed it in 1960 and I believe it even more in 1980 with its many exciting innovations, changes, and new features: indoor tennis club, golf club and courses, expanded clinic facilities and convention center, plus many new cottages and rooms.

The first room I did on my own at the Greenbrier was the Crystal Room, a large private-function room that was windowless. We hired a New York craftsman, William Cook, to make enormous chandeliers to grace the high ceilings, and we designed 15-foot French windows lighted from behind to give this windowless interior room a look of light, particularly in the evening, that was very much needed. These false French windows were installed into walls and draped in a coral-red damask—until the Greenbrier's top man, E. Truman Wright, decided the draperies were too orange. He was the gentleman-in-charge, and he knew precisely what shade of red he wanted. Mrs. D. had had yards of this silk damask imported from Italy at a cost of nearly $3,000, and in those days that was a lot of silk damask. Nevertheless, Mr. Wright would not have it. "I will not allow it in the Greenbrier," he said, and the yards and yards of silk damask were carefully rolled up and sent to the New York offices where they languished until I had the opportunity to bring them out again.

Soon after, while decorating restauranteur Patricia Murphy's living room in her Fifth Avenue apartment, I brought out the red-orange damask that had been banished from the Greenbrier and hung it on all the living-room windows for a charity function. Patricia walked into the room and said, "Those draperies are awful! I hate red-coral." I was disappointed, because I thought the shade was wonderful, like the brick red of the Southwest canyons reflecting the gold of the sunset. After a while, however, Patricia changed her mind. In fact, she kept the draperies up and learned to love and live with a new color.

After I had won the Greenbrier in the terrible Draper wars, there were a myriad of problems to work out and new projects to begin. One was the West Virginia Wing, a new building that houses a nationally known diagnostic clinic staffed with sixteen resident doctors. You check into the Greenbrier, pick a doctor, and undergo a complete physical examination; in two days' time you have all the results. Many State Department people go there for their annual checkups, and the so-called wing is more like a building in itself. I wanted to keep to the basic style of the main building, and designed it with the rhododendron wallpaper, apple green doors, and alternating corridor floors of red and green.

Although Mrs. Draper had designed some memorable spaces at the Greenbrier, I felt there could be some changes, for colors and attitudes do change as the years go by. The dining room, for instance, had been painted a pale sky blue. There was an emerald green carpet embellished with a pattern of ferns and fronds. The chairs were also green, and the draperies were aqua and sky blue. I wanted to soften the look of the room. The sky blue, I thought, was glorious and handsome by day but unflattering by night. I redecorated the room, beginning with a new wall color of cantaloupe. The columns are antebellum white, and the draperies are big white calla lilies, green leaves, yellow flowers, all on a melon-colored background. The portraits and paintings on the walls are individually lighted, and there are glittering candles on each table. The emerald rug and green chairs remain.

In those early days on my own at the Greenbrier, I became very friendly with lots of wonderful people, among them the executive housekeeper, Margaret Kappa. She has a long and impressive list of hotel credits, one of them being that she was the youngest executive housekeeper at the Plaza Hotel in New York. Margaret continues to be my on-site person at the Greenbrier, working with me in executing all our designs.

Dorothy Draper was always fearful of Mrs. Kappa. As far as she was concerned, all an executive housekeeper could do was get in her way and do things to rooms that she would never dream of doing. Life was no bed of roses for Mrs. Kappa when Mrs. D. was around demanding, "Move this ash tray here!" "Move that sand urn there!" Fortunately, Margaret was flexible enough not to let Dorothy get her down. My relationship with Margaret has been a fruitful one. While I covet the hotel, I never feel Margaret is trying to undermine my ideas. In fact, through her I've come to have a better understanding of the problems of maintaining a hotel. Hotel designers should understand hotel maintenance factors if they are to succeed, and the information I have learned from Mrs. Kappa has been invaluable to me.

I must admit that when I took over the Greenbrier on my own I felt somewhat insecure. Could I keep up that incomparable look Mrs. Draper had given the hotel? On one hand, maintaining that tradition was one of my goals; on the other hand, I thought the look was a bit stifling and wanted to freshen it up a little with some softness. And then there was the management—hard taskmasters if there ever were any. A certain inflexibility reigned at the Greenbrier that relied heavily on decorum, I thought, of people wearing the appropriate clothes in the appropriate places and saying the appropriate things. I thought the atmosphere was a big rigid, as if the Greenbrier were a gigantic cathedral rather than a resort.

In the early days, I made some mistakes that were all my own. I have an abhorrence of rooms without direct lighting from the great outdoors, hence my creating false French windows for the Greenbrier Crystal Room. A subterranean restaurant with the look of an English pub was another problem. I had designed the tavern room with brick and stone, striving for an Old English effect, and a section of the restaurant was to have a lighted greenhouse ceiling. Strip lights were installed behind tinted blue plexiglass to make you feel as though the sky was just overhead. When the lights went on, everything had a blue cast. The food on the plates had a gray cast, and the people eating it looked terminally ill. Out came the greenhouse, the strip lighting, the plants. Since then I've tented the lighted ceiling with beige canvas with a red and green trim.

Hotel management in the 1950s and '60s was of two minds when it came to the Greenbrier's image. On one hand, management wanted publicity, the more the better; but on the other hand it had to be the *right* publicity. Hotel staff scrutinized every scrap of information before it was released. If a Greenbrier interior was to be published in a magazine, Truman Wright himself liked to approve the text and the pictures. Perhaps Mr. Wright's idea of the right publicity was a four-page color spread in *Harper's Bazaar* of the entire British royal family proceeding in stately fashion toward the overwhelming front gate, the white enameled columns of the Greenbrier glistening in the sun like heaven itself.

Margo Coley, the hotel's enterprising publicity director, did not have her boss's image in mind at times. Her goal was simply to keep the name of the hotel in the society columns as much as possible. The most memorable moment was when she decided that one of the guests, Princess Grace of Monaco, was pregnant. She called me at my New York office one morning and said, "Princess Grace is here! She's in the State Suite and she's pregnant!"

"How do you know?" I said.

"Any fool can see it," she replied. "All she has to do is turn sideways. You've got to pass this on to Suzy."

Suzy Knickerbocker, then society columnist of the New York *Daily Mirror*, was thrilled to hear the news. However, she didn't run the story for a while. Meanwhile, Earl Wilson, another New York society columnist, had invited me on a radio program, and before we went on the air I let him in on Princess Grace's little secret as told to me by Mrs. Coley. He too was hot to run the story but first had to check the facts. When he called Margo Coley at the Greenbrier for confirmation, she was suddenly terrified. Deep in her entrepreneurial heart she knew that this was not the right kind of publicity for the staid old Greenbrier. Nevertheless, she confirmed the story. She wanted to see the name *Greenbrier* in italics in his column. The story came out the next morning, not in Wilson's column but in Suzy's. I have no explanation for the timing. All I know is that Earl Wilson has yet to forgive me for giving the scoop to Suzy, even when it turned out to be false.

Meanwhile, back at the Greenbrier, the management was not at all pleased. "We've invaded Princess Grace's privacy, and that is unforgivable," said one of them to a mollified Ms. Coley, unaware that she had done something contrary to the hotel's unwritten Code of Ethics.

Some six years ago John Lanahan became president and managing director of the hotel, and under his aegis I have done some of my best and most creative work. The hotel has a younger spirit now, and I credit Lanahan and his wife, Rosemary, with the new awareness at White Sulphur Springs. I redesigned the shopping colonnade and installed small boutiques with mullioned window fronts. There is a new coffee shop on the premises with a complete take-out bakery department. Gone is the churchlike atmosphere of old; "amen" has been replaced by "twenty-love" and "your serve" from the new indoor tennis courts.

The sulphur baths still bubble away, and I find a two-hour soak most relaxing. For those who don't want to spend their vacation waterlogged and want a little action as well, there's the nearby golf house and a discothèque. A disco at the Greenbrier? That's right, and why not? Not so long ago I would not have dreamed of suggesting such frivolity on the premises.

The Greenbrier is part of me. I am on the board of advisers for the hotel and conduct decorating clinics there each winter under the hotel's auspices. I love being at White Sulphur Springs. I consider Jack and Rosemary Lanahan very good friends, and I consider the hotel's young general manager, William Pitt, and his pretty wife, Sherry, good friends, too. I treat that enormous place as if it were my own house, and in a way it almost is, for I know the contents of the bottom drawer of Room 808 and what's on the mantel in 1432. The place has magic for me, and I love every minute I stay there.

Decorating hotels has become a passion of mine. In fact, when it comes to caring for my many inns, I have adopted a new credo, or rather an old one, found in Hebrews: "Be not forgetful to entertain strangers, for thereby some have entertained angels unawares."

Here's the family—Suzanne, Nicholas, Sebastian and yours truly at St. Croix in the Virgin Islands.

Going up! Suzanne and I watch the Waikiki Sheraton become a 1,900-room tropical palace by the sea.

My favorite place is the living room of our country house in the Hudson River Valley.

Photographed by Richard Champion

Chapter 12

There's No Place Like Home

At no time in the history of the human race have people lived such transient lives as they do today, and among the industrialized nations, Americans seem to be the most nomadic. How did it happen, this rootless wandering from town to town and home to home? The answer is too complex for the scope of this book, but our search for the peace and comfort that only a home can bring is not. In fact, change is *the* essential problem, the one that intensifies our already strong nesting instincts. We need, more than ever, to create an environment for ourselves— wherever we may be—that evokes a strong sense of belonging and the comfort and joy that connection brings.

Most of our Old World ancestors never left home. A few miles up the road was their limit, and the ancestral cottage or farmhouse remained the family birthplace and deathbed for centuries. These strong ties to a place and family were taken for granted until the settling of the New World and the profound shock of transplantation. Only then did people discover how much they needed the continuity of the family home.

America is a land populated by the descendants of those brave immigrants who made such a radical and permanent change in their environment. Homesickness was for their ancestors the prevalent malaise, and yearnings for home were passed on to descendants. But did the children and grandchildren stay put? Hardly. Once the tradition of uprooting had begun, it seemed that people were determined to continue it. First the move was directed westward, and when the frontier was gone, the tide went in other directions. Many children of the pioneers reversed the trend of pushing ever westward and living in isolated rural areas to moving in great numbers to the cities. "How

Can You Keep Them Down on the Farm After They've Seen Paree?" was a popular World War I song about the thousands of farmboys whose lives had been permanently changed by an exposure to new cultures. Then came the Lost Generation, the Nation of Strangers, and the Jet Setters. The car, that American dream machine, expanded to the trailer or "mobile home," certainly the last word in American rootlessness. When cities became overcrowded, people began expanding again, this time to the suburbs and the Good Life promised them by the giant developers who created mile after mile of bedroom communities.

All in all, the American search for home has been a restless, peripatetic, and often unsatisfying quest. Suburban living today is no more permanent than urban apartment dwelling. Corporations require a constant uprooting of their executives as they climb the ladder, each rung in a different, farflung city. Blue- and white-collar workers are also constantly on the move as many businesses and industries relocate. Will Americans ever stay put? Or is the pervasively rootless character of the average citizen a reflection of the ancestral call: "Just over the next ridge is the land we've come so far to find"? Or have the old sentimental songs about home sweet home been replaced by ones that tell us *anywhere* we hang our hat is home? In the constantly changing environment, most Americans simply try to re-create the last one, perhaps with a new color scheme, in the fond hope of someday recapturing that comforting feeling they experience only in their dreams of home.

But what is this *Home* we envision, the one that will make us happy and content, and why is it larded with an inch-thick layer of nostalgia? "I'll be home for Christmas," crooned Bing Crosby, and several generations of America responded with a misty-eyed recollection of sleigh bells and steaming plum pudding, the old homestead parlor with the upright piano and the dim photographs standing on the table next to Grandma's African violets. The power of the nostalgia for the old homestead is so great that even those who never had a Grandma who lived over the river and through the woods or rode a sleigh or ate plum pudding suddenly yearn for the whole scene. Norman Rockwell's great popularity as the artist who best depicted the American nostalgia for Home Sweet Home continues stronger than ever after his death. It was no surprise to me to find that he was an authentic, a man who lived his art.

When the country began playing musical houses, the old

songs about the delights of the family homestead were replaced with romantic songs about the open road. Home was something to dream about or view on the covers of the *Saturday Evening Post* while on that long, long trail a-winding. Gone was the passion to own land that brought many of our ancestors to this country. A new passion took its place, and the descendants of the immigrants were moved by a passion just as strong as the one for owning land and a permanent home, and that was the urge to fulfill the American Dream. After all, it was the logical continuance of the adventure begun by their ancestors. In vast numbers the new generation left the old folks at home and went on their grail-like quest not so much for a place as for the things to put in it.

As the generations of nomads move, move, and move again, with each new home they yearn to re-create . . . something. Many call in a decorator and ask for . . . something, a feeling, a look that will make them feel as if they really belonged. But what do they really want? I have discovered what most of us *don't* want, and that is to return home. We don't want to move back into our parents' house, but we do want those pleasurable feelings the memories of home gives us.

Creating an environment that will give us the kind of satisfaction childhood memories remind us we once had (or thought we had) becomes a lifelong search, and mine has been no exception. Being a decorator, I have probably gone through all the transitions with a little more self-confidence than most, but I really believe my changes have been every bit as soul searching and stressful as those of the person who approaches his surroundings with more emotion than knowledge of design and technical details. Being a decorator just means approaching change with a little less trepidation and a lot more confidence. But not less stress, for stress always accompanies change.

As you may expect, my very first apartment, the one I did myself after leaving college, was influenced by my upbringing. I brought New England with me. In New York that transplanted New England look was comfortable all right, but not for long. My life had changed too much for me to be satisfied with the past, and I went from replicating my parents' tastes to trying on my own. Eventually I took them to the limit, then reevaluated my surroundings once more, eliminated everything to the bare walls, and started over.

The metamorphoses have been long and interesting and not

at all untypical. After my Nouveau Boy period I began to get a little more sophisticated. I got into stripes, then into a strong English phase, then moved on to print-on-print and fabric-covered walls adorned with treasures—*things*, ever more complex and baroque, as if I had developed agoraphobia, a fear of open spaces. About the only station at which I did not stop and worship was the French. I couldn't live with that fussy style. I use it in my profession, and many a big window has been decorated by me with an Austrian shade. I have done my share of gilding lilies, but not for my home.

My most ornate period came just before I was married. I was living on Park Avenue and had become close friends with a Danish couple, Kaj and Inga Velden. Kaj was old enough to be my father, and my feeings for him reflected that of a son. He and his wife had been my hosts in their house on Shelter Island when I wrote my first book, and although he was a theater designer by profession, he had worked with me on several jobs, including a hospital in Connecticut I had designed and for which he had done the draperies. Fabric was his passion. When he found out I was thinking about redecorating my bedroom he said, "Let me do it for you. I'll make you the most wonderful bedroom you ever saw." I said, "Kaj, be my guest," and after telling him what colors I wanted in the bedroom, I took a summer trip to Sardinia.

What I came back to was a bedroom swathed in pale blue velvet. The bed had a big round moon canopy with shirring underneath. Delft blue side draperies were tied to the right and left, and the headboard was upholstered in matching blue velvet. The walls and windows were also covered in velvet. It was the most claustrophobic room I had ever seen. It was too small for all that fabric, and the windows that overlooked the courtyard did not allow in enough light even without draperies. I thought I would smother the first night I spent under that canopy of draped, shirred, and bow-tied velvet. It felt like the inside of a fancy coffin.

Kaj was a dear friend, as was Inga. He was thrilled with the way the room had turned out. Soon after, his life took a tragic turn when Inga drowned off Shelter Island. He died some years later in the hospital I had decorated with him. While he was alive it had been unthinkable to undo his gift, and I lived with all that velvet for about a year. I didn't want to hurt Kaj. He had accurately interpreted the direction in which I was going. He pulled out all the stops to give me the ultimate of what he thought I wanted.

After the velvet tomb I began to retreat from more and more, finding increasing satisfaction in less and less. All over the country people were evaluating their desires, having found that collecting externals is an unquenchable thirst. Nothing was ever enough, it seemed, until I experienced too much. The next direction had to be radically different.

Suzanne and I were hardly alone in our attempts at reevaluating the way we lived. A strong back-to-the-land movement had begun, and once again the country was full of nomads seeking new ways to fulfill old desires, this time repeating the directions of their ancestors in their search for Home Sweet Home. "California, here I come, right back where I started from" was an old popular tune that was making a comeback, only this time people were doing it, not singing about it. Suddenly the rage was all for wicker, cream cans, the look of old barn doors, gingham at the window, and patchwork on the bed and even the wall.

Those who weren't going back to nature were going minimal, and that was our new direction. The great American Dream of possession, the desire for more and more and the slogan "Progress is our most important product," was going out of style. The new slogans were "Less is more" and "Small is beautiful," ideas more un-American than the collective farm! Our discomfort with masses of possessions now had a new ethic behind it: it was more than acceptable to break the *More* habit—it was downright necessary. In our discovery that we no longer wanted or needed all those external valuables, we found out that *we* had to be the valuables; our worth now had to be determined by what we were, not by what we owned. Somewhere between the simplicity of the womb and the overly ornate Louis XIV drawing room was enough. *Enough* has become the litmus test, a reflection of my internal growth on my external environment. Right now that look is serenity. For the moment, as I cool out, I have forsaken the busy opulence of the West for the spare quietude of the East.

The Varneys live in an apartment in an elderly building in the East Sixties. According to Paige Rense at *Architectural Digest*, it looks like an uptown loft. So Ho moves north. We've stripped our rooms to the bare walls and started over. I've had it all, all the looks, over the years, and now I'm reevaluating what it all means. This thinking process is taking place in a radically pared-down environment I find soothing and easy.

Besides, there's a fleet of Tonka trucks coming down the hall driven by two small, rollicking boys, and I don't want any priceless Laotian jars in the middle of the road. Hawaiian Punch on the white suede sofa? Not on your life. Instead, there is one thing of value in my living room at the moment, a Sam Cady "Children's Tent" that stands on the floor. Not only does the living room reflect Suzanne's and my need for a simpler environment, it also must reflect the needs and interests of the two little boys who will grace our lives for such a few short years. My children are the collectors now. Gone are my records and arrowheads and Suzanne's collection of silver bottles. We have to make room for two little packrats with their collections of baseball cards, bubble gum wrappers, stuffed animals, buttons, stones, shells, and strange dusty items that regularly appear in the dust pile and are pulled out with an indignant "I've been looking all over for this, and you were going to throw it away!"

I can't live in a world of "don't touch," and I wouldn't want my children to live in it either. Consequently, the truck route that now serves as our living room is a sparsely furnished place with wide open spaces and a feeling of uncluttered openness with few distractions. I can't say serenity reigns very often around the house, but the environment itself is never chaotic. The living-room walls are painted in a marbelized and restful beige, and the ceiling is a soft melon. The diagonal floorboards are bleached white and coated with several coats of polyurethane. For the moment, I can't think of anything more I need. I've even put lights on the walls so I don't have to hang art. I have gone from covering every square inch of wall to leaving them bare and awash with light. There are two sofas upholstered in beige and a table and a green plant. That's all.

Outside my apartment walls, chaos and stimulation are everywhere, too much of it for my health and sanity. When I come home, I don't want to be stimulated. I can't be confused by having too many things around. I don't want clutter. I don't even want rugs underfoot. In other words, Suzanne and I are going through a "don't need" stage, an important part of the process of deciding how much is enough. We decided, for instance, that we don't need an empty room with a long table and twelve chairs that is used perhaps once or twice a week. We did away with the dining room, opened up the wall, and made another living room. We have a small table now, which opens up, and a banquette along the wall. We entertain on lacquer trays for light meals and give sitdown dinners for four or six. Sitting around a table gives you a chance to talk and be cozy without the danger of food falling in your lap. I try to avoid buffets because I find myself uncomfortable eating that way, all knees and where do I put my glass. That kind of eating is best in the country where chicken on the grass is one of my favorite forms of entertainment. In the city I'd rather have several small gatherings than one large buffet.

Throughout the apartment the look is Far Eastern with accessories like trunks used as coffee tables and lacquered trays. I find Chinese and Japanese living somehow easier. It's soothing, spatial, and not heavy. For me, it's the difference between the richly sauced *haute cuisine* of Louis XV and the new, light *nouvelle cuisine* with its inspiration from Oriental cooking. Somehow, in spite of its lightness, the Eastern approach is more satisfying in the end.

Light is a very important element in my new style. I want it architectural and indirect, sources that wash surfaces rather than lamps. I don't like to squint at a light source and see flashing rays of light. I want something softer and diffused that illuminates like the earth is lighted. Needless to say, sunlight and moonlight are hard to do, and we're only recently coming into the technology that will allow for a new, more natural, age of lighting. I can't live with objects wired for light bulbs. People turn wagon wheels into chandeliers and flowerpots into lamps—but they're not lamps. They're wheels and flowerpots, and the artificial quality of the light they beam into a room is even more artificial than their look. I want an invisible light that washes an area in a subtle way. The technology is not perfected by any means. Track lighting is going in the right direction, but it should be hidden behind moldings or backboards.

People think they have to have so much when in reality they need so little. What do they really need? A table, some places for people to sit, a comfortable bed, a shelf for books, and a phonograph—that plus an efficient kitchen and someone you love is enough for anybody, isn't it? I've always said that I could create a beautiful room for a couple of thousand dollars and a few gallons of paint. I would paint the walls bright green, the ceiling white, and the floor black. Then I'd put in some wicker furniture;

upholster the couch in green, black, and white print; put a wicker basket with an uplight on a coffee table; add a plant; and make it all look like magic.

My decorating jobs, particularly the commerical ones, are often of heroic scale. I've done herculean rooms, and in fact I am best working with big spaces. Big lobbies and big civic centers—these have been some of my best designs. But home is different. Another important difference is creating in collaboration with Suzanne. Her tastes intermingle with mine, and the result is a happy combination of our two tastes that makes for an interesting look. Suzanne is more subtle than I, and in our house we use a more refined color style. She likes things that are soft and understated, and I have a tendency not to want to play it safe. I think we've come to a mutual understanding of what we want. In fact, when a couple do interiors in which their thoughts successfully merge, surprisingly good looks can result.

My children are also aware of design, for they copy what they see, as all children do. When Suzanne is designing children's wallpaper, they bring her their sketches and ask her to use them in her designs. If I frame a crayon drawing for Nicholas, Sebastian is right behind with one of his own. I once walked into Sebastian's room and found him absorbed in moving his little chairs around. "I'm decorating," he said with all his four-year-old seriousness. I don't push their design interests, but I do encourage anything they do that expresses their creativity.

The strawberry wallpaper in the nursery, which Van Johnson remembered with such fondness, was put up for Seamus, who never came home to it. It was a cheerful room with white ruffled curtains at the windows, and we kept it as it was for a while, making it a sitting room with white wicker furniture. When Sebastian was born, we redid the room with one of Suzanne's wallpaper designs. She calls it "High Times," and it features abstract cutouts of clowns, white swings, stars, balls, and dogs. Both boys have beds that are miniature environments. I have always been fascinated by what can be done with a child's bed, and searched all over before I found the right ones. Nicholas, who is nine, has a double-decker English bus painted red with an upper and lower deck and lettering on the side that says *Visit London Zoo*. It has headlights and steering wheels on the upper and lower bunks.

Finding a bed for Sebastian that was equally as wonderful as his brother's but different was not an easy matter. I finally found it in Copenhagen and bought it right off the floor. It is a truck of white pine and oak that also has two levels. The upper level is his bed, and the lower is sectioned off into a desk area, a closet, and shelving. If he chooses, his entire world can be contained in one piece of furniture in the middle of his room.

Needless to say, my New York apartment is not an audition piece for my clients. It's as personal as an apartment can be, because we try to make it reflect who we are—even when we're in a state of transition. For the past few years we've been in an emptying process, having survived our suffocation period of valances, carpets, fabric walls, and possessions high and low, and we tend to take out rather than put in.

The colors in my own home are, above all, soothing. My office is a different matter. Considering how many hours I spend there, it's an important environment in my life and I treat it like another home, only this one is more stimulating. I find I am constantly changing it, right down to the windowboxes. Right now they are planted with geraniums. Later in the summer they will be filled with perennials, and in the fall with brightly colored mums. I need that sense of living around me, and the flowers are a moat between me and masses of concrete.

My country house is another entirely different matter. There I would never empty out and start over. Small, built in 1795, and still in its original wood frame condition, it reminds me of the house I grew up in in Nahant, Massachusetts, and has all the charming characteristics of Early New England without adding a single stick of furniture or dollop of paint. Outside is all the lush beauty of the Hudson River, which once inspired a whole school of painting, the first to celebrate a truly American look. The atmosphere of my farm is of gardens, birds, horses, roaming cats, and laughing children. I find that over the years we have had as much joy decorating the landscape as we have the interiors of our little house. I plant my cornfields not just because I want to eat the corn, which I do, but because I love the look of the fields. I like seeing the corn as I drive up every weekend, growing taller each week, and I love to hear it rustling in the wind. I love seeing the deer come down to eat the corn and the way it changes as the summer progresses into fall—all natural changes, and all things of beauty, even when the corn stalks turn stiff and brown.

Trees and plantings are chosen with the same care we devote to color and style in the interiors. Early each spring we take stock, literally. Do we need another apple tree? Why don't we have a magnolia? The season begins with a sunburst of forsythia and ends with the demise of the most frost-resistant mums. In between we enjoy and evaluate, making frequent trips into nearby Millbrook and our favorite nursery. This year we discovered quinces. Someone had sent us some, and we found the orange-red shade of the blossoms looked beautiful in a room with clay-colored walls. While we were at the nursery, we couldn't resist an andromeda tree or two. One of the reasons I could never sell the place is all those perennials and trees that we have planted, the events in the family's life each one calls up, and the constant reminder they bring of the passage of time. I can remember when each healthy tree was a mere stick in the ground.

In a very literal way I have put down roots at my farm. The greatest gifts I can give to my children are those roots, plus wings to fly with. The roots hold them down and make them secure, and wings will come later when it is time for them to create lives of their own—and roots of their own.

I want to build onto my farmhouse but have delayed doing so because there's something about the place in all its primitive natural self that greatly appeals to me. I have a strong attraction to all things primitive, and the best place to display them is at the farm. The environment there is a leap into the cozy atmosphere of brick, big sofas, fireplaces, and lots of wood furniture. It is a place that will never change much because its natural personality is so permanent and strong. My Manhattan apartment is more mercurial, and right now it's a growing situation. For the moment I prefer to leave it more empty than full and let my children do the filling up.

Roots and wings. Aside from the former, which give you the security to explore and change, travel has always been essential to me in determining how I want to live. On a trip to Ireland I may learn something about a gate or the color of a green field. A trip to the Southwest may expose me to new earth colors illuminated by the sun and the moon. This stimulation of the senses is the genesis of many a room and furnishings design. I find I need the mobility and exposure of travel in order to create, for it reveals to me all sorts of new environments—and after all, the creation of environments is how I make a living. Although I need the exposure, I always try to spend weekends in the country with my family. I will fly from Hawaii to New York just to be with the children for the weekend, for they're my major responsibility.

In my recent metamorphosis of traveling light, I would

gladly trade possessions for travel. If I wanted to take a trip to the Orient but didn't have the cash, I would not hesitate to sell something I once lusted after to go, just for the experience. Nobody can steal that from you, nor does it have to be insured. Another intangible that can't be taken from me is the fabulous education I earned for myself. I have spent my life, my decorating career in particular, avoiding the snobbery that is the prevailing attitude among people who have led isolated lives. In all my education and career choices I have made an effort to avoid that kind of exclusivity. I would never send my boys to an ultra chic prep school because the atmosphere there is nothing like the world. Instead I will choose a school that is a reflection of the diverse world in which they will have to live.

Isolated pigeonhole life styles are unsatisfactory to me because it often seems that very little thought goes into them. Even Park Avenue matrons wear uniforms. Their hair is a certain shade of blond, and it's carefully coiffed to look as if it had not been; and they wear full-length minks, shoes, handbags, and little shell dresses with matching jewelry that are so familiar they are practically interchangeable. It was no surprise to me when I found out that the homes of these Park Avenue matrons were equally interchangeable. I'm not criticizing the look if it's a conscious choice, but all too often I don't think it is.

My increasing awareness of the ephemeral nature of things has also increased my reluctance to be drawn into collecting them. The Russian or Iranian aristocrats with their palaces and their caviar, their blinis and vodka and jewelry and land—all that disappeared in the blink of an eye. It's better to concentrate on other values. In my avoidance of drop-dead chic, lunches at Grenouille, appearances at swanky cocktail parties and garden parties and the whole empty world people imagine is the decorator's milieu, I have drawn my share of criticism for my preferences for things primitive and strong. In fact, I have been told I look more like a football player than a decorator, whatever that means!

My favorite comment about my all-American anti-status image came from a midwestern newspaper reporter who wrote, "He looks like a choir boy who ate too much at the church supper." It's true I fight a never-ending battle with the calories, and it's also true I don't make any pretenses about who I am and what my chic has been. I've done all that, and I just didn't find it very satisfying.

Wherever I work, I am more interested in a sense of caring, something much harder to define, let alone accomplish, than laying on the status. Whether it's for a maid's room for Polly Bergen, a 1,900-room hotel for Sheraton, or a luncheon at the White House, I want the environments I create to convey warmth. After *Good Housekeeping* magazine ran an article on Rosalynn Carter's White House settings, they received many letters critical of her. "Why should anybody in this time of inflation be buying hand-painted napkins to serve at the White House?" wrote one irate reader. The answer was, I painted those napkins myself and gave them to the White House, as I had also donated my services, simply because it was something that gave me a great deal of satisfaction to do. I feel those occasions at the White House are an opportunity to make the country look its best in every aspect. I want the world to see that we have a sense of caring, a reverence for meaningful detail, and an ability to create a happy environment, beginning with the country's number-one residence. I have tried to warm up the often icy atmosphere of a formal state dinner through the use of color, texture, and the unexpected—much the same way I do at home.

Suzanne and I have lived in the same New York apartment for twelve years, and I hope we never have to move. When we talked about moving a few years ago, both the boys started to cry. They didn't want change. Basically, nobody does. On one level or another we fight change with all our resources. When I look back on my career, some of the most intense moments have been coping with people who were resisting change. I remember the famous songwriter who told me to drastically change her life and then hated me for it; Joan Crawford's collapse over the move from her beloved Fifth Avenue penthouse; Uncle Stewart's admonition to bolt down the lobby chairs at the Grand Hotel; Edie Beale's valiant attempt to hold on to Gray Gardens; Dorothy Draper's unwillingness to relinquish her firm after she had sold it; and my Iranian acquaintances who refused to see the impending revolution. All these people were going through the stress that inevitably accompanies change.

I have lived with other people's changes so much of my life that I believe I have become a little more adept at coping with my own. I too sometimes fight change, but I know it's inevitable that tomorrow will be nothing like today, and probably nothing like I expected either.

Tragedy provoked the most profound change in my life and

permanently affected my goals. My striving for perfection ended with the birth of my son Seamus. Afterward, I strove to fulfill more realistic goals and found them much more satisfying. Nevertheless, it was not at all an easy change. One of the cruelest comments directed my way came from someone who had just heard about the birth of our second child. "They deserved it. They were riding too high," this person had said. On the other hand, I have a soothsayer friend who predicts no more tragic events for me. She says I have paid my dues. Nevertheless, I'll always be in the precarious position of having much to lose, not of things, but of an enormous investment in living, the loss of which can be equally as devastating.

When I am on a lecture tour, I always begin my talk by saying that home is the most important place, and that people who go from watering hole to watering hole looking for some kind of mystique that is going to euphorically take them over and make their heads easy would be much better off staying at home and concentrating on the environment within their own four walls. That environment is sure to change through the years, but with a little courage those changes can be explored and can enrich one's life. They probably won't ever be the Big Answer, but that's part of the fun. For instance, it took courage to go minimal, and now that I've done it I've found minimal has its problems too. There never seems to be enough place to hide away the daily usables and consumables.

Sometimes I envision my future in an all-white room with no furniture, just something to set a teacup on and a place to put a few books and other necessary treasures, something warm under my feet, and something warm over me when I'm sleeping. In my most visionary moments I see myself in a quiet, womblike cave awash with mysterious light. Soft green moss grows on the floor, and a fire smolders in the corner. As I look at those bare walls I begin to get inspired. Pulling a stick from the fire, I approach the wall and say to myself, I wonder what this room would look like with a herd of beautiful horses galloping overhead. . . .